Romantic Wars

Studies in Culture and Conflict, 1793–1822

Edited by
PHILIP SHAW

Ashgate

Aldershot • Burlington USA • Singapore • Sydney

Published by
Ashgate Publishing Ltd
Gower House, Croft Road
Aldershot, Hampshire GU11 3HR
England

Ashgate Publishing Company
131 Main Street
Burlington, Vermont 05401–5600
USA

Ashgate website: http://www.ashgate.com

ISBN 1 84014 266 9

British Library Cataloguing-in-Publication Data
Romantic wars : studies in culture and conflict, 1793–1822.
 – (The nineteenth century series)
  1. English literature — 18th century — History and criticism
  2. English literature — 19th century — History and criticism
  3. Romanticism 4. War in literature 5. War and society in literature
  I. Shaw, Philip, 1965–
  820.9'358

Library of Congress Cataloging-in-Publication Data
Romantic wars : studies in culture and conflict, 1793–1822 / edited by Philip Shaw.
   p. cm.
    1. English literature—French influences. 2. France—History—Revolution,
  1789–1799—Literature and the revolution. 3. English literature—19th century—History
  and criticism. 4. English literature—18th century—History and criticism.
  5. France—History—Revolution, 1789–1799—Influence. 6. Napoleonic Wars,
  1800–1815—Literature and the wars. 7. France—Foreign public opinion, British.
  8. Napoleonic Wars, 1800–1815—Influence. 9. Romaticism—Great Britain.
  10. Romanticism—France. 11. War in literature. I. Shaw, Philip.

PR129.F8 R66 2000
820.9'358–dc21

00–34842

This volume is printed on acid-free paper.

Typeset by Manton Typesetters, Louth, Lincolnshire, UK and printed in Great Britain by TJ International Ltd, Padstow, Cornwall.

L
10.1.08

University of
Chester

This book is to be returned on or before the last date stamped below. Overdue charges will be incurred by the late return of books.

WITHDRAWN

Romantic Wars

Contents

List of figures

All measurements are in millimetres, height before width.

The Nineteenth Century
General Editors' Preface

The aim of this series is to reflect, develop and extend the great burgeoning of interest in the nineteenth century that has been an inevitable feature of recent decades, as that former epoch has come more sharply into focus as a locus for our understanding not only of the past, but also of the contours of our modernity. Though it is dedicated principally to the publication of original monographs and symposia in literature, history, cultural analysis, and associated fields, there will be a salient role for reprints of significant texts from, or about, the period. Our overarching policy is to address the spectrum of nineteenth-century studies without exception, achieving the widest scope in chronology, approach and range of concern. This, we believe, distinguishes our project from comparable ones, and means, for example, that in the relevant areas of scholarship we both recognize and cut innovatively across such parameters as those suggested by the designations 'Romantic' and 'Victorian'. We welcome new ideas, while valuing tradition. It is hoped that the world which predates yet so forcibly predicts and engages our own will emerge in parts, as a whole, and in the lively currents of debate and change that are so manifest an aspect of its intellectual, artistic and social landscape.

Vincent Newey
Joanne Shattock

University of Leicester

Notes on contributors

Simon Bainbridge is Senior Lecturer in the Department of English at Keele University. He is the author of *Napoleon and English Romanticism* (1995) and of a number of articles on the interrelations of literature and culture of the Romantic period with the Revolutionary and Napoleonic Wars. He is currently working on a monograph entitled *British Poetry and the Revolutionary and Napoleonic Wars*.

Stephen C. Behrendt is George Holmes Distinguished Professor of English at the University of Nebraska. His publications include *Shelley and his Audiences* (1989), *Reading William Blake* (1992), *Royal Mourning and Regency Culture: Elegies and Memorials of Princess Charlotte* (1997) and a collection of poems entitled *A Step in the Dark* (1996). A co-edited collection of essays, *Romanticism and Women Poets: Opening the Doors of Perception*, appeared in 1999.

David Collings teaches at Bowdoin College in Brunswick, Maine. He has published *Wordsworthian Errancies* (1994) and articles on Coleridge and Mary Shelley. He is currently working on a book about the transformations of the idea of the common body in Britain in the late eighteenth and early nineteenth centuries.

Jacqueline M. Labbe is Senior Lecturer in English at the University of Warwick where she specialises in poetry of the eighteenth and early nineteenth centuries. She is the author of *Romantic Visualities: Landscape, Gender and Romanticism* (1998) and *The Romantic Paradox: Violence and the Uses of Romance, 1760–1830* (forthcoming), as well as articles on women's writing in the Romantic period and nineteenth-century children's literature. She is currently working on a study of gender dynamics and the development of the persona in the poetry of Charlotte Smith.

Geoff Quilley is Lecturer in History of Art at the University of Leicester. His research concentrates on eighteenth-century British art and the maritime nation, and he has published articles on art and colonialism, and art and national identity in eighteenth-century Britain.

Mark Rawlinson is Lecturer in English at the University of Leicester. His main research interests are in nineteenth- and twentieth-century poetry and prose and the literature of European urbanization. He is the author of *British Writing of the Second World War* (2000) and has written articles on twentieth-century literature, film and representations of the Holocaust.

Diego Saglia has taught at the University of Wales, Cardiff and the University of Bath and is now Lecturer in English at the University of Parma. He has written two books, *Byron and Spain* (1996) and *Poetic Castles in Spain: British Romanticism and the Figurations of Iberia* (forthcoming) and has published articles on Byron, Southey, Hemans, Mary Russell Mitford, the Alhambra in British Romantic Poetry and British Romantic translations of Spanish ballads. He is a collaborator with the Centre for Interdisciplinary Romantic Studies at the University of Bologna and is currently researching the discourse of luxury in Romantic-period writing.

Philip Shaw is Lecturer in English at the University of Leicester. His main research interest is in Romantic poetry and British culture during the Napoleonic Wars. His recent publications include articles on Wordsworth, Southey, Leigh Hunt and the cultural significance of the Revolutionary and Napoleonic Wars. With Vincent Newey he is co-editor of a collection of essays called *Mortal Pages, Literary Lives: Studies in Nineteenth-Century Autobiography* (1996). Forthcoming in 2001 is a book-length study of Waterloo and British Romanticism.

Eric C. Walker is Associate Professor and University Distinguished Teaching Professor in the English Department at Florida State University. His most recent publications include accounts of previously unpublished letters by Wordsworth, Coleridge and Johnson and studies of Wordsworth and the culture of Romantic heroism. The essay in this volume is part of a work in progress on marriage and Romanticism.

CHAPTER ONE

Introduction

Philip Shaw

This collection of essays is the first of its kind to address the relations between warfare and literary and visual culture in Great Britain between the years 1793 and 1822. It is no accident that this period is roughly coincident with the 'golden age' of Romanticism. As the Revolutionary and Napoleonic Wars raged across Europe, writers as diverse as Wordsworth and Thelwall, Charlotte Smith and Lord Byron, responded to the violence of their times with a mixture of ardent protest and measured acceptance. More often that not, the cline of criticism and advocacy may be traced in the career of a single observer. Wordsworth, mentioned above, is a case in point. From the anti-war polemics of *Salisbury Plain*, composed in the wake of Britain's entry into the war in 1793, to the establishment rhodomontides of the 'Thanksgiving' poems, published in the aftermath of Waterloo, the poetry embraces a complex of feelings. It is curious, then, given the impact of warfare on British consciousness in this period, that comparatively few studies have sought to address this issue. The significance of the French Revolution, by contrast, has loomed large in recent critical writing. Spurred on, no doubt, by the unparalleled success of Marilyn Butler's and Jerome McGann's revisionary accounts of Romanticism, a generation of scholars has reminded us that the culture of this period was forged within a context of social unrest. The key players in this new history are no longer Kant and Schelling, Fichte and Hegel (the grand advocates of 'the powers inherent in human consciousness'; Abrams, 1971, pp. 169–95) as filtered through the revisionary lens of the *Biographia Literaria*, but Burke and Paine and the polemical charge of *The German Ideology*. The resultant shift in emphasis, away from the 'metaphysics of integration' (Abrams, p. 182) towards the politics of antagonism, has rendered afresh the material realities that Romanticism would ideally obscure.

Yet as self-reflexive and historically fulsome as these studies undoubtedly are, one is hard-pressed to find any evidence of the material effects of history on the age other than those which encompass the revolution debate. Rarely, if ever, do we encounter a reading of Romanticism that takes seriously the impact of war, both on its participants – the men who are sent to war and who engage in the business of killing – and on those who remain behind, the families and communities blighted by socio-economic decline and political instability. All too often, as Stephen Behrendt notes in this volume, the evidence of individual trauma and its subsequent emergence in literary and visual culture is subsumed beneath a deluge of numbers. The historian Clive Emsley estimates that the casualty rate of serving soldiers was proportionately higher than in the First World War (1979, p. 169), but this is a figure that fails to take account of the vast numbers of those who suffered as a result of the conflict's aftermath. By any reckoning, the full scale of the disaster is unquantifiable, but still this does not explain why warfare has failed to capture the attention of critics of this period. How, then, are we to account for this neglect?

One explanation, proffered by Mary Favret in an important essay first published in 1994, is pointedly historical: 'in strictly empirical terms, the displacement of fighting onto foreign lands and waters meant that the immediate activity of war ... remained for the most part outside the visual experience of the English population' (1994, p. 539). At the same time as the threat of internal conflict was discharged abroad, so a number of discursive institutions conspired to 'produce an aphasia about war'; the actuality of 'reciprocal injuring' (Scarry, 1985, p. 63) thus became literally unspeakable. Following on from this we might add that the invisibility of warfare in contemporary analyses of the Romantic period may well be a consequence of an historical act of suppression. But Favret goes on to claim that the resources for a thoroughgoing investigation of the culture of conflict are available, albeit in distorted form, in the 'familiar landscape' of Romantic culture as well as in less established forms (1994, p. 539).

As a case-study, we would do well to consider the pervasive image of the destitute and grieving widow in war poetry of the 1790s. Dismissed by many readers as a product of the age of sensibility, the evocation of female suffering, as Stephen Behrendt points out, was in fact a highly politicized trope, one that enabled women writers in particular to criticize the effects of war (though crucially not *the* war) without fear of censure. More subtly, their manipulation of the trope of the nation-family emphasizes 'by analogy how the devastation of the family parallels the inevitable destruction of the state'. To this extent, the representation of familial decimation proved to be a powerful and effective tool against the state, a reminder of the flimsy barrier separating domestic security and individual conflict. Jacqueline Labbe, writing here on the poetry of Charlotte Smith, makes a related point when she observes that in 'The Emigrants' the horror of war and the horror of masculine culture are intertwined. When women write of the violation of the vulnerable feminine body their protest is directed against a system that promulgates war as the apogee of male oppression.

But what of the primary victims of war? In the literature of the period direct evidence of masculine pain – what statistical knowledge means when translated into human terms – is noticeable by its absence. To be sure there are passages that speak of the soldier's wounds, the blood-drenched fields and the costs of human sacrifice, but one looks in vain for records of personal suffering. If, as Favret claims, the war was mediated and channelled through sources that sought to expunge the terrible realities of combat, then we should not be surprised at the relative dearth of explicit descriptive material. It is for this reason that the representation of the widow and her children offers what Walter Benjamin calls a 'dialectical image': progressive in so far as protests against the collapse of domestic security are concerned, reactionary in its sentimental displacing of the male body in pain. Yet in many ways, as Favret explains, the ruined family provides an effective means of exposing the gender politics that divide the body of the 'immortal' public soldier from the vulnerable private world he fights to protect. In this respect, the act of displacement, of portraying the wounded or dying body through feminine eyes alone, is itself a demonstration of the extent to which suffering remains a private affair, unrelated to the greater needs of the warring state.

In 'The Field of Battle', a ballad published in the *Gentleman's Magazine* in 1794 and reprinted in the *Courier* in 1800 (Bennett, 1976, pp. 112–13), we encounter an interesting example of this effect. A young woman is depicted searching for her lover on the eve of a grisly battle:

> The field, so late the hero's pride,
>   Was now with various carnage spread;
> And floated with a crimson tide,
>   That drench'd the dying and the dead!
>
> O'er the sad scene of dreariest view,
>   Abandon'd all to horrors wild,
> With frantic step, Maria flew;
>   Maria, sorrow's early child!

Maria, 'by duty led', is the embodiment of disciplined femininity, bound by chains of love to Edgar, the 'gallant' soldier of popular myth. As in 'dire amaze' she wanders the field of battle, the hope of romantic reunion is checked by the news of her Edgar's death. Eventually, of course, Maria discovers the body of her beloved: 'Half buried with the hostile dead, And bor'd with many a grisly wound'. Now, if there is a logic of sacrifice at work here, the reader is left in no doubt as to the pitiful truth that such fictions conceal, for in death the heroic warrior has become, once more, the private man of feminine longing: no longer the impregnable citizen-soldier but a vulnerable human being, subject to the effects of 'reciprocal wounding'. Concentration on the women's grief (in the concluding lines she suffers a fate 'worse than death') means that it is no longer possible to view the soldier as a functionary of the national will. Bereft of the domestic security that is the lifeblood of the state, the story of Maria 'undermine[s] the fiction motivating the war effort: that it will keep violence from coming home' (Favret, 1994, p. 547).

One problem with Favret's conception of the representation of war resides in her assumption that exposure of the wounded and dying soldier makes visible 'a counter-public sphere, a space which recognizes the violence that the public sphere alone cannot, constitutively accommodate' (p. 543). Orrin Wang, in his response to Favret's essay, argues that the notion of a 'counter-public sphere' is romantic (and therefore benighted) in so far as it must assume the existence of a reading public and a set of discursive institutions 'in some way distinguishable from that of the bourgeois private and public spheres' (Wang, 1994, p. 585). There is considerable support for this observation when we recall that the audience for the 'Field of Battle' was likely to be confined to the highly literate supporters of the Whigs, a party unable to muster, out of fear of the return of revolutionary violence, an effective opposition to the bellicist policies of the Pitt administration. A reader of the poem could well shed a tear for Maria whilst maintaining tacit support for the pursuance of the war. Favret herself, in response to Wang's response, is quick to qualify her use of the term, noting that rather than 'positing this "other" space, the body of the dead soldier simply introduces cracks or discontinuities in the concept of the public sphere' (1994, p. 543). One is led, therefore, to the grim conclusion that such exposure is politically ineffective, so strong is the identification of the public sphere with the desires of the state.

There is, however, some evidence for the existence of a counter-public sphere, based on the findings of critics such as Nicholas Roe (1988), Chris Jones (1993) and David Worrall (1992), to name but a few. Moreover, in support of this argument, we might well reconsider the notion that women become the sole filter for representations of the conflict. There is a wealth of occasional verse, collected in Betty Bennett's *British War Poetry in the Age of Romanticism* (a volume first published in the 1976, now coming into its own as a vital resource), which takes the effacement of male suffering head on. A number of these poems reflect the ideological contours of the nascent peace movements, motivated in large part by the combustible alliance of Painite radicalism and dissenting Christianity (Roe, 1988; Ceadel, 1996, pp. 166–221). The anti-war poetry published in such journals as the *Cambridge Intelligencer*, the *Cabinet* and the *Protestant Dissenter's Magazine* is un-flinching in its portrayal of the contradictions of battle. The Quaker John Scott, for example, notes in his poem 'The Drum' (1793) the discrepancy between the allure of '*Ambition's*' 'tawdry lace and glittering arms'; and the 'mangled limbs, and dying groans' of the hapless soldier (Bennett, 1976, p. 80). The fatal lie of war is a subject on which the radical Southey, in the controversial poem 'The Battle of Blenheim' (Bennett, 1976, p. 245), is no less explicit:

> They say it was a shocking sight
> After the field was won,
> For many thousand bodies here

> Lay rotting in the sun;
> But things like that you know must be
> After a famous victory.

Southey presents a suave opposition between the painful truth of war (what Scarry would deem the ontological gulf separating the violated body of the combatant from his peaceful counterpart) and its fictional representation. This point applies equally to the early writings of Coleridge. In 'Fears in Solitude' (Coleridge, 1969), a poem which in many ways contributes to the gender confusion noted by Favret (1994, p. 543), the reality of the injured masculine body seems to undermine the bellicist imaginings of the nation-state:

> Boys and girls,
> And women, that would groan to see a child
> Pull off an insect's leg, all read of war,
> The best amusement for our morning meal!
> The poor wretch, who has learnt his only prayers
> From curses, who knows scarcely words enough
> To ask a blessing from his Heavenly Father,
> Becomes a fluent phraseman, absolute
> And technical in victories and defeats,
> And all our dainty terms for fratricide;
> Terms which we trundle smoothly o'er our tongues
> Like mere abstractions, empty sounds to which
> We join no feeling and attach no form!
> As if the soldier died without a wound;
> As if the fibres of this godlike frame
> Were gored without a pang; as if the wretch,
> Who fell in battle, doing bloody deeds,
> Passed off to Heaven, translated and not killed
>
> (ll. 104–21)

By linking the 'poor wretch' of line 108 with the 'wretch' killed in battle, Coleridge underscores the vacuous concord of domestic life. But ultimately his poem is an exercise in linguistic re-education; as the discourse of the public sphere undoes the consubstantiation of word and flesh, Coleridge works hard to remind his audience of this vital connection. That this passage is building up to a justification of holy war against an impious other is underlined when we consider the echoes of Hamlet's ruminations on the frailty of man (IV. iv 55–6; Shakespeare, 1992). Like Hamlet, Coleridge is moved to the position where the mindless courage of war – 'The imminent death of twenty thousand men / That for a fantasy and trick of fame / Go to their graves like beds' – summons up thoughts of personal and national integrity. It is not anti-war polemic that Coleridge produces but a paean to the pleasures of pure war. In short, as David Collings suggests in his essay for this volume, by bowing to 'harsh', idiotic 'duty', the poet is released from the burden of self-consciousness and, one might add, from the struggle to maintain allegiance to the harsh demands of the counter-public sphere.

Coleridge's poem raises some disturbing questions about the role of fantasy in war and, in particular, the extent to which pacificism (a position that does not rule out the use of armed force for defensive purposes) and militarism (the belief that all war is a positive good and should never be shirked; Ceadel, 1996) converge in images of virtual suffering. By placing 'Fears in Solitude' in the context in which it first appeared, namely the cultural significance of the invasion threat in the period 1797–1803, Mark Rawlinson reminds us that readings such as the one outlined above 'beg the question of how war imagined makes possible both bellicose and ethical thinking'. It is not enough, in other words, to read the poem as an attempt to negotiate between pro- and anti-war sentiments since the reasonableness of this dualistic approach obfuscates the extent to which such positions converge in symbolic representations of alarm. Since both attitudes fall back on violent imaginings – on fantasies of destruction, against others and against the self as nation – it is important that critics take account of the moral ambiguities that such fantasies present. Moreover, as Rawlinson concludes, the fact that military strategy has as much to do with sign systems as with the brute empirical truth of reciprocal killing, should encourage us to reappraise approaches to war that claim to recover a level of reality untainted by symbolization.

Rawlinson's reference to Walter Benjamin's observation about the pleasure of contemplating one's self-destruction is a further reminder of what is at issue in shifting from a pacificist to a bellicist stance during a period of alarm. Under such conditions, is it at all possible for the radical intellectual to find a language that will speak through the call of duty and of discipline? Here again, one might profitably turn to the example of Coleridge, whose attempts to create a language appropriate to the subject of opposition have been well documented (see Roe, 1988; Leask, 1988; Morrow, 1990). What recent studies leave unsaid, however, is the way in which Coleridge's growing disillusion with the politics of opposition shaded into a growing admiration for the bracing effects of international war. The shift from the anti-war stance of *The Watchman* to the more nuanced, equivocal writings of the *Courier* period provides us with an insight into Coleridge's personal battle to reconcile a rational objection to waste and ruin with an imaginative response to conflict's harsh delights. As successive articles in the *Courier* vacillate between these extremes, Coleridge turned to the philosopher Immanuel Kant to provide theoretical support for the idea of a 'just' conflict (De Paolo, 1985, p. 10). But, as Diego Saglia observes in his essay for this collection, it was the narrative resources of romance rather than the philosophical reflections of Kant that allowed Coleridge to effectively sublate the 'actualities of war'. This rendering of military campaigns into chivalric expeditions marks the point at which high Romanticism joins with the state in cloaking the activity of reciprocal injuring. As bodies disappear from the text of Romanticism (even imagined ones) so, too, does the chance of any realistic opposition to military activity.

It is for this reason that Geoff Quilley introduces us to another ambivalent presence in the representation of war: the body of the sailor. Like the soldier, the tar was widely portrayed in anti-war propaganda as an unwilling participant in his nation's cause, his body subject to impressment and crimping and thus a confirmation of the abuse of constitutional liberties (Bennett, 1976, p. 122). The mutiny at Spithead in 1796 confirmed the tar as a source of potential rebellion. In a popular song, reprinted in the *Morning Post* and the *Courier*, the mutineers are attended by 'The Genius of Britain' who rejoices in the seamen's devotion to 'Freedom'. It is clear, however, that the call for liberty is bounded by the sailor's 'Loyalty' to his country; the mutineers are acting in accordance with the traditional ideals of the commonwealth's-man and should not be identified with the threat of Jacobinism. But freedom of another kind was to taint the official view of the tar as Britain's valiant 'heart of oak' (Bennett, 1976, p. 294; pp. 434–5). Whilst conservative pundits gloated over the success of the fleet in the war against Napoleon, they were quick to remind their audiences of the sailor's reputation for drunkenness, violence and sexual excess (Bennett, 1976, pp. 436–7). As long as the tar remained overseas, his threat to the integrity of the body politic could be kept in check.

Quilley's representation of the ambivalent iconography of the British tar has as its verbal analogue the Wordsworthian encounter with fugitive seamen and discharged soldiers. What do these strange meetings signify, if not the return of the repressed? Consider, first of all, the role of the sailor in figuring the connection between culture and conflict in *Guilt and Sorrow; or, Incidents Upon Salisbury Plain* (1842; Wordsworth, 1975). In his book *Wordsworthian Errancies* (1995), David Collings argues that the sailor's crime evokes a deeper level of cultural violence, one that is repressed in the transition from a Hobbesian state of war to the civilized antagonism of the public sphere. War, as it is experienced in the revolutionary turmoil of the 1790s, is thus best understood as an expression of the failure of the state to substantiate the fiction of social unanimity. In this sense, war is profoundly invisible in so far as it nominates the failure point of all attempts to legitimize authority, including that of the self. For Wordsworth, war is precisely that which takes place on the borders of vision, disturbing the poet's affirmation of the stabilizing influence of nation and, crucially, of 'home'.

This much is shown in the incident involving the discharged soldier in book 4 of *The Prelude* (1805; Wordsworth, 1984). Wandering along the public way, the poet's 'self-possession' (l. 398) is checked by the sudden appearance of a 'ghastly' (l. 411) figure wrapt in 'solitude', uttering 'murmuring sounds' (ll. 418–31, *passim*); a double, no less, of the rootless would-be poet, William Wordsworth. When questioned, the soldier troubles the poet with his sublime indifference; the division between memory and feeling (ll. 477–8) runs against the conventional current of Wordsworthian doctrine, as outlined in the preface to *Lyrical Ballads* (first published in 1802). Here, the indifference of memory makes a mockery of the restitutive aims of emotion recollected in tranquillity. But more importantly, the soldier's realm of objectivity, of 'hardship, battle, [and] pestilence' (l. 471) remains stubbornly 'sublime' (l. 473), suggesting a level of experience that queries the progress of the originating consciousness to terminal self-consciousness. War is not blotted out in this vision, rather it returns to haunt the poem as its irreducible, impossible other, an effect of what the neo-Lacanian theorist Slavoj Žižek would call the Real: 'that which makes every articulated symbolic truth for ever "not all" ... [and] makes it impossible to "tell everything"' (1997, p. 216). If, like Conrad's Kurtz, the soldier has seen it all, he teases the poet with his possession of this unconveyable knowledge. And, in the end, it is this registering of 'the horror' – that which marks the end of civilization – that encourages the errant youth to make his way home. As Coleridge and Thelwall were also to realize, in the state of war the place of retirement is a covering fiction available only to those who withdraw from the arena of revolutionary debate.

Just as Wordsworth presents a darkly ironic reflection on the ontology of war, so Byron in his post-Waterloo writings speaks of its ethical considerations. What emerges in Simon Bainbridge's discussion of siege warfare in *The Siege of Corinth*, *The Deformed Transformed* and *Don Juan*, is the sense in which Byron's awareness of the pleasures of war – the Coleridgean desire to extinguish self in the service of another – adds conviction to his critique of its total impact. Rather oddly, Byron in his later poetry is not unlike the early Southey; at least in so far as his verse juxtaposes the brutal realities of war with its aesthetic representations by inquiring sardonically, as in *Don Juan* (1980–93, vol. 6), 'if a man's name in a *bulletin* / May make up for a *bullet in* his body?' (VII. 21). What makes Byron's verse appealing to contemporary critics is the way his writing consistently reflects on its own potential to revel in the intoxicating glamour of combat. No pacifist, as Tim Webb (1990) has argued, Byron knows that men engage in warfare because of its direct appeal to the death instinct. Hence the constant recourse to the equation of the martial and the erotic, to 'Fierce loves and faithless wars' (VII. 8). But if, in invoking the parallel of the taking of the town with the conquest of women, the poetry comes close to celebrating the very thing it would denounce, the reader is made aware that 'the use of force to attain either territory or the object of desire is destructive and self-defeating'. Again in common with Wordsworth, Byron attests to the way in which warfare emerges out of a desire to realise the unattainable.

If the official culture of what we might call, in the light of Rawlinson's suggestion, revolutionary and Napoleonic Britain seems preoccupied with the disturbing appeal of war, what then are we to make of those who maintain an anti-war or pacificist stance? It is Philip Shaw's contention, in his essay for this volume, that Byron's fascination with military power points towards a problem that resides at the heart of Romantic politics and aesthetics. By way of a close examination of Leigh Hunt's post-war writings, Shaw argues that the inability of liberal thinkers to produce a coherent response to the fall of Napoleon Bonaparte is a consequence of their failure to provide a rational alternative to the poetics of oppression. With Byron, Keats and Hazlitt predisposed to representations of politics that emphasize its violent and tragic aspects, the realization of a progressive alternative seems remote. But for Hunt, the way forward is clear: a revolution in society must be accompanied by a revolution in poetic language. Post-war society, that is, must overcome its fascination with the degraded and war-like forms of the Miltonic sublime and must learn instead to embrace Milton's lesser forms, chiefly the pastoral, the sonnet and the masque. That the ensuing history of Britain and, indeed, of British poetry does not, on the whole, follow Hunt's recommendations suggests that culture is more intimately connected with the spectacle of conflict than nineteenth-century liberalism and utilitarian pacificism would allow.

How, then, is culture to compose itself in the aftermath of war? One answer, supplied by Eric Walker in the final essay in this volume, is that peace is imagined as a restitution of the order that conflict destroys. If we begin with the premise that war contributes 'to the construction of domestic sphere ideology by building a myth of the (virtuous) public male warrior defending the (virtuous) female home' then the answer to the question, why war? is straightforward: 'To make the world safe for conjugality'. Given the expectations stored in this response to the absurdity of conflict one would expect the ensuing period of peace to be characterized by images of happy union, 'a matrimonial paradise regained'. Yet, as Walker goes on to state, post-war writing is notoriously 'antithalamic' in the sense that it is frequently 'perplexed, stymied, or otherwise balked by the nuptial'. The inscrutability of modern marriage, as presented in Wordsworth and Austen, arises therefore 'at precisely the moment when the conjugal myth fails to supply the justification for a war nominally fought to restore it as triumphant'. A war fought in the name of national unanimity has opened up a void in the social that the forms of cohesion – marriage in Austen, the clerisy in Coleridge, liberal constitutionalism in Hunt – may never fulfil.

Walker's reading of the depiction of marriage in post-war British culture returns this book to its origins in the destruction of familial relations that is the theme of the essays by Behrendt and Labbe. Without wishing to overstate the issue, one might claim that the restoration of war as a context within which to situate Romantic writing provides the impetus for a reconsideration of other matters, hitherto disregarded in studies of the period. In a recent essay, Jerome Christensen has suggested that the poetry written by Blake, Wordsworth, Coleridge and Southey, during most of the last decade of the eighteenth century and the first decade or so of the nineteenth, 'ought to be

named wartime poetry, for it was written under the threat of imminent invasion, during the state's emergency suspension of dailiness, amidst the din of
official exhortations to unity, and in the face of brutal and systematic repression' (1966, p. 603). Implicit, then, within Christensen's statement, is a
judgement concerning the efficacy of the literary-historical classification,
Romantic. By replacing the 'pure concept' of Romanticism (Perry, 1998, p.
3) with an empirical alternative, one that acknowledges the fact that writers
and artists did, indeed, respond to the pressures of war, the culture of the
period becomes open, once again, to constructive questioning. As these essays demonstrate, a focus on the imagining of conflict and its aftermath
enables us to reconfigure our understanding of a number of issues, from the
relation between private and public in wartime journalism, to the symbolization of the returning soldier in poetry and painting, or from the portrayal of
gender and sexuality in writing by women, to the significance of militarist
rhetoric in Romantic writing and contemporary criticism.

One final point. In an important reading of Carl von Clausewitz's *On War*
(first published in 1832), Jacqueline Rose suggests that the division between
the theory and practice of war 'corresponds to the philosophical opposition
between the ideal and the empirical ... It also reflects the clash between the
Enlightenment philosophy of war as reason and an emergent romanticism
which stresses the unique and singular instance, the place of the incalculable
and imaginative in the human mind' (1993, p. 28). Rose might have added
that it is precisely the clash between the totalizing understanding of the
Enlightenment and the new age's fascination with the exceptional, the contingent and the unquantifiable that constitutes the Romantic. Of course, Romantic
criticism has for some years now been vacillating between a desire for totalizing
theory (from Abrams to de Man) and a wish to recover the untheorized
primacy of empirical events (see Klancher, 1989). The conflict between these
respective schools constitutes, no doubt, the recent history of our own Romantic movement. But given that this is indeed the case, should we then
strive to speak from a position that is beyond this history? Writing in the
awareness that the 'attempt to theorize or master war, becomes a way of
perpetuating or repeating war itself' (Rose, 1993, p. 23), the contributors to
this volume would seek to distance themselves from all such claims to retro-
spective purity.

Bibliography

Abrams, M. H. (1971), *Natural Supernaturalism: Tradition and Revolution in
    Romantic Literature*, New York and London: Norton.
Bennett, B. (ed.) (1976), *British War Poetry in the Age of Romanticism:
    1793–1815*, New York and London: Garland.

Byron, G. G., Lord (1980–93), ed. McGann, J. J., *Lord Byron, Complete Poetical Works*, 7 vols, Oxford: Clarendon Press.

Ceadel, M. (1996), *The Origins of War Prevention: The British Peace Movement and International Relations, 1730–1854*, Oxford: Clarendon Press.

Christensen, J. (1996), 'The Detection of the Romantic Conspiracy in Britain', *South Atlantic Quarterly*, 95 (3).

Clausewitz, C. von (1986), trans. Graham, Col. J. J., ed. Rapoport, A., *On War*, Harmondsworth: Penguin Books.

Coleridge, S. T. (1969), ed. Coleridge, E. H., *Poetical Works*, Oxford and New York: Oxford University Press.

Collings, D. (1994), *Wordsworthian Errancies: The Poetics of Cultural Dismemberment*, Baltimore: Johns Hopkins Press.

De Paolo, C. (1985), 'Kant, Coleridge, and the Ethics of War', *Wordsworth Circle*, 16 (1).

Emsley, C. (1979), *British Society and the French Wars, 1793–1815*, London: Macmillan.

Favret, M. A. (1994), 'Coming Home: The Public Spaces of Romantic War', *Studies in Romanticism*, 33 (4).

Harvey, M. D. (ed.) (1986), *English Literature and the Great War with France: An Anthology and Commentary*, London: Croom Helm.

Jones, C. (1993), *Radical Sensibility: Literature and Ideas in the 1790s*, London and New York: Routledge.

Klancher, J. (1989), 'Romantic Criticism and the Meanings of the French Revolution', *Studies in Romanticism*, 28 (3).

Leask, N. (1988), *The Politics of Imagination in Coleridge's Critical Thought*, London: Macmillan.

Morrow, J. (1990), *Coleridge's Political Thought: Property, Morality, and the Limits of Traditional Discourse*, London: Macmillan.

Perry, S. (1998), 'Romanticism: The Brief History of a Concept', in Wu, D. (ed.), *A Companion to Romanticism*, Oxford: Blackwell.

Roe, N. (1988), *Wordsworth and Coleridge: The Radical Years*, Oxford: Oxford University Press.

Rose, J. (1993), 'Why War?', in Rose, J. (ed.), *Why War? Psychoanalysis, Politics, and the Return of Melanie Klein*, Oxford: Blackwell, pp. 15–40.

Scarry, E. (1985), *The Body in Pain: The Making and Unmaking of the World*, New York: Oxford University Press.

Shakespeare, W. (1992), ed. Hoy, C., *Hamlet*, New York and London: Norton.

Wang, O. N. C. (1994), 'Romancing the Counter-Public Sphere: A Response to Romanticism and its Publics', *Studies in Romanticism*, 33 (4).

Webb, T. (1990), 'Byron and the Heroic Syllables', *Keats–Shelley Review*, 5 Autumn.

Wordsworth, W. (1975), ed. Gill, S., *The Salisbury Plain Poems of William*

Wordsworth, Cornell Wordsworth Series, Ithaca and New York: Cornell University Press; Brighton: Harvester Press.

Wordsworth, W. (1984), ed. Gill, S., *The Oxford Authors: William Wordsworth*, Oxford and New York: Oxford University Press.

Worrall, D. (1992), *Radical Culture: Discourse, Resistance, and Surveillance, 1790–1820*, London: Harvester Wheatsheaf.

Žižek, S. (1997), *The Plague of Fantasies*, London and New York: Verso.

CHAPTER TWO

'A few harmless Numbers': British women poets and the climate of war, 1793–1815

Stephen C. Behrendt

If a maim'd soldier meets thy wand'ring eye,
Ne'er turn disgusted, but his wants supply;
Think how he lost his *limbs*, his *health*, his *home*;
Perhaps his *children*, to secure *thy own*!
    Catherine Upton, *The Siege of Gibraltar* (1781)[1]

My epigraph predates the period with which I shall be concerned in this essay, as does the military action it commemorates. What remained true throughout the years of warfare against revolutionary and Napoleonic France, however, was the plight of the veteran and his family – to which Upton alludes already in 1781 – which often resulted in the decimation of that family. The casualties of war are not to be reckoned simply by a body-count of the fallen, therefore, nor even by the larger numbers of wounded who subsequently perish, whether in field hospitals, back home, or somewhere between. Nor is the full story told even when we add the number who succumb to disease or mischance. Chastening as these numbers unquestionably are, the full scope of the disaster only becomes apparent when we consider also the immediate families of the wartime dead and when we contemplate the effect of these numbers (and the real people they represent) upon actual communities. The individual conflict – and the killing it involves – marks only the most central of the rings of social, political and economic impact that radiate out from that point of origin. This essay examines some of these rings, but it does so within the context of poetry written and published by British women during the period of the French revolutionary and Napoleonic conflicts, a period during which 'war was the single most important fact of British life' (Bennett 1976, p. ix).[2] It does so, moreover, with an appreciation that the stuff of poetry is not necessarily the stuff of historical fact, or vice versa. I do not mean to suggest that these women wrote exclusively – or even primarily – about war and its effects: they did not. At the same time, though, poetry (and art in general) is often a good indicator of both cultural assumptions and individual experience during periods of crisis, when broadly-shared preoccupations reveal themselves repeatedly in the artifacts of culture, including literature. That being so, we may reasonably expect a look at this limited body of poetry to reveal something about the nature both of the experience of women in particular and of the nation generally, in light of the protracted conflict in which England found itself in the aftermath of the French Revolution.

This essay examines what was unique both about the women poets' perspective on war and about the circumstances of their authorship and publication.[3] It must be noted immediately that few women wrote either a great deal about the war or engaged in explicit criticism of the war effort. Even those whose associations with radical and anti-war associations are known tended to be circumspect and indirect in their approach to the subject – and for very good reason. For even though by 1793 women were firmly-established members of the literary community – widely published and widely read – their gender still exposed them to anti-feminist attacks like those in T. J. Mathias's *Pursuits of Literature* (1794–97) and Richard Polwhele's *The Unsex'd Females* (1798), which used politics as a pretext for attacking women's literary and intellectual activities. More important, though, women historically were rendered particularly vulnerable by their legal dependence upon men – husbands, sons, fathers, brothers – for their social and financial welfare. For a woman to engage in explicit anti-war writing was as dangerous economically and socially as it was politically; left 'on her own', her known public stance could result in the denial of even minimal assistance, which she might otherwise receive, from a community prone to reading into her misfortune divine retribution for her 'disloyalty'. This meant that the women poets typically stressed the suffering inflicted upon individuals (and their families) by war-making, concentrating on sentiment and pathos to carry their argument against not this particular war, but rather against war in general. Thus, as we shall see, when Christian Gray relates the tragic history of the generically named Julia and Alexis who are ruined by war, the situation itself is sufficiently familiar to ensure that readers can easily substitute for Gray's unfortunate lovers the names of others in their own communities. The same is true of poems by Anne Hunter, Isabella Lickbarrow, Mary Leadbeater and Amelia Opie, all of whose poems invite their readers to recognize in them the outlines of other 'actual' stories located within each reader's personal experience. In other words, these poets frequently adapt for their own rhetorical purposes in their poems the trope of the nation-family to emphasize by analogy how the devastation of the family parallels the inevitable destruction of the state.

Let me begin by sketching some of the demographic context for the detailed examination of the poetry that follows. First, the numbers. It is never easy to establish precise demographics, even in our own times; culling reliable information for a moment some two centuries ago is even more difficult. But we need a sense at the outset of the numbers involved on England's side in the conflict with France (and indeed with others), in order to situate more accurately the sort of things that the poems tell us. When war was declared in 1793, England was ending a period of military engagement that had included the Seven Years War and, more recently, the war with the American colonies. Although hostilities in the latter ceased in 1781, the effects continued to be felt, both in economic terms and in human ones, well into the 1790s. This was one reason why there was considerable resistance in many quarters to a renewed engagement with France, especially when that new conflict seemed to many to represent, like the recent American one, a struggle against those who were essentially in search of liberty, however defined. As the egalitarian principles of the French Revolution gave way increasingly to the imperialist aspirations of the Napoleonic period, the initially mixed response of the 1790s began to give way to greater solidarity with British aims (and British nationalism) after the collapse of the Peace of Amiens and the subsequent coronation of Napoleon as Emperor, which provided both official and sym- bolic verification of his totalitarian ambitions. By the time of the Peninsular campaign, women poets like Felicia Hemans were not only extolling the virtues of dashing soldiers ('That gallant band, in countless danger try'd') waging war against empire-builders, but they were in fact marrying them.[4]

England's military preparedness at the outbreak of war with France in February 1793 was questionable at best.[5] While the navy had been expanded by some thirty ships of the line in the previous ten years, and ample stores had been stockpiled to provision them once sailors had been recruited (or impressed) to man them, the army was in sad shape. Its small force of 50,000 was ill-equipped and even worse trained. Half of this number was needed for domestic garrison and police duties, and most of the rest was scattered widely throughout the empire. Mercenaries were again employed, as they had been in the campaign against the American colonies: 14,000 Hanoverians and 8000 Hessians were put on army payrolls to augment the British force, which as late as the beginning of the Duke of York's incompetent campaign in Flanders in April 1793 still included only some 7000 native British soldiers, many of them actually too young or too old for active service. When this motley force, expanded by the often unreliable mercenaries, was finally hunted into Bremen by the French General Pichegru after he had defeated the Allies at Fleurus, the relatively small number of men actually killed in action was augmented to such an extent by the numbers who perished on account of unsanitary conditions on the fields and in the field hospitals in the particu- larly brutal winter of 1793–94, that the British populace learned that those 'killed or dead in service' numbered an astonishing 18,596. While no British forces landed on the Continent during the next four years, they were de- ployed elsewhere, as we shall see.

By 1801, in spite of the losses it had sustained in the West Indies and elsewhere, the army had reached a force of some 150,000. When the Peace of

Amiens was signed in 1802, however, Britain reduced its regular army to some 40,000 men, an action which the nation rued when the war's resumption in 1803 made it necessary abruptly to mobilize a whole new armed force. That Napoleon seemed about to invade England made it somewhat easier for the government to muster support to defend the native shores, in part by mounting a remarkably successful alarmist campaign, so that by 1804 England had in place some 75,000 regular infantry, 12,000 regular cavalry, 80,000 militia, and 343,000 yeomanry and volunteers. This last large number were essentially for local 'home defence', however, and not intended for actual service in the theatre of war. Still, this left a total of roughly 167,000 men, of whom 87,000 were soldiers of the line available specifically for the Continental conflict. It has been estimated that in 1804 as many as 20 per cent of all adult males were serving either in the regular army or in one of the other defence forces, including the volunteers (Christie, 1991, p. 170).

But England's was a global military presence, not just a localized one. By 1809 (the year of the ignominious Convention of Cintra that marked for many the nadir of British military competence) nearly 700,000 soldiers served Britain. The garrison for the United Kingdom alone comprised some 108,000 regular infantry and cavalry, along with 65,000 militia, 200,000 local militia and 190,000 volunteers. Some 110,000 troops served abroad, including some 22,000 each in the Mediterranean and the West Indies, 24,000 in India and an additional 4000 in Ceylon, 8000 in North America, 6000 at the Cape of Good Hope (to safeguard this strategic point on the route to India) and 900 in Madeira. An additional 1300 fighting men were required to guard the penal colonies in New South Wales (Australia). Finally, the troops at sea (who represented both artillery and the corps of engineers) accounted for an additional 18,000, while the expeditionary army in Portugal was made up of some 22,000 more. By 1814, the regular troops and foreign and colonial troops together numbered more than a quarter of a million.

This is the picture of the army. The navy represents yet another set of numbers. At the outset of the war with France, in February 1793, the total number of seamen and marines, including officers of all ranks, was some 45,000. By October 1801, on the eve of the signing of the Treaty of Amiens, the number had swollen to approximately 135,000. By the end of 1803, when hostilities resumed, the total number had dropped to about 100,000, and when the war ended in 1815 it was 90,000. But the intervening years saw considerable fluctuations. When the fledgling United States entered the scene in the war of 1812, for instance, the number reached some 145,000.

Numbers and statistics like these have an inevitable sanitizing (and perhaps anaesthetizing) effect, for they permit us to avert our eyes from the ruined faces and bodies of the participants and see only the depersonalizing curtain of numbers. We are spared the actuality, the individual persons these numbers represent: Private William Wheeler of the 51st Battalion (who survived), Sergeant John Donaldson (the Scot who served with Wellington in the Peninsular campaign and whose memoirs offer a picture of army life), the young rifleman John Harris who in an extraordinary gesture of pity proposed to the widow of his close friend Cochran who had perished in battle, or the unfortunate Duncan Stewart. Stewart, another Scot, enlisted after being made drunk by a recruiting party; his wife Mary, who was in an advanced stage of pregnancy, was sent for but when she arrived she learned that she would not be permitted to accompany her husband. The traumatic separation that followed brought on labour, and mother and child both died. Crushed, Stewart sailed with his regiment and was one of the first of that unit to die in action (Gleig, 1825, pp. 9–19; see also Harris, 1928 and Wheeler, 1952). Tales of this sort were rich sources for poets and prose writers alike, who could capitalize on their pathos precisely because by the time of Waterloo there were few Britons who were not acquainted with stories of this sort. Not the stuff merely of sentimental writing that could be confined to the exercise of the imagination, war was the defining reality of British life, and its victims were real people who suffered and died in remarkable numbers.

The devastation wrought by the death abroad of husbands, sons, fathers and brothers was naturally a common theme among women writers, who appreciated especially well the precarious social and economic situation which such deaths inevitably precipitated.[6] The plight of these victims of war would now be traced in large part by women writers, who no longer represented the higher classes (as the bluestockings had done), but who instead embodied the voices of the middle and lower classes, and whose themes therefore reflect mundane, quotidian realities (Ross, 1989, p. 192). Not surprisingly, many poets adopted the sentimental mode in mounting an implicit appeal to shared experience. Writing after Waterloo, for instance, Charlotte Richardson deftly juxtaposes in a poem called 'To-Morrow' the external concord produced by the war's end and the conflict that continues for women who have lost the men dearest to them:

> Soft Peace our happy land had blest,
>   And Britain's gallant Sons returning,
> Each clasp'd some fav'rite to his breast,
>   And fondly hush'd the voice of mourning.
> When lovely Anna, hapless maid!
>   Thus pour'd the melting strain of sorrow,
> 'My Edward, may thy gentle shade
>   'Direct my wand'ring steps to-morrow.'
>
> The morn that calls a world to joy,
>   With grateful sounds of triumph swelling,
> Shall see the wretched Anna fly
>   Far distant from her peaceful dwelling.
> I'll seek the turf that Edward prest,
>   There sigh my last adieu to sorrow,

And pillow'd on his clay-cold breast,
  We'll wake in happier scenes to-morrow.
          (Richardson, 1818, pp. 88–9)

Brief as it is, this poignant poem nevertheless reflects how the deaths of loved ones transformed the domestic scene – the traditional site of tranquillity – into a site of intolerable anguish. The new morning, filled with 'grateful sounds of triumph', is more than Anna can bear; it drives her from 'her peaceful dwelling'. For Anna there is no returning soldier to hush 'the voice of mourning' by the happy fact of his survival. Her empty arms share no embrace. Anna's recourse is to leave both 'her peaceful dwelling' and the British nation for which it stands as symbol, and to seek the foreign – and therefore inherently alien – 'turf that Edward prest'. Unlike the women in the reunited couples whose temporary sorrow is dispelled by actual, physical embraces, Anna can dispel her sorrow only by embracing the earth with which Edward is symbolically and semantically merged in the penultimate line's figure of 'his clay-cold breast'. Life is intolerable for Anna without the living, breathing Edward, and the final line implies that the distraught woman will join the dead Edward in death, whether by suicide (the unstated but clear suggestion) or as a result of a fatal overflow of grief precipitated by her locating Edward's grave. For Anna, only death holds the possibility of happiness. This is not mere hyperbole, however, but a representation of human grieving that is both culturally and emotionally recognizable for many in our own time – just as it would, of course, have been for Richardson's readers.

   Comparable social and psychological extremity figures in 'Lines Written at Norwich on the First News of the Peace', which appeared in Amelia Opie's *Poems* of 1802 (pp. 81–6), and which employs the simple, accessible and egalitarian ballad stanza that in the 1790s had become a favourite choice for poems of social consciousness and social protest. The peace in this case is that which was signalled by the Treaty of Amiens; as in the later Richardson poem, that cessation of hostilities produces joy for those who are reunited with their male loved ones whose lives are now seemingly spared:

And you, fond parents, faithful wives,
Who've long for sons and husbands feared,
Peace now shall save their precious lives;
They come by danger more endeared.
          (ll. 29–32)

Peace here participates in the action, literally saving the lives of these returning warriors. But peace is not universally benevolent, nor of course could it be, for war has exacted its grisly toll. Thus, for the one 'shrunk form' (l. 34) who appears amid the public general rejoicing there is neither joy nor peace. This 'poor mourner' declares in her own voice 'Alas! Peace comes for me too late … / For my brave boy in Egypt died!' (ll. 39–40). Only a year earlier, the Egyptian expeditionary campaign under Sir Ralph Abercrombie that routed

the French forces from Egypt had resulted in 650 deaths at the Battle of
Aboukir Bay (7 March 1801) and another 1500 (including Abercrombie
himself) two weeks later at the Battle of Alexandria (21 March). These losses
were still fresh in the public mind when the Peace of Amiens was signed in
1802, and Opie's poem effectively reveals the particular bitterness that en-
sues when one's son (in this instance) is lost so near what seems to be the
resumption of peace. The first line spoken by the bereaved woman says it all:
'Talk not of Peace ... the sound I hate' (l. 37).

This bitter and largely inconsolable grief characterizes much of British
writing of the war years. We recognize these elements, for instance, in Mary
Darby Robinson's 'The Widow's Home', which appeared in her *Lyrical Tales*
(1800), in Mary Leadbeater's 1808 poem, 'The Widow' (*Poems*, 1808), and
in Dorothea Primrose Campbell's 'The Distracted Mother' (another lament
for a son killed in battle) and her 'The Soldier's Widow, at the Grave of Her
Only Child' (which poem records the double tragedy of two losses), both of
which appeared in her *Poems* of 1816. The latter poem was written before
Campbell was seventeen and published in an effort to aid her own family, of
which she was the eldest child.[7] In it, her speaker deplores the uselessness of
summer to one whose

> world is yonder little grave,
> My all its narrow space;
> My only Child reposes there,
> Lock'd in Death's cold embrace.
> (ll. 13–16)

Somewhat surprisingly, when it comes to mourning her lost husband the
speaker seems to take death in war as a given and does not wish him alive
again, but instead only buried near their child:

> Why didst thou go, my only love,
>   The bloody war to wage?
>
> Bless'd had I been had'st thou repos'd
>   Beside our infant son;
> Not buried in a field of strife,
>   Where bloody deeds were done.
> (ll. 39–44)

This resignation in the face of bereavement reflects one strategy – however
inadequate it may have been in individual instances – for coping with the
seemingly endless cycle of killing and the social dysfunction it was producing on every side. The question in Campbell's lines was framed by many
women speakers in the poetry written throughout the period. It features, for
instance, in Elizabeth Moody's 'Anna's Complaint':

> Ah, William! Wherefore didst thou go
> To foreign lands to meet the foe?

> Why, won by war's deceitful charms,
> Didst thou forsake thy Anna's arms?[8]

We shall return to Moody shortly.

In the meantime, Mary Leadbeater's poem, like Richardson's, treats the compound distress produced by a slow, lingering death far from the attentions of the widowed spouse:

> 'Nine days the mortal wound thou bore,
>   'And Death with Nature strove;
> 'And I was on this distant shore,
>   'Thou husband of my love.
>
> 'Denied to me each sacred rite
>   'Of mourning love to pay;
> 'Denied to me the last sad sight: –
> 'Oh! thou wert far away. –
>   (ll. 1–8)

Leadbeater's speaker laments the deceptive illusion of security held out to those who thought their role in the militia or the volunteers would keep them on English soil:

> 'Why did he trust the promise vain,
>   'That he should *here* abide;
> 'Should stay to guard his native plain,
> 'And guard his hapless bride?
>   (ll. 21–4)

They are betrayed by their own government 'who honour's just demand / So lightly can forego, / Who tear him from his native land' (ll. 25–7). She recounts how she gave birth in his absence to a child, and how she is now driven obsessively to journey to India, having sold the 'garments fair' he had left for her to sell to support herself in his absence (ll. 73–4) and having parted even with his 'watch of silver fine' which he had admonished her to keep until the last necessity (ll. 77–80). Now she is left to mourn from afar her husband who fell at the Bay of Bengal during the Indian campaign, 'On Coromandel's coast; / When Cuddolore the force withstood / Of Britain's warlike host' (ll. 114–16).

This poem raises the issue of the global nature of Britain's military involvements during this period. While the situation in India had begun to stabilize somewhat, for instance, Holland's fall to the French required military engagements to wrest from French control the former Dutch positions in Ceylon and the Cape of Good Hope, the primary staging points on the route to India. Then there was the Egyptian campaign mentioned above, as well as the considerable activity in the West Indies to which destination some 35,000 soldiers were sent between August 1795 and May 1796, and where engagements under difficult tropical conditions likewise played havoc with the troops.[9] Despite British military successes in the West Indies and elsewhere outside the Continent, the human toll was terrific. In the eight years between war's outbreak and the Peace of Amiens, for instance, England sent some 89,000 officers and men to the Caribbean and lost approximately 70 per cent of them (Mackesy, 1989, p, 160). The years 1795–96 alone saw more than 40,000 fighting men discharged as a result of wounds, disease and infirmity, and plain mishap (Traill and Mann, 1914, vol. 5, p. 526). One such victim is recounted in Anne Hunter's two-part ballad 'The Song at Maria's Grave', which poem, significantly, concludes Hunter's 1802 collection (pp. 114–22). Like so many of the poems couched in the sentimental vein, this one centres upon the demise of its female sufferer in the wake of her beloved's death; her 'charms exist no more', we are told, and 'soon their memory shall cease' (ll. 11–12). And although we are told that the poem is 'founded on a true story' that 'took place in 1785, or near about that time' (according to Hunter's footnote, p. 122), its obvious continued relevance in 1802 is underscored by the poem's placement as the final text in Hunter's volume.

Falling prey to the seductive illusion of glory in war, Henry 'Resolv'd to dare the hostile wave':

> Dauntless to see his country's foes,
>   And bravely to guard her injur'd rights,
> Warm from the heart his courage flows,
> For love and honour Henry fights.
>   (ll. 32–6)

We learn that although 'Long absent on the wat'ry waste', Henry was successful at sea: 'vanquish'd foes his fame increas'd, / While with his fame his fortune grew' (ll. 57–60). Indeed, his last letter to Maria ominously tempts fate in the confidence with which he declares that

> 'For thee I live, for thee could die.
> 'For thy dear sake I still pursue
>   Unceasing toils, and think them sweet;
> For now the time appears in view,
>   When we again shall meet.
> 'Fly fast, ye hours! With winged haste,
>   Propitious gales, come waft me o'er!
> Swift let me cross the wat'ry waste,
> To meet my love! and part no more!'
>   (ll. 76–84)

The second part of Hunter's poem intimates the inevitable:

> Gay, glitt'ring hope! How bright you seem,
>   Gilding some joy beyond the hour!
> A painted cloud, a fairy dream,
>   A rainbow in a summer's shower.

> Sudden distracting terrors rise,
>   Unthought-of ills their hopes assail;
> A dark and dreadful rumour flies,
> And time confirms the horrid tale.
>
> (ll. 93–100)

Not surprisingly, the winds prove anything but propitious, and Henry's vessel is wrecked in a terrible storm that 'rises on the water's roar, / And death and desolation brings' as the inevitable result of 'The warring elements at strife' (ll. 105–9). In an ironic turn on the theme of war, Hunter makes Henry the immediate victim not of warring armies, but rather of warring elements, though his fatal attraction for the former is what has placed him at the mercy of the latter.

The deadly burden of all this worldwide war-making fell with particular devastation upon those least able to cope with it: the poor.[10] For many, going to war (on land or on the sea) offered a small and temporary financial opportunity for the family, in the form of the enlistment bonus that was variously offered over the course of the war years, and some veterans were able to parley their war experiences into further profit by publishing memoirs and the like. But these were the exceptions, for those who participated in the wars experienced on the whole little benefit to outweigh the often fearsome losses they and their families sustained (Emsley, 1979). Even when the deplorable circumstances of returning British soldiers and seamen (and their families) brought about passage in 1795 and 1796 of legislation that allowed military men to allocate some of their wages directly to their families, usually that money was still woefully inadequate to their needs, especially when foul weather forced severe price rises (a fact that informs poems like Wordsworth's 'The Female Vagrant', published in 1798 in *Lyrical Ballads*). The aforementioned enlistment bounty figures in the work of many other poets; among canonical male poets, for instance, Wordsworth mentions it in 'The Ruined Cottage'. The meagre bonus is of little use, ultimately, when its recipient is killed, wounded or otherwise incapacitated. Nor, for that matter, was it even relevant (since it was never paid) to the families of the countless men who fell victim to the ruthless press-gangs, leaving their families both impoverished and often ignorant even of the men's fate.[11] Therefore, many writers turned to the theme of philanthropy, and to appeals to the wealthy and powerful to assist the less fortunate.

Such an appeal appears in Isabella Lickbarrow's 'Written after the News of a Battle' (quoted entire):

> Pale lamp of night, on this low world
>   How canst thou look so wond'rous fair?
> How canst thou on its horrors smile,
>   Its scenes of misery and despair?
>
> Thou shin'st on many a lowly cot,
>   Where widow'd mothers wake to weep,

And wearied nature vainly tries
  To lose awhile its woes in sleep –

Thou seest full many a soldier brave,
  Expiring on the field of death,
Imploring mercy for his babe
  And widow with his latest breath.

Oh! turn thee from the dreadful plains
  Where Europe's sons unburied lie,
The view would thy pale lustre stain,
  And give thy beams a crimson dye.

Ye sons of wealth! On beds of down
  Who undisturb'd by grief repose,
Pity the fallen soldier's child,
  Pity his friendless widow's woes.
                              (1814, pp. 106–7)

Lickbarrow exploits for all its sentimental effect the haunting image of the moon shining on the uncollected dead who litter the battlefield after combat ceases. Interestingly, her pity extends not just to the British dead but to all of 'Europe's sons', all of whom the last stanza invites the reader to regard as the victims (in death as in life) of the 'sons of wealth' for whose political, ideological and economic interests protracted wars seem perpetually to be fought, largely at the expense of the common soldiers and sailors for whose fate no grief disturbs the well-to-do. This concern reflects a common theme in anti-war discourse: the war is being conducted by 'an aristocratic class indifferent to the suffering of the poor' (Bennett, 1976, p. 13). The point was apparent early on in the stark dualisms that drive Mary Darby Robinson's 'January, 1795':

Pavement slipp'ry; People sneezing;
Lords in ermine; beggars freezing;
Nobles, scarce the Wretched heeding;
Gallant soldiers – fighting! – bleeding!
                              (ll. 1–4)[12]

This dualism – and the hostility toward the privileged it reflects – is never far from the surface in poetry on the war, by men as well as by women.

For all her ostensible concern for the less powerful, the less privileged, expressed in 'Written after the News of a Battle', Lickbarrow was nevertheless a thoroughgoing nationalist, as is apparent from her 'Invocation to Peace'. Lickbarrow expects that the war's end will leave England as the undisputed moral and economic leader of post-Napoleonic Europe:

Oh come! on Albion's plains for ever dwell,
Thy sacred temple let our island be,
Then arts and manufactures would revive,

And happy Industry rejoice again;
Then friendly Commerce would unfurl her sails,
No hostile natives arm'd with bolts of death,
Would meet in dreadful conflict on the deep,
But freighted vessels, laden with the fruits
Of ev'ry varied clime, would crowd our ports

(ll. 31–8)

The universalized appeal for pity and compassion for all of war's victims – as opposed to a strictly nationalistic focus on England only – figures in other poems written by women during the period. It reflects, among other things, the difficult rhetorical situation in which anti-war writers found themselves. Loyalist sentiment was predominant for most of the period, stoked by England's historical antipathy toward France. Rather than protest the war's objectives, therefore, anti-war writers tapped the widespread hostility to yet another bloody and protracted war by stressing that war's terrible consequences for individual citizens and family units. In this way, they were able to rhetorically and symbolically align the experiences of the family with those of the nation-state, and to argue by analogy that the destruction of the former is inextricably linked to the erosion of the latter. Relevant here is Anne Mellor's observation that what she calls 'feminine romanticism' constructs upon the trope of the 'family politic' an image of a nation-state 'that evolves gradually and rationally under the mutual care and guidance of both mother and father' (1993, p. 65). Nothing is more destructive to this healthy partnership, of course, than protracted and bloody war, which devastates the family and enervates the nation. The point was made brilliantly by Anna Letitia Barbauld in her controversial long poem *Eighteen Hundred and Eleven*, which foresees the decay of a Britain whose stature and influence have been eclipsed by America (Behrendt, 1997).

Perhaps nowhere does the strategy of universalizing the experiences of war figure so fully as in the extraordinary poems of Elizabeth Moody. Little seems to be known about Moody, whose unmarried name was Greenly, who seems to have been married to a clergyman, died in 1814, and reviewed for the *Monthly Review* between 1789 and 1808 (*Feminist Companion*, 1990). This last fact is interesting, however, in light of the policy of Ralph Griffiths (editor from 1749 to 1803) of hiring a staff of experts to review books in their particular fields (Sullivan, 1983, p. 233). The *Monthly Review*'s identifiably Whig and dissenting orientation seems like a good 'fit' for Moody, whose poems offer some of the strongest – and best-written – moral and intellectual opposition not just to England's war with France but to war generally.

In her preface to *Poetic Trifles* (1798) Moody writes, 'I am well aware that this is no period favourable to the Muse', 'when the monster WAR is sounding his terrific alarms; – when the spirit of discord is in the air, and pervades every Atmosphere, – when it not only stimulates the combatants in the field of *battle*, but in the field of *Literature*, – when the fiend POLITICS is sharpening the pen to make it a two-edged sword'. 'How I presume to ask,' she continues, 'may the compilation of a few harmless Numbers be expected to engage the public attention?' (pp. i–ii). In the context of the remarkable numbers involved in the war effort – cited earlier in this essay – Moody's phrase, 'the compilation of a few harmless Numbers', assumes a special poignance beyond the irony the poet intended.

While the rest of Moody's preface in fact appears self-deprecating – and engagingly witty – in the fashion of later eighteenth-century prefaces (especially by women), there is no escaping the fact that a collection that begins (as *Poetic Trifles* does) with the frankly contestatory poem 'Thoughts on War and Peace' is unlikely to have been viewed as either inoffensive or 'harmless'. The poem goes directly to the moral issue of European militarism generally in the age of deepening nationalism:

> But chief in Europe flow'd, and ever flows,
> The baneful current of war's crimson tide:
> Where despots heedless of a nation's woes,
> Unsheathe the sword to guard the regal pride.
>
> Trophies of victory surround the throne;
> Monarchs survey them with deluded eyes;
> Lost is the pageant in the people's groan;
> Humanity before ambition flies.
>   (ll. 21–8)

As always, it is not the mighty but the humble who suffer most, for it is they whose meagre lot makes their losses the more dramatic, unbearable and irreversible, especially when severe food shortages follow crop failures as they did in 1794–96 and 1799–1801:

> When Rapine's cruel unrelenting hand,
> Beggars the tenant of each little field;
> Bids the poor cottager resign his land,
> And his reap'd harvest to a stranger yield.
>
> Bids hostile troops invade the cultur'd soil,
> And desperate steeds o'erwhelm the bearded grain,
> Rend'ring abortive agriculture's toil,
> And vain the labours of the peasant train.
>   (ll. 49–56)

Renouncing this woeful vision, Moody calls upon her muse now to 'Reverse thy theme to images of Peace, / And let her scenes contrast the scenes of woe' (ll. 67–8). This rosier prospect reveals for Moody, as it would for Lickbarrow in 1814, a flourishing 'Commerce' (appropriately and allegorically capitalized) reinforced by a burgeoning sea trade and a regenerated agriculture ('Her fertile valleys destin'd now no more / To feed the robber and entomb the slain'; ll. 87–8). Swords are exchanged for ploughshares, if not actually fashioned into them:

> Her sons now lab'rers of the peaceful field,
> The fearful instruments of War resign;
> More pleas'd the tools of husbandry to wield,
> Than on their brows the sanguine wreath to twine.
> (ll. 89–92)

In short, England is transformed under the aegis of this new peace, and it is interesting to note the twin guides that Moody sets up to direct this new and humane traffic:

> Britain shall rise in new refulgent day,
> And brightest rays on her horizon shine;
> Morals reform'd shall rule with milder sway;
> And Genius all her schools of art refine.
> (ll. 93–6)

Morals and Genius: the moral/spiritual/ethical life and the spark of inspiration that both reflects and builds upon that foundation; the two interpenetrate inseparably in Moody's formulation. The clear implication is that these are precisely the qualities that are absent in the state of war, which explains why war is, by definition, inhumane.

'Anna's Complaint; or, The Miseries of War; written in the Isle of Thanet, 1794' is interesting on several accounts, including its foreshadowing already in 1794 of themes and preoccupations that characterized much of the writing on the war for the following two decades. As noted earlier, Moody's poem details Anna's grief over the death in war of her beloved William. The poem is shrewdly insightful about the seductive nature of war and the nationalistic jingoism through which it is popularized among the people:

> Alas! full little didst thou know,
> The monster war doth falsely show;
> He decks his form with pleasing art,
> And hides the daggers in his heart.
>
> The music of his martial band,
> The shining halberd in his hand;
> The feather'd helmet on his head,
> And coat so fine of flaming red.
>
> With these the simple youth he gains,
> And tempts him from his peaceful plains;
> And by this pomp was William led,
> The dangerous paths of war to tread.
> (ll. 17–28)

'War' cannot do all this alone, however; the powerful, the influential, and the greedy are all complicitous in the deadly seduction of the innocent, the idealistic, the gullible:

Fair-sounding words my love deceiv'd
The great ones talk'd, and he believ'd,
That war would fame and treasure bring,
That glory call'd to serve the king.

                                                    (ll. 29–32)

How many believers were disabused of their illusions may be seen by the
rolls of casualties for the next twenty-plus years, by the numbers of displaced, dispossessed and indigent citizens (widowed or otherwise), and by
the haunting images of physically and emotionally maimed individuals (men
and women alike, but especially men) who people the widely circulated and
grim war caricatures by artists like Gillray, Woodward, Heath and Cruikshank
in the succeeding years. These pictures especially, like Cruikshank's *He
Would Be a Soldier* (1793) or Gillray's *John Bull's Progress* (1793; figure
2.1) make visible for a popular audience images that would become ever
more common in England as the human wreckage of war accumulated everywhere. Still, Elizabeth Moody's increasing anti-Gallicanism, visible in an
anti-Napoleonic poem like 'On Hearing that Buonaparte was landed in Egypt',
mirrors that of many her fellow citizens (including canonical male poets like
Coleridge and Wordsworth). As the war proceeded and the ferocity of the
French regimes became increasingly apparent, direct criticism of the British
government (and the motives that inspired it) diminished, while resistance to
war on principle became ever less relevant as the issue seemed increasingly
to be the survival of England.

The note struck by Moody about war's seductive veneer of glory was
echoed later by Anne Hunter in a brief song called 'The Farewell' from her
Poems of 1802:

Far from hope, and lost to pleasure,
    Haste away to war's alarms!
Sad I leave my soul's dear treasure
    For the dismal din of arms.

But, ah! for thee, I follow glory,
    To gain thy love I dare to die;
And when my comrades tell my story,
    Thou shalt lament me with a sigh.

All my griefs will then be over,
    Sunk in death's eternal rest:
You may regret a faithful lover,
    Though you refuse to make him bless'd.

Bestow a tear of kind compassion
    To grace a hapless soldier's tomb;
And, ah! forgive a fatal passion,
    Which reason could not overcome.

2.1 James Gillray, *John Bull's Progress* (3 June 1793), engraving, each section 140 × 185.

The ending of the third stanza suggests that this is the posthumous song of a jilted (or simply refused) suitor who foolishly went off to war to impress the woman who had scorned him. Was his dare worth the cost, one wonders? Or does he hope in death to secure through guilt the woman whose heart he could not turn in affection? The self-indulgent tone of most of the poem (particularly the melodramatic third stanza) is nicely countered by the astringent final stanza, rich with puns and double meanings. Is the soldier hapless – unfortunate – because of his failed romance or because of his misfortune in dying in war? Or is he hapless because he leaped into war without considering its reality, its dangers? Likewise, is the 'fatal passion' what he felt for the woman, or what he believed about the glory to be won in war? The (deliberately) ambiguous final line leaves the ending 'open' and multi-stable: whether it was his love for the woman, his illusions about the war, or the irrational train of thought that led him from the former to the latter, its imperviousness to the sobering influence of reason did, indeed, prove fatal.

The reality of war and its consequences, even when filtered through the vehicle of sentimental fiction, was unquestionably terrible, and perhaps all the more so for its awful familiarity. Barbara Hofland published a series of Minerva Press novels about broken families struggling (often with surprising success) to survive the loss of the male head of the family. Perhaps none bears such topical relevance as *The History of an Officer's Widow, and Her Young Family*, published in 1809 and reprinted frequently. In this tale the young husband and father of five, Captain Charles Belfield, is ordered (presumably in 1794) 'to join the ill-fated expedition to Holland', where he is wounded. His wife, Maria, travels to Whitby to meet him on his return, only to find a dying wreck typical of the many wounded who returned home only to perish:

> Having been wounded early in the engagement, and fainted through loss of blood, his wounds had been wholly overlooked, and he had lain for many hours on the sea-sands, exposed to the heat of the mid-day sun, and afterwards the chilling sea-breeze. He had afterwards crawled to a cottage, where he was denied even a drop of water to allay the feverish thirst which preyed upon him, or a rag to defend his smarting wounds from the midnight air. At length his wearied limbs lost their power of motion, and he fell on the ground in the forlorn hope of soon terminating his sufferings by death.

Rescued temporarily by a poor woman who tends him 'in despite of her own poverty, and the malice of her neighbors', he revives sufficiently to escape by sea.

> But here again misfortune pursued: he was tempest-tost, and obliged, notwithstanding his exhausted state, to work so hard upon the water, that his strength was entirely exhausted, and all that remained of hope was, to see his wife and die.

> (Hofland, 1846, pp. 25–8)

For countless British women and children during these years, this account was more fact than fiction.

Indeed, war's fatal consequences are nowhere presented with more pathos than in the poem called 'The Victims of War', published in 1811 by the blind poet Christian Gray. Her long poem traces the history of Julia and her young lover Alexis, a rural pair whose love cannot survive war's horrors. When Alexis is ordered to enlist ('The lord of the manor commands, I obey'; l. 61), Julia, who has previously pretended indifference to him, now weeps at the prospect of what may come and resolves to accompany him ('And if, far from his dear native land, / He must sail to the Continent, face the dread foe, / Then to share his every danger shall Julia go'; ll. 72–4). This course of action was not unusual, especially in the years after 1800, when surprising numbers of women (and even children) accompanied their husbands to war.[13] In Wellington's army, for example, while the number of wives was nominally restricted to six per hundred men, chosen by lot, others occasionally managed to join the party in one way or another, and they were normally allowed to move forward with the army (though they were expected to stay with the baggage so as not to become involved in the fighting), rather than being billeted behind (Page, 1986, pp. 17, 27, 49 and *passim*). After battles, however, women frequently wandered amid the carnage, searching for their loved ones. One such scene at the Battle of Nivelle in November 1813 was described thus:

> In one place you could see a lovely young woman supporting the head of her dying husband on her bosom, anxiously awaiting the last gasp of life, then again your eye would meet with one in bitter anguish, bewailing her loss, fondly clinging to the cold remains of all that was dear to her, and many more were running about mad, unconscious of where they were going or what they were doing, these had received the news of their husbands' deaths in some distant part of the field.
>
> (Wheeler, 1952, pp. 160–61)

Many contemporary visual works document terrible scenes of this sort.[14]

In Gray's poem, Alexis is in service for a year (during which time the couple has a child), before he faces an engagement. Refusing to remain behind the lines when Alexis goes into his first combat, Julia 'follow'd him ev'n to the fight', and when 'a ball pierced his bosom, he sunk on the plain!' she 'swoon'd at the sight' (ll. 112–15). Alexis dies, and Julia is borne, disconsolate, to a tent, from whence she attempts to make her way back to England, enduring great hardship. In a scene reminiscent of Wordsworth's 'An Evening Walk' of some twenty years earlier, she reaches her physical and emotional crisis alone, in the dark, after frequent rebuffs to her pleas for charity:

> Cold charity sometimes her wants did supply,
>   But as often rejected her prayer;

Till one night, quite exhausted, a storm threat'ning nigh,
To a forest for shelter the wand'rer did fly;
   For ah! where can the wretched repair.

The country around was dark, barren, and bleak,
   And keen darted the thick driving hail;
She press'd her cold lips to her child's colder cheek,
But feeling no motion, she utter'd a shriek,
   O my child! and sunk senseless and pale.
                      (ll. 126–35)

She recovers and tries, distracted, to revive the child but not even the intervention of a charitable rider who gives her shelter avails, and child and mother perish among strangers, their fate invisible to the parents and friends in England who 'ne'er knew of her fate' (l. 154).

It is not surprising, in some ways, that women were anxious to accompany their husbands, even if they understood (which many did not) the rigours that faced them. Competition was keen, and numerous visual works document both the sorrow of parting and the activities of those who did manage to go with their husbands (Hunter, 1802, pp. 81–2).[15] A brief ballad by Anne Hunter, 'William and Nancy, A Ballad', suggests the lengths to which some women would go to try to follow their husbands.[16] As William embarks for naval duty his wife Nancy, having failed to secure the ticket to accompany her husband ('chance denied the wish'd-for prize, / The envied lot another drew;' ll. 13–14), watches from the quay. Finally, she risks all in a remarkable gambit:

But when the shouting seamen strove
   To tow the vessel on its way,
Wak'd from despair by anxious love,
   She rush'd along the crowded quay.

The sails unfurl'd, as gliding round,
   The parting cheers still louder grew,
She flew, and with a fearful bound
   Dropp'd in her William's arms below.
                (ll. 17–24)

Such happy anecdotes, recorded in simple songs and rhymes, do occur in the writing of the war years but they are the exceptions to the rule. In reality, the returned veterans were in many cases ignored, discarded, forgotten; many ended up in debtor's prisons or in workhouses where their impoverished families struggled to eke out a subsistence existence. Prophetic as it is of the fate of many twentieth-century veterans of unpopular wars like that in Vietnam, their experience was even then not a new phenomenon, as may be seen from Maria Barrell's 1788 poem called *British Liberty Vindicated*, which laments the fate of the families of war veterans imprisoned for debt. The incarcerated soldier asks the rhetorical question: 'Did I for this in distant climates bleed? / None need my help, and none relieve my woe' (ll. 282, 284). So, too, the sailor's fate:

> For debts contracted in his Country's cause,
> He lives imprison'd by that country's laws!
> For whom he oft had fought and oft had bled,
> For whom he mourns a more than brother dead.
> Nor brother, services, or worth avails,
> His wealth exhausted, all his merit fails:
> In vain the horrors of the war are o'er,
> In vain the sailor hails his native shore.
>
> (ll. 303–10)

The war in Barrell's poem may be that with the American colonies, but the impecunious warrior's fate – and that of his family – was little better twenty or thirty years later.

The poems of Catherine Upton and Maria Barrell from the 1780s, with which this essay begins and ends, point toward a theme that would be repeated again and again in the decades that followed, when the voices of women entered fully into the poetic discourse over both the principles and the costs – the human costs in particular – involved in war. That they so often came down on the side of humanity and the toll for the nation of the terrible bloodletting offers an illuminating point of comparison to the writing of many male poets who alternately promoted and sensationalized war. The poetry written by British women in the wartime culture consistently engages issues of the quotidian reality that was for so many of them and their countrywomen the only reality, in a society in which the survival of the persons about whom – and for whom – they wrote was so frequently in question. In the process it discloses an important thread of oppositional poetic discourse whose power was not diminished, but in fact effectively enhanced, by the poets' strategy of arguing their case through both familiar example and rhetorical analogy. Both the effectiveness and the ubiquity of their approach, from their engaging and accessible poetic forms to their sophisticated rhetorical strategies, indicate the very considerable literary skill they brought to their task, and to their readers, both then and now.

Notes

1. Published anonymously in 1781, *The Siege of Gibraltar* was subsequently included in *Miscellaneous Pieces, in Prose and Verse*. Mrs. Upton, as she is styled on the title-page, is identified as 'Governess of the Ladies Academy, No. 43, Bartholemew Close' (Upton, 1784). She was married to a lieutenant in the army and seems to have had first-hand experience with coming under fire; see Jackson, 1993, pp. 355–6.
2. Bennett's collection of some 350 poems, drawn from the literally thousands

published during the period on various aspects of war, remains a rich resource. See also Scrivener, 1992.

3. I do this also in the wake of the wholesale reassessment of Romantic poetry that has attended the efforts of literary and cultural scholars during the past decade to recover the works of women writers and restore them to their historical centrality in the Romantic literary community. This ongoing project is, in fact, rewriting 'English Romanticism' and the Romantic intellectual and artistic milieu in a way that has the potential to return it to a shape that was at least recognizable for readers until perhaps two-thirds of the way through the nineteenth century, and which was subsequently lost to view in the late Victorian and, especially, the twentieth-century formalist views of Romantic poetry as a poetry of the masculine sublime.

4. See, for instance, 'To My Eldest Brother, with the British Army in Portugal', from which line 27 is quoted here. This poem was placed, significantly, just before the long poem 'The Domestic Affections', with which the collection of that title concludes (Browne, 1812). In 1812 she married Captain Alfred Hemans, himself a veteran of the Peninsular campaign.

5. The figures in the following paragraphs are derived from a number of sources. Principal among these are: Traill and Mann, 1914; Christie, 1982; Emsley, 1979; and Mackesy, 1989.

6. For a study of the British government's efforts during this period to create the nation's first social welfare system to assist the families of common soldiers and seamen, see Lin, 1997.

7. This information appears in the pleading preface, which declares that the publisher (presumably J. Young, who first published the poems in 1811) was so impressed with the naive beauty of the poems and so struck by his 'feeling for the helpless situation of one who seemed so unconscious of their value' that he published the poems for the Campbells' sole benefit (1816, pp. 7–9).

8. The poem first appeared in the *Universal Magazine* in March 1795 and in the *Scots Magazine* in May 1795. It was reprinted (pp. 63–4) with an anti-war essay attributed to one George Miller, writing under the pseudonym of 'Humanitas', called *War a System of Madness and Irreligion, to which is subjoined by way of a conclusion, The Dawn of Universal Peace, Wrote on the late Fast Day, 1796.* The British Library copy bears no printer's information, but it does contain a handwritten inscription: 'Presented by the Author to the editor of the *Philanthropist* with best wishes that his efforts to put an end to the horrid and barbarous custom of War may be crowned with the most complete success.' The editor of the *Philanthropist* was the radical publisher Daniel Isaac Eaton, whose *Politics for the People* had ceased publication in March 1795, the month in which the *Philanthropist* began a run that lasted until early 1796. The poem subsequently appeared in Moody's *Poetic Trifles* (1798).

9. See also Duffy, 1991, where deployments to Ireland are considered in addition to those to the Americas.

10. H. T. Dickinson observes that this disproportionate burden on the lower classes had consequences for the poor rates and overall public order. See his 'Introduction: The Impact on Britain of the French Revolution and the French Wars, 1789–1815', in Dickinson, 1989, p. 16.

11. Among the later fictional works that examined some of the consequences of the press-gangs' activities was Elizabeth Gaskell's 1863 novel, *Sylvia's Lovers*.

12. This is the opening of the poem as it appeared in the *Morning Post* on 29 January 1795. It was signed 'Portia', one of the immediately transparent pseu-

donyms under which the poet published in the popular press. The revised poem appears in Robinson, 1806, rpt. 1824. The original 'Nobles' of the 1795 version is replaced by the less pointed term 'Misers' in the reformulated opening stanzas (p. 222).

13.   Mary Darby Robinson's rollicking, noisy poem 'The Camp', published in the *Morning Post* under her pseudonym 'Oberon', effectively captures the chaos which these camp-followers endured (albeit often willingly) already before 1800.

14.   William Blake, for instance, includes such a scene at the base of the title-page of his illuminated poem, *America: A Prophecy* (1793), and in the background of a painting known as *A Breach in a City, the Morning after a Battle* (c. 1790–95).

15.   See, for instance, the engraving of the melancholy parting of a uniformed man from his wife and three children (one of whom wears a child's replica of the uniform), who have not secured a ticket to follow him (not surprisingly, having children worked against wives' petitions to follow their husbands), or the prints of activity along the march, reproduced in Page, 1986, between pages 40 and 41.

16.   A prefatory note announces that the poem is 'Founded upon an interesting incident which took place on the embarkation of the 85th Regiment for Holland at Ramsgate, August 10, 1799'.

Bibliography

Barrell, M. (1788), *British Liberty; or, a Delineation of the King's Bench*, London: W. Justins, M. Barrell.

Behrendt, S. (1997), 'British Women Poets and the Reverberations of Radicalism in the 1790s' in Behrendt, S. (ed.), *Romanticism, Radicalism, and the Press*, Detroit: Wayne State University Press, pp. 83–102.

Bennett, B. (ed.) (1976), *British War Poetry in the Age of Romanticism: 1793–1815*, New York: Garland.

Blain, V., Clements, P. and Grundy, I. (eds) (1990), *The Feminist Companion to Literature in English*, New Haven: Yale University Press.

Browne, F. D. (1812), *The Domestic Affections, and Other Poems*, London: T. Cadell and W. Davies.

Campbell [of Zetland], D. P. (1811), *Poems*, Inverness: J. Young; rpt. 1816 with additions as *Poems*, London: Baldwin, Cradock, and Joy.

Christie, I. R. (1982), *Wars and Revolutions, 1760–1815*, Cambridge, MA: Harvard University Press.

————. (1991), 'Conservatism and Stability in British Society' in Philp, M. (ed.), *The French Revolution and British Popular Politics*, Cambridge: Cambridge University Press.

Dickinson, H. T. (1989), 'Introduction: The Impact on Britain of the French Revolution and the French Wars', in Dickinson, H. T. (ed.) *Britain and the French Revolution, 1789–1815*, London: Macmillan.

————. (ed.) (1989), *Britain and the French Revolution, 1789–1815*, London: Macmillan.

Donaldson, J. (1852), *Recollections of an Eventful Life*, Edinburgh: Martin.

Duffy, M. (1991), 'War, Revolution, and the Crisis of the British Empire', in Philp, M. (ed.), *The French Revolution and British Popular Politics*, Cambridge: Cambridge University Press, pp. 118–45.

Emsley, C. (1979), *British Society and the French Wars, 1793–1815*, London: Macmillan.

Gleig, G. R. (1825), *The Subaltern*, Edinburgh: W. Blackwood; London: T. Cadell.

Gray, C. (1811), *Tales, Letters, and Other Pieces, in Verse*, Edinburgh; for the author.

Harris, J. (1848; rpt. 1928), *Recollections of a Rifleman*, London: Peter Davies.

Hofland Mrs. [Barbara Hoole] (1809; rpt. 1846), *The History of an Officer's Widow, and Her Young Family*, New York: Saxton and Huntington.

Hunter, A. (1802), *Poems by Mrs John Hunter*, London: T. Payne.

Jackson, J. R. de J. (1993), *Romantic Poetry by Women: A Bibliography, 1770–1835*, Oxford: Clarendon Press.

Leadbeater, M. (1808), *Poems*, Dublin: Martin Keene; London: Longman, Hurst, Rees, and Orme.

Lickbarrow, I. (1814), *Poetical Effusions*, Kendal: Braithwaite; London: J. Richardson.

Lin, Y. C. E. (1997), 'Extending Her Arms: Military Families and the Transformation of the British State, 1793–1815', Berkeley, University of California: unpublished PhD dissertation.

Mackesy, P. (1989), 'Strategic Problems of the British War Effort', in Dickinson, H. T. (ed.), *Britain and the French Revolution, 1789–1815*, London: Macmillan, pp. 147–64.

[Mathias, T. J.] (1794), *The Pursuits of Literature*, London: Becket.

Mellor, A. K. (1993), *Romanticism and Gender*, New York: Routledge.

Miller, G. ['Humanitas'] (1796), *War a System of Madness and Irreligion, to which is subjoined by way of a conclusion, The Dawn of Universal Peace. Wrote on the late Fast Day, 1796*; published together with 'Anna's Complaint' by Elizabeth Moody. The British Library copy bears no printer's information.

Moody, E. (1798), *Poetic Trifles*, London: T. Cadell, Jun., and W. Davies.

Opie, A. (1802), *Poems by Mrs. Opie*, London: T. N. Longman and O. Rees.

Page, F. C. G. (1986), *Following the Drum: Women in Wellington's Army*, London: Andre Deutsch.

Philp, M. (ed.) (1991), *The French Revolution and British Popular Politics*, Cambridge: Cambridge University Press.

Polwhele, R. (1798), *The Unsex'd Females: A Poem*, London: Cadell and Davies.

Richardson, C. C. (1818), *Harvest, A Poem, in two parts; with other Poetical Pieces*, London: Sherwood, Neely, and Jones.

Robinson, M. D. ['Portia'] (1795), 'January, 1795', *Morning Post*, 20 January 1795.

———. (1800), *Lyrical Tales*, London: T. S. Longman and O. Rees.

———. (1806; rpt. 1824), *The Poetical Works of Mrs. Mary Robinson*, ed. Robinson, M., London: Jones and Co., 1824.

Ross, M. B. (1989), *The Contours of Masculine Desire: Romanticism and the Rise of Women's Poetry*, New York: Oxford University Press.

Scrivener, M. (ed.) (1992), *Periodical Verses from the English Democratic Press, 1792–1824*, Detroit: Wayne State University Press.

Sullivan, A. (ed.) (1983), *British Literary Magazines: The Augustan Age and the Age of Johnson, 1698–1788*, Westport, CT: Greenwood Press.

Traill, H. D. and Mann, J. S. (eds) (1914), *A Record of the Progress of the People*, 5 vols, London: Cassell and Co.

Upton, C. (1784), *Miscellaneous Pieces, in Prose and Verse*. London: T. and G. Egerton and G. Robinson.

Wheeler, W. (1952), *The Letters of Private Wheeler*, ed. Liddell Hart, B. H., Boston: Houghton Mifflin.

CHAPTER THREE

The exiled self: images of war in Charlotte Smith's 'The Emigrants'

Jacqueline M. Labbe

How difficult it is to uncouple women from domestic life

Joan Landes

In 1784, Charlotte Smith published her first book of poetry, *Elegiac Sonnets*, partly as a wifely response to her husband's need: Benjamin Smith, ever the profligate husband, finally contracted enough debt to land himself in prison, and Smith's publication was a money-making venture. Smith went with her husband to prison, as she later accompanied him on a debt-dodging move to France, but she signed her title-page not only with her name – itself an unusual move for a first-time female author – but with a residence: 'Charlotte Smith, of Bignor-park, Sussex'. Allowing the preposition both its directive ('of') and originary ('from') functions, she places herself as a lady and as a sheltered women, her gentility apparent from the title-page on.[1] By the time of 'The Emigrants' (1793) Smith, now separated from Benjamin, is an established and respected poet and novelist; she signs herself from Brighthelmstone, and opens her poem 'on the cliffs to the Eastward of the Town', a self-placement remarkable for its danger and risk, both physical and poetical (Smith, 1993, p. 135). The purpose of this sketch of Smith's move from housed to homeless is not to contradict Joan Landes, but rather to reiterate her point; for even in 1784 Bignor Park is not Smith's home, but her younger brother's (the legal heir), and her claim resonates with its own impossibility. But it also reveals Smith's own dependence on – or awareness of – a woman's need for a domestic identity, especially in the public eye. In 1793, the problem is not that Smith is now unhoused; the irony is that, once married, she lost her domestic sphere even as, culturally, she was placed firmly in it. Her desire for Bignor Park reflects as much a gesture towards her pre-marriage identity as it does an affirmation of personal gentility despite her husband's inadequacies. By the time of 'The Emigrants', she has moved from country to town, from private to public; from the restricted and enclosed sonnet to extended blank-verse ruminations; from a poet whose persona wanders 'cheerless and unblest' (*Elegiac Sonnets*, LXII, l.1) to one whose sympathy for French *émigrés* masks a rage against the privations imposed by a 'masculinist' bourgeoisie (Landes, 1988, p. 7). In this essay, I will discuss 'The Emigrants' as a poem that subtly but firmly calls not just for a 'REVOLUTION in Female Manners' (as Wollstonecraft phrased it), but for a revolution in English (read: human) culture. The *émigrés* function not merely as representatives of victims of the French Revolution, but as metaphors for Smith's own sense of marginality, personal and cultural. The violent uncoupling suffered by the *émigrés* mirrors Smith's own exile from a society that simultaneously requires her domestic identity, and renders its sphere uninhabitable.

Landes describes a 'specific, highly gendered bourgeois male discourse that depended on women's domesticity and the silencing of "public" women', and goes on to note that while a 'public man is one who acts in and for the universal good ... a public woman is a prostitute, a commoner, a common woman' (1988, pp. 2–3). Although she is concentrating on French society, the public–private dichotomy structures British society of the time as well, spiced with more than a little complacency of the 'we in enlightened England' variety. Smith herself appeals to this nationalistic self-pride when she describes the 'just compassion' of 'English hearts', a feeling as natural as the obedience of 'our element, the deep' to 'the mild dominion of the Moon' ('The Emigrants', I. 360–63). The feminine associations of the moon are not unknown to a poet who elsewhere calls it the 'mute arbitress of the tides' (*Elegiac Sonnets*, XLIV, l. 1); here, the virtues of being English find their definitive origin in a trope of femininity. And to a certain extent Smith rewrites English culture to a feminine template, insisting on the public validity and political viability of, for instance, motherhood, or rejecting the masculine 'marring' of what was once 'fair' ('The Emigrants', I. 33).[2] Her strategy, however, is not one of simple reversal: Smith displays a disarming awareness of the complexities of class, gender and nationality in 'The Emigrants', and her development of the metaphorics of exile reveals a simultaneous exploration of the theme of alienation. For Smith, exile is both ejection and rejection, and alienation is both felt and performed. Her continual deployment of her name and personal circumstances on the title-pages and in the prefaces, dedications, parentheses and footnotes, as well as (more poetically) in the body of her poetic works, not only mark her ownership of her own experiences and texts; they not only create a coherent self-portrait; they also show Smith to be manipulating the gendered nature of the 'public' remarked by Landes. For as soon as Smith steps into the publishing sphere, named, she is a public woman, always at risk that the selling of her body of work may be interpreted as the selling of her body (Labbe, 1994). Her awareness of the connotations of her own publicity creates the paradox that Smith's self-declared marginality becomes central to her work; she exemplifies Suzanne Desan's description that 'women's position [is] on the border between the public and private spheres' (1994, p. 20). The paradox is exploited by Smith when she poeticizes her own movements as 'straying' from marked paths (a common image in the *Elegiac Sonnets*), or on cliffs and eminences (as in

'The Emigrants') or on 'stupendous summits' (as in *Beachy Head*, 1807).
Smith thus secures our attention: the readerly eye is caught by an 'I' whose
separation from domestic life has resulted in personal, intellectual and poetic
rupture.

In 'The Emigrants' Smith manages to reconcile a pro-revolutionary sentiment with a deep and extensive sympathy for the *émigré* priests and aristocrats
the Revolution has spent most of 1791–92 persecuting. Curran notes one
aspect of her identification in his opening note to the poem:

> As the Revolution unfolded in France, a great many who had enjoyed
> power and privilege under the *ancien regime* sought refuge in England
> ... to the numbers of unprotected women who had been sent abroad with
> their children for safety were added others whose husbands had emi-
> grated with them but had then returned to France to fight and die ... The
> extent to which the rules made by men at once keep women dependent
> and leave them no recourse when left alone links these distressed emi-
> grants and the poet who observes them.
>
>   (Smith, 1993, p. 131)[3]

And it is quite true that Smith concentrates her most moving imagery on the
plight of the mothers whose role has been denaturalized by revolutionary
violence, from Marie Antoinette down. But Smith's keen observations are
placed in time as well as location: we open in November 1792, just two
months after the abolition of the monarchy and imprisonment of the royal
family, while book I moves forward to April 1793, after both the execution of
the King and the founding of the Society of Revolutionary Republican Women.
In the meantime, Smith herself moves from a sheltered and buried position in
book I of her poem – the *scene* is 'on the Cliffs', a spectacular position, but
the 'I' enters only in line 42, 'half-adjur[ing] Society / And sigh[ing] for
some lone Cottage, deep embower'd / In the green woods' (I. 42–4) – to the
authoritative Eminence of book II, 'which afford[s] to the South a View of the
Sea; to the North of the Weald of Sussex' and which sees the 'I' enter in line
5.[4] Smith's achievement of a respectable, yet highly politicized and visible
self-placement comes about partly through her facility with grammar – before we reach the first-person in line 42 of book I we have travelled from the
omniscient, and disembodied, third-person, to the docile and co-operative
first-person plural ('[God] surely means / To *us*, his reasoning Creatures,
whom he bids / Acknowledge and revere his awful and, / Nothing but good'
(I. 29–32, emphasis added)). Smith's desire to 'hide' herself in the 'lone
Cottage' further functions to disarm the powerful cliffside position she has
manifestly claimed, while her description of her powerful feelings – 'my
swol'n heart ... bursting with its sorrows' (I. 62) – confirm her feminine
sensibilities.[5] In an important way, Smith claims both femininity and masculinity in the first ninety-three lines of 'The Emigrants', and it is this doubleness
that figures throughout the poem, allowing Smith a consistently layered

approach that enacts and confirms the dualities – masculine–feminine, exile–alienation, sympathy–critique – only hinted at so far. Underpinning Smith's complicated self-representation is a manipulation of established conventions of gender and culture that can be contextualized and explained in terms of another revolution: the invention of psychology.

The return of the uncanny repressed abject

The development of proto-psychological tools and theories in the nineteenth century uniformly followed the given that men and women occupied emotional territory as separate as their social spheres. Whether because of her tendency to hysteria, to melancholy, to lust, to chastity, to heat, to coolness, to earth(li)ness, to angelicalness, woman provided the disorder against which men defined their own order. The psychological untrustworthiness of women grew out of and was contingent on their irrationality; this, coupled with a woman's potential to achieve reason – usually suspended – constructed her as the not quite but almost human figure whose weaknesses justified her restrictions. Smith, for instance, signals her knowledge of her pre-prepared social position when she states publicly, in print, her awareness that 'for a Woman, "the Post of Honor is a Private Station"' (preface to the sixth edition of *Elegiac Sonnets*, 1792), ignoring the inherent contradiction her impossible public–private self-place-ment poses. Freud inherits this tradition of defining woman through her body, and relationally – as mother, as daughter, as sister, and so on – and refines a theory that depends on the physical difference of women to the standard of humanity – men. What men have, women lack; men fear women's lack; what men fear, they invade: the sexual act, then, in part re-enacts the birth process, and functions as a man's attempt to conquer that which he does not understand. Freud explains this with terms like the 'uncanny', the 'repressed', the *unheimlich*: for him, the female and the feminine is not necessarily foreign, but rather forgotten. As he says, the uncanny only appears that way: 'this *unheimlich* place [the female genitals], however, is the entrance to the former *Heim* of all human beings … In this case too, then, the *unheimlich* is what was once *heimisch*, familiar; the prefix "*un*" is the token of repression' (qtd. Zerilli, 1992, p. 52). The uncanny – the unknown, the odd – is associated with a lack, the unfamiliar nature of women's bodies: this is, paradoxically, an expression of recognition of a common home. The return of the repressed can be seen as the return to the familiar, the acceptance and understanding of difference. And yet, because the standard is still the male understanding, the female mind remains, notoriously, defamiliarized to itself; it has no home. Freud's solution is that women accept their repressed desire to fit the pattern, which involves, of course, an acceptance of their own essential *unheimlich* nature. They are only whole if, confusingly, they accept they are incomplete.

The *heimlich*, then, is akin to the home: it is the place by which one defines oneself as female (on a literal and cultural level). Kristeva, in her exploration of the individual's need to erect barriers between self and (m)other, implicitly redraws the uncanny as the abject; she realigns the unknown as the unknowable, the undefined. Where Freud's *heimlich* is the entry to the *unheimlich*, Kristeva's abject is a 'boundary':

> abjection is above all ambiguity. Because while releasing a hold, it does not radically cut off the subject from what threatens it – on the contrary, abjection acknowledges it to be in perpetual danger … Abjection preserves what existed in … the immemorial violence with which a body becomes separated from another body in order to be.
>
> (Zerilli, 1992, p. 54)

The abject is that by which the One defines him/herself against the Other – for Kristeva, the (m)other, the origin. For both Kristeva and Freud the originary point is, more accurately, an edge – door or boundary – and human beings work very hard to keep from falling off. For both, as well, the maternal, the metaphoricized act of mothering is key. What this sketch allows is the introduction into Smith's self-marginalized world of a dense weaving of exile, identity, the *unheimlich/heimlich*, and the abject. Smith deploys the uncanny: in 'The Emigrants' she reveals the *unheimlich* nature of the *heimlich* by showing the disfamiliarity between the preparation for life and the living of it. In this she explores the very definition of alienation, the legal as well as cultural ramifications of which her own long-running lawsuit had made her familiar.[6] She creates a knowing, chosen marginalization that bears its own uncanny relationship to a kind of self-conscious abject, an exile from an *unheimlich* culture to the boundary of the *heimlich*, a flight which in itself figures a new *heimlich*. And she reconstitutes gender boundaries as themselves uncanny. In discussing Burke's *Reflections*, for instance, Linda Zerilli defines 'abjection' as 'attest[ing] to the instability of borders, of the demarcating line that separates the feminine beautiful from the masculine sublime' (p. 56). Smith's reflections on the revolution in France also focus on separation, on gender and on the maternal, as she considers and condemns the deadly and deadening effect of war; but it is in her exploration of boundaries and her embracing of the margin that she locates peace.

(M)othering

Before the margin can be (b)reached, Smith suggests, layers of cultural assumptions must be explored. In 'The Emigrants', she begins with her manipulations of rank, depicting the priests whose aristocratic connections and religious beliefs led to their exile, and moves from them – representatives of fatherhood – to mothers, and for Smith mothers and the maternal provide a

signal instance of the uncanny. In writing of Helen Maria Williams, Mary
Favret remarks that for Williams, 'the experience of revolution is only realised as the experience of spectators, foreigners, and strangers' (1994, p. 157).
Smith's emigrants are also 'foreigners and strangers', but rather than distancing them from her speaking self, Smith sees their strangeness as uniting them
with herself: 'I too have known / involuntary exile', she says, and so can
'mourn [their] sorrows' (I. 55–6).[7] Again in Favret's words, 'her heart and
soul understand the French people precisely because she is a woman and [to
them] a foreigner' (p. 159). In Smith's case, the 'people' function as representative types, 'banish'd for every and for conscience sake / From their
distracted country, whence the name / Of Freedom misapplied, and much
abus'd / By lawless Anarchy, has driven them far to wander' (I. 97–101).[8]
Book I opens on 'a Morning in November, 1792', a contextualizing date that
allows her readers to understand that 'lawless Anarchy' does not necessarily
characterize the Revolution itself, but rather its turn to Terror; the 'name of
Freedom' suffers under this harsher regime, but as Smith will make clear, not
the original desire for freedom and equality that, she understands, drove the
Revolution heretofore. On the beach, then, the boundary between land and
sea, wander a group hostile by role to the new republic. Smith's sympathy is
not unalloyed; even as she introduces the 'group' she deplores their 'prejudice', their 'Bigotry (the Tut'ress of the blind)' and 'errors' – that is, their
Catholicism – that teaches them narrow ways: the monk who seeks to please
God by 'renounc[ing] God's works', the cardinal 'dwelling on all he had
lost', the abbot 'lighter of heart than these, but heavier far / Than he was
wont' (I. 119, 128, 147–8). These men 'hang / Upon the barrier of the rock'
(I. 109), their position replicating their marginality, and Smith watches them
and remembers her own 'involuntary exile':

> while yet
> England had charms for me, [I] have felt how sad
> It is to look across the dim cold sea,
> That melancholy rolls its refluent tides
> Between us and the dear regretted land
> We call our own
>
> (I. 156–61)

By associating the *émigrés*' exile with her own, Smith introduces the idea
that marriage dislocates women in the way that the Terror phase of the
Revolution has dislocated the clerics, an unpicking of the threads of culture
that she presses still further.

    The exiled churchmen represent one form of *émigré*;[9] Smith now turns to a
'softer form' who 'reclines' 'where the cliff, hollow'd by the wintry storm, /
Affords a seat with matted sea-weed strewn' (I. 202, 200–201). This figure,
the first in a sequence of mothers, mourns her lost lavish lifestyle; sheltered
not on, but in the margin, she watches her children playing and finds in

'Fancy' some respite. This first mother embodies the dissolute aristocracy; she imagines the crowds that 'paid [her] willing homage' since 'Beauty gave charms to empire' (I. 225–6). Smith's observing self cannot identify with this careless mother; like her 'fellow sufferer', her husband, she represents arrogance, conscious haughtiness and an inability to recognize 'that worth alone is true nobility' (I. 240). Unlike the mothers to follow, this one, 'lost in melancholy thought', lacks maternal care; her error is a concern with self at the expense of deep mother-love. Smith's stance is sympathetic, yet judgemental; from her vantage point, she characterizes this mother as unfamiliar with her maternal duty, as in exile from her appropriate position of care. All these emigrant figures are in error – religious, class-based – and in this way their exile mirrors their moral position. Smith's own position is double: she both identifies with, and condemns, the *émigrés*, in the same way that she both supports the Revolution's principles, and deplores its current 'distraction' from those principles. To this point, her engagement with the *émigrés* is openly textual, observational – she watches them, sympathizes, empathizes, and critiques, but she does not interact with them.

This allows Smith to conclude book I with a rousing paean to British liberty, albeit in a roundabout way. Having approached and then defamiliarized the emigrants, Smith uses their situation to 'other' England itself. Even as the French rose up against tyranny, and cast out the corrupt, so too, she warns, those 'who feed on England's vitals', 'whom Britons pay / For forging fetters for them', court trouble (I. 316, 330–31). As she says to her readers, 'trembling, learn, that if oppress'd too long, / The raging multitude, to madness stung, / Will turn on their oppressors' (I. 333–5). The progress from indolent, careless mother, to proud aristocrat, to an England teeming with injustice, shows that Smith's *émigrés*, in book I, serve to illuminate the weaknesses of English culture as much as the violence of the French Revolution. Her persona judges on a personal and a political level – the inattentive mother serves as a representative of inattentive England, and this, once linked back to Smith's covert association of her marriage with the Terror, serves to import a distinctly politicized tone not only to Smith's ruminations of war, but also to her understanding of that microcosm of the social order, the family. The rapid and unsignposted movements from individuals to classes to institutions to governments builds into book I a desire to associate the personal with the political and, further, to reveal the hollowness of each sphere. Even as book I ends with a (not entirely convincing) celebration of English compassion towards the emigrants, it also straightforwardly denounces war for its personal cost:

> 'Bloodless laurels'
> Far better justify the pride, that swells
> In British bosoms, than the deafening roar
> Of Victory from a thousand brazen throats,

That tell with what success wide-wasting War
Has by our brave Compatriots thinned the world
                            (I. 369, 378–82)

Smith roundly condemns war just as Britain is entering into one; she expresses (guarded) support for the Revolution just when its turn to terror was losing it many ardent supporters; she maintains an identification with *émigrés* who yet provoke her criticism. The 'Cliffs to the Eastward' of Brighton are required to loom over a carnivalesque landscape, the confusion of which arises from Smith's desire to present a pro-revolution, anti-war, personally politicized, objectively-subjective point of view. Like the chaos arising from the Terror, the mixture of stances and attitudes pervading book I threaten to overshadow its strength: an underlying sense of structure that needs the addition of book II to clarify itself. Smith builds into book I an alienating unconcern with its potential incoherence; while her presentation of events and vignettes is straightforward enough, it is the rationale behind it that destabilizes and defamiliarizes the reader. I would suggest that this is not inadvertent, but rather a kind of poetic of unknowability: even as Smith invites complex readings, she disallows easeful comprehension.

In many ways it is the mothers that bind together books I and II: the *émigré* mother of book I foreshadows a collection inhabiting book II, and it is here that their (m)othering function becomes more sustainable. It is as if, occupied with the conflicting techniques of sympathy and judgement, desire and repression that characterize book I, and mirrored in her liminal self-placement 'on the Cliffs', Smith uses book I to populate her polemic and suggest the directions of book II, as many of her character-types reappear. Smith herself moves from cliffs to 'an Eminence', a manifestly authoritative and visionary placement, and she advances the calendar from November to 'an Afternoon in April, 1793' (see Labbe, 1998a). This allows her to react to the execution of Louis XVI in January, and take on board the founding of the Society of Revolutionary Republican Women in February. The society endorsed women as publicly revolutionary figures despite conclusions, that, 'in the ideal Republic, women were meant to be "mothers" not writers ... women were expected to remain in the private sphere ... rather than play a public role, be it political or literary' (Montfort and Allison, 1994, pp. 3–4); as Desan elaborates, however, 'in both ideology and practice, women's newfound role as citizens stood in tension with the ideal patriotic role of women as republican mothers and moral guardians of the revolution within the home' (1994, p. 20). In book II, Smith responds to this clash of ideologies, encoding in her own self-placement a rejection of strictly domesticated femininity, but also exposing the effect of the revolution – of war – on the domestic ideal: her mothers are prevented from guarding the nation's morals by that very nation's immoral assault on their bodies.

Smith bolsters her more assertive physical self-placement with a number of literary props: her epigraph, in Latin, from Virgil, displays her knowledge

of the (masculinized) classics and her detestation of war, while the choice of
April carries echoes of Chaucer, and hence embeds in the poem ideas of
pilgrimage and moral storytelling. Unlike book I, book II begins in the first
person:

> Long wintry months are past; the Moon that now
> Lights her pale crescent even at noon, has made
> Four time her revolution; since with step,
> Mournful and slow, along the wave-worn cliff,
> Pensive I took my solitary way,
> Lost in despondence, while contemplating
> Not my own wayward destiny alone,
> (Hard as it is, and difficult to bear!)
> But in beholding the unhappy lot
> Of the lorn Exiles; who, amid the storms
> Of wild disastrous anarchy, are thrown,
> Like shipwreck'd sufferers, on England's coast,
> To see, perhaps, no more their native land,
> Where Desolation riots: they, like me,
> From fairer hopes and happier prospects driven,
> Shrink from the future, and regret the past.
>   (II. 1–16)[10]

The reader senses a new firmness in Smith's explicit identification with the
émigrés; no longer merely an observer, she is now a kind of participant in
exile. In book II, the personal–political link will be both cemented and more
fully explored: the defamiliarizing process of book I results in a new ability
to express the repressed, to unhouse the *heimlich*. And so Smith moves from
a statement of her personal sorrows, through four lines decrying the behead-
ing of the King, to a more sustained reverie on war's violent effect on the
landscape (for Smith, this April is indeed a cruel month – spring hesitates to
enliven a countryside 'stain'd with blood' (II. 71)). Smith devotes some sev-
enty-five lines to describing the historical uselessness of war in her movement
from beheaded father (King) to imprisoned mother (Queen), via the 'unhappy
heir / Of fatal greatness', whose 'baby brow' is too young to comprehend 'the
savage howl of Murder' heard daily in his 'sullen prison' (II. 127–8, 130, 150,
149). For Smith, the child allows her access to the mother, here divested of
Burkean sexual allure and transformed into a 'wretched Mother, petrified
with grief, / [Who] views [her son] with stony eyes, and cannot weep!' (II.
152–3). Like the aristocratic mother of book I, Marie Antoinette suffers for
past folly, but unlike that careless mother, she is focused on her son, petrified
not with fear her herself, but grief for what – who – has been lost. Constructing the Queen as mother, Smith 'mourn[s] thy sorrows, hapless queen! /
And deem[s] thy expiation made to Heaven / For every fault, to which
prosperity / Betray'd thee, when it plac'd thee on a throne / Where boundless
power was thine, and thou wert rais'd / High (as it seemed) above the envious
reach of destiny!' (II. 154–60). Perversely fulfilling republican ideals, the

Queen has been transformed from a public to a private woman, from frivo-lous to responsible, from error-laden to a moral guardian, from Queen to mother. That she has also been imprisoned creates a paradox that Smith exploits; even as she makes clear the Queen/Mother's fears are 'for those / More dear to thee than life!' (II. 173–4), she also links her personal feelings of loss and despair to the Queen's: the earlier subtextual association of the violence of the Terror with her own marriage is here rendered an overt identification of mother with mother, persecuted by 'sad experience' (II. 170). The Queen's 'eminence of misery' (II. 173–4) proves a metaphorical analogue to Smith's position 'on an Eminence': for Smith, the eminence is both proof and cause of alienation. That the home – the protected domestic space – is, for the Queen, exchanged for a prison, only emphasizes the contradictions of a culture that requires a femininity exemplified by mother-hood yet fails to protect mothers. By recasting a dissolute Queen as a despairing mother, Smith questions easy assumptions of guilt while further defamiliarizing motherhood itself.

Smith makes use of such imagery to further her subtle exposure of how England fails its citizens (through apathy and neglect), but she continually returns to mothers and their special victimization by war: the nightmare landscape created by battle, when 'the flames of burning villages illum[e] / the waste of water' (II. 226–7), echoes with 'the frantic shrieks / Of mothers for their children' (II. 229–30). Smith moves from the general to the specific, cutting into her description of horrors the tale of a 'wretched Woman, pale and breathless'. This latest mother, 'clasping close / To her hard-heaving heart her sleeping child, / All she could rescue of the innocent groupe [sic] / That yesterday surrounded her' (II. 264–7), proves a culminatory figure: driven from her home by 'lawless' soldiers, she exemplifies the wrongness of war. If the Revolution idealizes mothers, how comes it to kill them, asks Smith? This mother is doubly victimized – she lacks a protector in the home since he has gone to fight; she is at the mercy of soldiers who do not recognize her motherhood. Smith makes it clear that war destroys what it purports to uphold. The mother dies, pursued by the soldiers' 'hostile foot-steps' (II. 260), but, 'in Death itself, / True to maternal tenderness, she tries / To save the unconscious infant from the storm / In which she perishes / ... / But alas! The Mother & Infant perish both!' (II. 280–84, 290–91). Even as Marie Antoinette's motherhood will not save her from the guillotine, neither will this woman's protect her from violence. The homeliness, the refuge of maternity, in Smith's handling, reveals its own emptiness.

Considering that 'The Emigrants' concerns itself in part with the errors of the French, it might be expected that Smith would turn to England for relief, but even as her representations of English politics have been equivocal, so too her experience of its culture proves alienating. Invoking memory, Smith finds she can locate personal happiness only in her childhood: the advent of adulthood and almost immediate motherhood mean only 'never-ending toil / ... terror and ... tears!' (II. 350–51). Having dwelt for so long on the terrors of war, on the Terror itself, it is significant that when Smith turns to herself as mother she uses such diction. Like the mother who died in the wilderness, Smith attempts

> To save my children from the o'erwhelming wrongs
> That have for ten long years been heap'd on me! –
> The fearful spectres of chicane and fraud
> Have, Proteus-like, still chang'd their hideous forms
> (As the law lent its plausible disguise),
> Pursuing my faint steps
>
> (II. 353–8)

Smith, having presented us with a series of mothers victimized by war, now links her own situation with theirs: where they are persecuted by violence, she is by chicanery and fraud. There is a sense that the entire poem has been building to this point, that Smith declares herself an emigrant from a violent and terrible social evil, that she declares that not even motherhood can withstand its force. Underlying Smith's imagery is an accusation: even as the Revolution has betrayed its allegiance to Liberty, so too English law has betrayed its commitment to equality – or rather, Smith's experience has proved the hypocrisy of that commitment. Her 'mother's efforts' find as little support as a French mother's, despite a cultural insistence on its necessity, but part of the thrust of 'The Emigrants' has been to 'vindicate [Smith's] humble fame' (II. 383); given the 1792 publication of Wollstonecraft's *Vindication of the Rights of Woman*, this word is as evocative as Smith's earlier, personalized use of 'terrors'. To be a 'mother' is to be the 'other'; the home is invaded and destroyed by violence; social forces collude to push women to its margins. Smith's self-placement on the eminence allows her to see this and to embody this. Her delineation of mothers exiled from the protective family space by the very society that insists on the primacy of motherhood underscores her critique of 'the variety of woes that Man / For Man [or Woman] creates' (II. 413–14). The repressed – the social violation of the maternal – returns to take up a central space in 'The Emigrants'.

The abject, the object, the subject

Having placed mothers on the boundary, having relentlessly defamiliarized the familiar spectacle of hearth and home, Smith embeds in 'The Emigrants' a further critique: a horror of war becomes a horror of culture itself. Far from using the imagery of exile to 'redefine ... culture or subjectivity from [a] (middle-class) wom[an's] point of view' (Chu, 1992, p. 100) – in that way participating in culture – Smith underscores the impossibility of such a move.

For her, culture itself remains an Other, intent on ejecting *differance*. She rejects the notion of 'a compliant form of femininity' either as 'the demarcating lines of gender identity' or 'as a necessary form of political artifice' (Zerilli, 1992, p. 55), and she does this by shadowing her victimized mothers with an authority literally marginalized – that is, in the margins, in the footnotes to the poem. Elsewhere I have argued that the footnotes to *Beachy Head* create a choric sub-voice that allows Smith to infiltrate her own poetic voice with history (Labbe, 1998b); in 'The Emigrants' the footnotes perform a similar function, allowing the poet to form an alternative identity that revolts against the victim's voice dominating the poem. The footnotes function as the textual object, a boundary at which Smith straddles gender as well as culture. In the footnotes, she reinterprets the dependence she both exposes and embraces in the poem-proper. It is there that we find the poem's emigrant, the voice in exile from itself, a self-conscious exploration of the marginality to which that poem's persona is exiled. In the footnotes, gender itself is revealed as a margin, as the abject: Smith declares a revolution to shadow and accompany her poetic exploration of the effects of revolution.

Mary Favret has argued that 'in the context of home, family, and friends, the outsider/woman occupies the central position' (1994, p. 160). Centrality, however, is precisely what Smith rejects; she constructs layers of margins that represent the liminality of her – and by extension, the female exile's – life. In her notes, she furthers this marginality: the notes are textually marginal, and the voice in which they speak asserts dangerously rebellious sentiments. For example, the first substantial note follows Smith's introduction of the cleric-emigrants; she has just referred to the monk's 'pious prison, and his beads' (I. 124). At this point the reader is directed to a note:

> Lest the same attempts at misrepresentation should now be made, as have been made on former occasions, it is necessary to repeat, that nothing is farther from my thoughts, than to reflect invidiously on the Emigrant clergy, whose steadiness of principle excites veneration, as much as their sufferings compassion. Adversity has now taught them the charity and humility they perhaps wanted when they made it a part of their faith, that salvation could be obtained through no other religion than their own.
>
> (Note to I. 124)

This voice, prosaic and personalized, expresses impatience at the potential misreading of the poet's intentions she has experienced before; responding to the ambiguity – the multiple interpretations – resident in poetic language, the speaker imports into the notes her awareness of the dangers posed by wayward readers. In addition, she allows herself a straightforward critique of the clerics' religion that anticipates, and eventually authorizes, the more veiled, self-consciously poetic stance taken by the poem's speaker. The next note pushes further:

Let it not be considered as an insult to men in fallen fortune, if these
luxuries (undoubtedly inconsistent with their profession) be here enu-
merated – France is not the only country, where the splendour and
indulgences of the higher, and the poverty and depression of the inferior
Clergy, have alike proved injurious to the cause of Religion.

(Note to I. 129)

As Curran glosses it, 'the ambiguity of Smith's prose seems meant to imply
that such inequality exists as well within the Anglican establishment' (Smith,
1993, p. 140). However, at this point in the poem itself, Smith has not yet
moved beyond sympathizing with the emigrants. The footnotes seem to function as the space wherein Smith rehearses her more radical, critical assessments
of her own culture that, eventually, she expresses in the poem (England's
politics, its law), but that are also embedded in patriotic celebrations of
England's probity, clemency and valour. Even as the poem's body internal-
izes its rebellion, so too the footnotes provide an outlet on the margin for
Smith's articulations of her alienation: this becomes explicitly when, in
sourcing the lines 'amid the sons / Of Reason, Valour, Liberty, and Virtue, /
Displays distinguish'd merit, is a Noble / Of Nature's own creation!' in
Thomson, she adds 'these lines ... are among those sentiments which are
now called (when used by living writers), no common-place declamation, but
sentiments of dangerous tendency' (note to I. 244). The 'dangerous tendency'
towards social breakdown threatened by a pro-revolutionary stand, Smith
implies, is turned back on the repressive culture that can rewrite 'Patriot
Virtue' (I. 346) as its own obverse; as Smith notes, 'this sentiment will
probably *renew* against me the indignation of those, who have an interest in
asserting that no such virtue any where exists' (note to I. 346; Smith's
emphasis).

Smith's notes both assert a sympathy for revolutionary principles and stand
as evidence of its strength in the face of continuing social disapproval; her
notes reveal a voice that reiterates what her readers already know about her.
They attest to an individuality that nonetheless exiles itself to the margin, a
complicated position of assertion and retreat that suggests, perhaps, the 'structural impossibility' of the 'female citizen or enlightened feminine subject'
remarked upon by Vivien Jones (1993, p. 301). Are we meant to applaud
Smith's audacity or decry her timidity? The poem itself offers a resolution:
even as the revolutionary voice of the notes in book I authorize an increasingly critical poetic persona whose strength of mind is fully utilized in the
text of book II, if we explore the notes to book II we see that, while fewer,
they maintain an easy authority that seems an outgrowth of the increasingly
strong subject position developed in book I. The poem's journey from the
chaos of book I to the resolution of book II is a corollary to the progress of
the notes. Besides sourcing a number of allusions to Shakespeare, and writing feelingly of the virtues derived from an 'education in the School of

Adversity', Smith focuses her two major notes on further condemning the
effects of war, following swiftly on in the poem itself with the vignette of the
third, dead, mother. It is as if she is informing her readers, before the fact,
that war turns men not into soldiers, but into marauders, existing on inadequate food ('unripe corn ... mashed into a sort of paste') and forced into
'disappointment and humiliation' (notes to II. 223 and 245). Reading between the lines, or rather under them, one begins to get a fuller picture of the
culture that has created a world in which mothers die at the hands of soldiers.

   And it is important, again, to note timing: in February 1793 war was
declared between England and France, rendering an anit-war polemic as
politically suspect as a pro-revolution argument. In book I, in November
1792, Smith offers to her readers a persona not merely sympathetic to, but
marginally supportive of the Revolution. In book II, in April 1793, Smith
condemns 'destructive war' (II. 215). This is itself a politically marginalized
opinion; Smith further enacts the unsayability of her critique by using the
margins to expose the wretched conditions endured by the French emigrant
soldiers and the dehumanizing effect of dishonourable war. Again, the margin
authorizes the body of the text, freeing the poetic voice to expose fully the
destructive and maddening effects of battle: dead mothers, murdered children, maniac husbands:

> Woes such as these does Man inflict on Man;
> And by the closet murderers, whom we style
> Wise Politicians, are the schemes prepar'd
> Which, to keep Europe's wavering balance even,
> Depopulate her kingdoms, and consign
> To tears and anguish half a bleeding world!
>   (II. 319–24)

   The notes, then, textualize the abject subject-position – the boundary-voice –
that in turn allows for the increasing pacifism of 'The Emigrants'. Locating the
abject in the margins allows Smith to defamiliarize both pro-revolutionary
fervour and standard anti-French posturing, creating instead a revoluntionary
sympathy that fully recognizes, exposes and condemns the ravages and inequities perpetrated by that revolution, and subsequent war. Negotiating the borderline
of the unspeakable, Smith fashions a subject-position that, by the poem's end,
allows her to direct – not plead, or even bargain with – God to reinstate peace,
in a series of imperatives: 'view', 'cause', 'restrain', 'teach' and 'drive'. The
interactions between note-voice and poem-voice result in an authoritative, politicized Smith who skirts the alternatives of 'sexual object or asexual
"respectability"' (Jones, 1993, p. 305). Jones argues that Wollstonecraft, Helen
Maria Williams 'and other women writers of their generation' sought in the
representation of revolution a release from the strictures of gender: 'they struggle to construct a new subject position, a feminine agency, but the repressive
binary categories on which nationalist identity, gender, and, it would seem,

emergent Romanticism are constructed are essentially unbroken' (p. 305). By utilizing the margin, however, Smith exiles herself from the binary; she observes its destructiveness and simply opts out. She explores and enlarges the borders, a self-effected alienation that, paradoxically, strengthens her subject-position. In this way, Smith energizes the abject; she reveals an awareness of the constructedness of the margin; and she allows herself to occupy, simultaneously, the centre and the borderline. War becomes the catalyst which activates Smith's exploration, and performance, of her persona.

Outside history[11]

Smith's persona – poet, mother, liberal, pacifist, revolutionary – is self-consciously constructed; readers become spectators in a drama played out on the very edge of the nation. As she does in *Beachy Head*, Smith extrapolates from a physical margin – the edge of a cliff, the coast – a symbolic alienation from her culture. But 'The Emigrants' offers a specific moment that crystallizes Smith's self-exile, a moment in history that proclaimed a self-evident centrality. The revolution, the overthrow of a monarchy, the violence of the Terror, the declaration of war with an historic enemy – the events of 1792–93 constituted 'history' even as they occurred, and Smith's understanding of this embues 'The Emigrants'.[12] But Smith's engagement with history masks a deeper disaffection; even as her opposition to war with France encompasses but goes beyond the 'humanitarian reasons' described by Matthew Bray (1993, p. 155), so her creation of historic 'spots of time' function as much to separate Smith from history as to facilitate her participation. Bray, for instance, argues that in *Beachy Head* Smith rejects the 'ideological Anglo-Saxon yoke' of history 'that allows English people to support an untenable division with France': *Beachy Head*'s version of history is one that realigns misplaced Anglo-French hostility, substituting a Humean history and denying the Anglo-Saxonesque perception of the Norman invasion as the introduction of a foreign tyrant (p. 158). Bray calls this Smith's 'seditious historiography' (p. 157). Smith lays out the groundwork for *Beachy Head*'s sedition, however, in her challenges to authority contained in 'The Emigrants': maintaining the morality of peace in the face of a cultural emphasis on the patriotic value of war constitutes one aspect of this challenge.

Allying herself with peace in 'The Emigrants' is suggestively akin to her later alliance with a French-friendly version of history in *Beachy Head*. What both show is a poet ill at ease with dominant voices of her own culture. To redraft English history in order to emphasize kinship with France works to place Smith *outside* English history; it functions to make her country's favoured version of history alien to the poet, who seeks for union rather than competition. By exiling herself from a position where she can support the

Anglo version of history, Smith re-enacts her cultural alienation: in exile from her country's history, she substitutes a rewritten one. Similarly, in 'The Emigrants' Smith's humanitarian representation of the *émigrés* supports, on the one hand, English compassion (the *émigrés* find to their surprise that 'we [English] for them / Feel as our brethren' (I. 359–60)), but on the other allows for pointed and open critique of English 'venalities'. Moving from depicting the *émigrés* 'homelessness' to the 'wide-extended misery' that contradicts Britain's self-image as a 'land of highly vaunted Freedom' (I. 307, 245), Smith uncovers the inequities that infect her own nation; the footnoted challenges described earlier authorize the anger that is at the centre of the text:

> Pensioners
> Of base corruption, who, in quick ascent
> To opulence unmerited, become
> Giddy with pride, and as ye rise, forgetting
> The dust ye lately left, with scorn look down
> On those beneath ye ...
> ...
> Ye pamper'd Parasites! whom Britons pay
> For forging fetters for them; rather here
> Study a lesson that concerns ye much;
> And, trembling, learn, that if oppress'd too long,
> The raging multitude, to madness stung,
> Will turn on their oppressors; and, no more
> By sounding titles and parading forms
> Bound like tame victims, will redress themselves!
> Then swept away by the resistless torrent,
> Not only all your pomp may disappear,
> But, in the tempest lost, fair Order sink
> Her decent head, and lawless Anarchy
> O'erturn celestial Freedom's radiant throne; –
> As now in Gallia; where confusion, born
> Of party rage and selfish love of rule,
> Sully the noblest cause that ever warm'd
> The heart of Patriot Virtue!
>   (II. 316–21, 329–46)

These lines are plainly revolutionary: not only are the basic tenets of the French Revolution upheld, but England's 'highly vaunted Freedom' is revealed as an empty show, and an English revolution is actually threatened as an appropriate, if not inevitable, action. As if to collect herself, Smith pauses after 'throne': the long dash builds in a deep breath and a deliberate turn away to 'Gallia'. The subsequent return to 'compassionate Britain' is less than convincing, if expedient; it allows Smith to end book I with a decorous praise of English virtue and a plea to avoid 'wide wasting War' (I. 381) – three months before war was openly declared.

Smith plants in 'The Emigrants' an anti-war stance that does not preclude the need for radical change in England. Her technique in book II is more guarded, but the careful reader can see her denunciations of 'Party Rage' and 'base Venality' references not only to a blind following of Robespierre and his policies but also to an equally blind veneration of leaders closer to home: allusions to 'private vice / [That] makes even the wildest profligate recoil' (II. 120–21) are as applicable to, for instance, the Prince of Wales as they are to Jean-Paul Marat.[13] But the trajectory of book II is not geared towards an ever more explosive exposé of British cultural shortcomings, nor even, despite the almost rhapsodic closing invocation of divine interference, a dismissal of this world in favour of God's; rather, the significance lies in the turn to the personal I noted earlier when discussing Smith's mother-imagery. 'The Emigrants' witnesses Smith's growing alienation from her society; her presentation of the *émigrés* fosters her identification with them; and her rejection of history is catalysed by her immersion in another version of it: her own personal history, her private sorrows that have, paradoxically, become a public property through Smith's frequent poeticization of them. The existence and continuation of her sorrows provoked by cultural indifference and hypocrisy, Smith decides to quit that culture; for her, the turn to the personal from the historical does not constitute trivialization, but rather a recognition that the personal is political. Smith's circumstances provide a micro-instance of the unhappiness and dissatisfaction that resulted, in France, in revolution, and by forging a direct bond between herself as dogged, victimized mother and the victimized mothers of war, she completes her image. Even as Smith-as-woman follows 'the rugged path, / That leads at length to Peace! – Ah! Yes, my friends, / Peace at least will be mine; for in the Grave / Is Peace' (II. 370–73), so Smith-as-poet proclaims that, with God's intervention,

> the fierce feuds,
> That long have torn their desolated land,
> May (even as storms, that agitate the air,
> Drive noxious vapours from the blighted earth)
> Serve, all tremendous as they are, to fix
> The reign of Reason, Liberty, and Peace!
> (II. 439–44)

Personal peace foreshadows historic peace: the woman's and mother's resolution inexorably allows for that of 'fierce feuds'. The turn to personal history thus creates the conditions for a return to a natural and cleansed culture. War has been rejected, but not, it is important to note, revolution.

Smith achieves this conclusion by placing herself outside history. She thus observes, but also maintains an attachment to, the culture of revolution. For Smith, her marginalization as a married woman and mother – culturally revered yet voiceless – offers an opportunity to embrace that marginalization and explore its territory. What she finds is an area of flexible boundaries, characterized by what has been culturally forgotten – repressed – and sidelined – made abject. Playing with these 'entities', she repopulates the margin, making visible the repressed and utilizing the abject, until the edge becomes central, becomes unavoidable, and the familiar becomes strange, and the strange becomes homely. By representing the invisible, by voicing the unspeakable, Smith transforms 'The Emigrants' into a polemical document, not merely anti-war or pro-revolution, but rather anti-cultural and proactive. From her position on the headland, Smith overlooks the *émigrés*, their adopted refuge, the country they have fled, and she notes the *unheimlich* nature of all three. But the deepest revolution is the one Smith herself embodies: in this poem, she takes up a complex involvement with conventions of gender and culture. As she concentrates on war and exile, she also manoeuvres her persona, performing gendered stances and roles as suggested by her construction of scenarios, vignettes of revolutionary import, and use of theatrical language. 'The Emigrants' is a poem about war, about being at war; it is a rejection of war; and it is a declaration of war on a culture that continually seeks to marginalize and cast off – abjectify – segments of itself. The repressed returns seeking vengeance, and Smith herself assumes the *unheimlich* stance of a woman on the verge: 'and all the various pain / I now endure shall be forgotten there' (II. 374–5).

Notes

1. It is important to keep in mind when noting Smith's self-naming that to do so in the late eighteenth century was to counter strict notions of feminine propriety; from the title-page, Smith is implying her departure from cultural inhibitions of female self-expression. In addition, the 'home' indicated on the title-page – Bignor Park – functions as an ironic foil to the homelessness of the sonnet 'I', who most often 'wanders' unhoused through the landscape. Here, as elsewhere, all references to Smith's poetry and prose will be to the texts printed in Smith, 1993.

2. Smith fully exploits the meanings suggested by 'fair': both 'beautiful' and 'balanced'. Only a few lines later she parenthetically dwells on the 'vain board / Of equal Law' as 'mockery' (I. 37–8). 'Man' mars the fairness of natural law, which is defined by equality, when he creates his own laws.

3. Although Curran implies that Smith's emigrants are only women, in fact only one of the five is: she describes three clerics, an aristocrat and his wife.

4. In the period in which Smith writes, achieving the eminence is of high political and literary importance; see Labbe 1998a for a full discussion.

5. In a typical Smithian move, the very lines that indicate a desire for seclusion also maintain the energy of individuality: 'there do I wish to hide me' (I. 48), she says, infusing her gesture towards domesticization with both agency and division.

6. Smith's involvement in the lawsuit that resulted from the flawed will of her father-in-law is detailed in Curran's introduction to Smith, 1993, p. xxi. As Curran notes, 'a sense of the legal system as an arbitrary machine of power operating without any essential relation to equity runs deep in Smith's writing' (p. xxi). See, for instance, note 2.

7. In 1784, Smith's husband Benjamin fled England to France to escape further imprisonment for debt. Smith, as the dutiful wife, accompanied him there, and regarded her six months' stay in France as 'exile'. However, it is part of the thesis of this essay that Smith saw marriage itself as exiling her from autonomy and personal freedom – which, of course, in legal and social terms, it did.

8. As with 'fair', Smith uses a word that carried multiple meanings: 'distracted' means 'mad' and 'preoccupied'.

9. Of all the clerics, the one who garners Smith's most sympathetic lines is the parish priest:

> Even such a Man
> Becomes an exile; staying not to try
> By temperate zeal to check his madd'ning flock,
> who, at the novel sound of Liberty
> (Ah! Most intoxicating sounds to slaves!),
> Start into licence
> (I. 190–95)

The priest's 'temperate zeal' is matched by his flock's enslavement to the tyranny of class; it is in lines like this that Smith reveals her pro-revolutionary stance.

10. One should also note the 'Tintern Abbey' resonances of the first lines of book II:

> Long wintry months are past; the Moon that now
> Lights her pale crescent even at noon, has made
> Four time her revolution; since with step,
> Mournful and slow, along the wave-worn cliff
> Pensive I took my solitary way …

says Smith

> Five years have passed; five summers, with the length
> Of five long winters! and again I hear
> These waters, rolling from their mountain-springs
> With a sweet inland murmur …

says Wordsworth (1984). As Wordsworth does in 'Tintern Abbey', Smith deliberately defers the introduction of the 'I' in order to solidify the effect of the passage of time on her self-construction: although, given that 'The Emigrants' is published five years before 'Tintern Abbey', perhaps what should be noted is Wordsworth's use of Smith's trope of memory. For a further discussion of Smith–Wordsworth interweavings, see Labbe 1998b.

11. I acknowledge my debt to Eavan Boland, whose collection of poetry, *Outside History*, inspired the title for this section of my essay.

12. Wordsworth's 'Tintern Abbey', of course, familiarly elides revolutionary history to concentrate instead on the history of the poet's development; yet, as Marjorie Levinson has shown, history is inevitably present. See Levinson, 1986. In the context of this essay, it might be said that history constitutes Wordsworth's repressed.

13. Curran's note to these lines remarks that 'this attack appears directed at Jean-Paul Marat, the most violent of the Jacobin propagandists, who was assassinated by Charlotte Corday later in 1793' (Smith, 1993, p. 153).

56   JACQUELINE M. LABBE

Bibliography

Boland, E. (1990), *Outside History*, Manchester: Carcanet.
Bray, M. (1993), 'Removing the Anglo-Saxon Yoke: The Francocentric Vision of Charlotte Smith's Later Works', *Wordsworth Circle*, 24 (3).
Chu, P. (1992), '"The Invisible World the Emigrants Built": Cultural Self-Inscription and the Antiromantic Plots of *The Woman Warrior*', *Diaspora*, 2 (1).
Desan, S. (1994), 'Women's Experience of the French Revolution: An Historical Overview' in Montfort, C. R. (ed.), *Literate Women and the French Revolution of 1789*, Birmingham, AL: Summa Publications, pp. 19–30.
Favret, M. A. (1994), 'Spectatrice as Spectacle: Helen Maria Williams at Home in the Revolution' in Montfort, C. R. (ed.), *Literate Women and the French Revolution of 1789*, Birmingham, AL: Summa Publications, pp. 151–72.
Jones, V. (1993), 'Femininity, Nationalism and Romanticism: The Politics of Gender in the Revolution Controversy', *History of European Ideas*, 16 (1–3).
Labbe, J. M. (1994), 'Selling One's Sorrows: Charlotte Smith, Mary Robinson, and the Marketing of Poetry', *Wordsworth Circle*, 25 (2).
———. (1998a), *Romantic Visualities: Landscape, Gender, and Romanticism*, Basingstoke: Macmillan.
———. (1998b), 'Charlotte Smith, *Beachy Head*', in Wu, D. (ed.), *A Companion to Romanticism*, Oxford: Blackwell; pp. 204–10.
Landes, J. (1988), *Women and the Public Sphere in the Age of the French Revolution*, Ithaca: Cornell University Press.
Levinson, M. (1986), *Wordsworth's Great Period Poems: Four Essays*, Cambridge: Cambridge University Press.
Montfort, C. R. and Allison, J. J. (1994), 'Women's Voices and the French Revolution' in Montfort, C. R. (ed.), *Literate Women and the French Revolution of 1789*, Birmingham, AL: Summa Publications, pp. 3–17.
Outram, D. (1987), '*Le Langage Male de la Vertu*: Women and the Discourse of the French Revolution' in Burke, P. and Porter, R. (eds), *The Social History of Language*, Cambridge: Cambridge University Press.
Smith, Charlotte (1993), ed. Curran, S., *The Poems of Charlotte Smith*, Oxford: Oxford University Press.
Wordsworth, W. (1984), ed. Gill, S., *The Oxford Authors: William Wordsworth*, Oxford and New York: Oxford University Press.
Zerilli, L. M. G. (1992), 'Text/Woman as Spectacle: Edmund Burke's "French Revolution"', *Eighteenth Century*, 33 (1).

CHAPTER FOUR

The harsh delights of political duty: Thelwall, Coleridge, Wordsworth, 1795–99

David Collings

Various claims about the political and historical engagements of English Romantic poetry pivot upon the writing of the final years of the 1790s, when Samuel Taylor Coleridge and William Wordsworth began their turn away from political radicalism. Both M. H. Abrams, who argues that after the disappointment of revolutionary expectation radical energies were channelled into an equally cataclysmic literature, and Jerome McGann, who argues that romantic writing turned away from political engagement to construct a 'romantic ideology,' point to evidence from the late years of the revolutionary decade (Abrams, 1971, pp. 112–19; McGann, 1983, pp. 81–92). Such critics take for granted a fairly simple account of political and literary agency, assuming that these poets could move beyond a stable or continuous domain of political action into a domain of primarily aesthetic action. Such a mapping of the discursive situation in England during the years in question disregards the possibility that the forms of political agency available then were under severe threat. Indeed, given the polarization of public opinion, the hostile relations between the British government and its dissidents, and the state of war between England and France, one cannot claim that the public sphere even survived in its familiar form. In the late 1790s, radical writers like John Thelwall, Coleridge and Wordsworth, friends and fellow dissidents, were faced with a wholesale anti-Jacobin onslaught and the active persecution of the Pitt government. While they remained committed to radical positions, by 1797 they found themselves in a nation increasingly dominated by loyalist associations and Francophobic enthusiasm, and surrounded by government informants and suspicious neighbours. To persist with an open avowal of radical opinion was to risk attack, imprisonment, exile, perhaps death. A mode of debate that had once allowed for a certain latitude in opinion had given way to something quite different, a form of total social violence which, like war, attempted to legitimize its fictions through violence against actual bodies, the privileged site of substantiation (Scarry, 1985, p. 62). Thus, the radical authors of that era found themselves in what can only be called an illiberal society, one in which 'the constitutive controversy of the public sphere dwindled as the public effectually identified with the desires of the State' and transformed 'the public man into a man of war' (Favret, 1994, pp. 541–2).

These three authors wrote the lyrics of the late 1790s not to retreat from, but to think through the problem of political duty. Rather than embarking on a mystified project, they examined the absence of options available to them, the stark limits of either heroic resistance or domestic retreat, the cost to themselves of participating in such a violent public debate and of losing the familiar sources of political agency, and the way that they might come to take an inhuman pleasure in the very violence they feared. In varying ways, they were thus fashioning a new kind of discourse, written from within radical traditions, that asked what one should be willing to bear or desire for the sake of social transformation. Thelwall set forth many of the terms for these poems, representing himself as traumatized by public hostility but incapable of finding refuge in domestic life, and Coleridge and Wordsworth worked out their own statements in response. Perhaps the most difficult challenge they faced was how to imagine a space for subjectivity not already invaded by the violence of war or of state harassment. Such lyrics invoke one tradition in anti-war poetry, including such poems as Wordsworth's *Salisbury Plain* and its revision, *Adventures on Salisbury Plain*, that depicts how war injures private bodies, whether abandoned women or wounded, non-privileged men (Favret, 1994, pp. 544–5; Collings, 1994, pp. 18–49), but as they do so they bring such conventions closer to home, pointing to the effects of total social war on the public man himself, on the very author of such poetry. If the battle was being conducted within oneself or on one's own body, how best should one go on?

As the 'Spy Nozy' episode of *Biographia Literaria*, chapter 10, demonstrates, Coleridge and Wordsworth recognized that they shared common cause with Thelwall, one of the most (in)famous radicals of their day. The evidence of Coleridge's correspondence with Thelwall, the careful reconstructions of scholars, and the writings of the principal participants demonstrate that they saw themselves as sharing similar histories, similar investments in poetry and an urgent interest in each other's survival during the late 1790s. The significance of such solidarity is lost if we glance too quickly at Thelwall. Literary biographers at times tend to regard him as a lesser poet-radical who passed quickly through the lives of his famous friends; in contrast, a historian of British radicalism like E. P. Thompson characterizes Coleridge as 'a sort of little Bristol Thelwall' (1969, p. 159). The latter statement better reflects the attitude of contemporaries. Thanks to his being tried and acquitted during the Treason Trials, and to his courage in defying the Two Acts of late 1796, Thelwall was a nationally known figure, the very embodiment of the English Jacobin – a term he did not shrink from applying to himself. But he was as original a radical tactician and theorist as he was a man of courage. Along with several others, he served as a liaison between the London Corresponding Society and the Society for Constitutional Information (Thelwall, 1989, p. xxvii), setting the pattern for the London-based organizational activists who flourished in the post-Napoleonic radical period. In his political lectures, he emphasized the decreasing real wage for workers, the staggeringly high rate of taxes that fell upon the poor, and the political illegitimacy of the unreformed House of Commons (Claeys, 1995, pp. 245–84), handing down a set of obsessions that would reappear most famously in the work of William Cobbett. He served as the leading speaker at the mass rallies held near London in October and November 1795 (effectively outlawed by the Two Acts that December), wearing a white hat during his orations (Corfield and Evans, 1986, p. 231), thereby creating the role later filled by Henry Hunt of Peterloo fame, though he goes unmentioned by Hunt's major biographer (Belchem, 1985). In a recent edition of his Jacobin prose works, Gregory Claeys argues that by 1796 Thelwall pushed beyond the familiar civic republican discourse to place novel interpretations on the economic rights of British citizens, at once welcoming ideas from David Hume and Adam Smith while challenging their conception of the effects of commercialism upon the poor (1995, pp. xlii–lvi; Hampshire-Monk, 1991); in this way he anticipated the radical political economists of the 1820s, who similarly appropriated natural law traditions and Smithian economics to rewrite economic orthodoxy. Even his cleverness in giving radical lectures after the Two Acts by disguising them as lectures in Roman history anticipated the resourcefulness of later activists. However neglected by certain historians, he looms large as a figure in the British political tradition and was clearly a potent force for his fellow radicals.

Neither Coleridge nor Wordsworth would have been cowed in his presence. As Nicholas Roe emphasizes, Coleridge's political career resembled Thelwall's. In 1795, both were independent lecturers, advocating reform and an end to the war with France (Roe, 1988, p. 148). After the failure of his Roman history lectures in London, Thelwall made a lecture tour of cities in East Anglia, circumventing the Two Acts in yet another way. In the same season, as Roe notes, Coleridge delivered lectures in western districts to drum up support for the *Watchman*, an experience also recounted comically in chapter 10 of the *Biographia* (1988, p. 155). Thelwall ceased publication of the *Tribune* one month before Coleridge ceased publication of the *Watchman* in May 1796 (p. 156). The two men had very different views on Christianity and on the value of Godwin's philosophy, as their correspondence reflects. But Roe is right to correct Thompson's belittling of Coleridge as a lesser Bristol Thelwall; Coleridge, too, had his influence and a major radical reputation (p. 154).

What about Wordsworth, the least known to his contemporaries? Even if one sets aside his experiences at Cambridge and in France, not to mention the radical poetry he wrote during the period, one can still follow his movements in the radical public sphere of the day, although he kept a much lower profile. Significantly, although he did write the *Letter to the Bishop of Llandaff* in 1793, he never saw it into print. His participation in radical London circles of the period seems similarly cautious. Kenneth Johnston suggests that members of the Godwin circle in London published a periodical, the *Philanthropist*, during 1795. Its first issues contain the essays most likely to have been written by him or Matthews, covering topics such as the use of talent, the British constitution, the freedom of the press, and the effects upon both rich and poor of the war with France. But Wordsworth took great care to obscure his role on the periodical both during and after its appearance (Johnston, 1998, pp. 427–67). Thelwall and Wordsworth must have shared many political opinions during that year, since both were influenced by the tradition of civic republicanism, defended the French Revolution in mid-decade, followed many of Godwin's teachings and moved in his London circle and, to follow Johnston's account, were associated with similar arguments against the war. However, Roe shows that, like Godwin, Wordsworth 'condemned public meetings and lectures' and as a result probably disapproved of Thelwall's convening large meetings (1988, p. 183). When Godwin went public with his disapproval of Thelwall's 'role in the London Corresponding Society' in 1795 (Claeys, 1995, p. xxix), Thelwall broke with him and continued his public activities. Wordsworth's disapproval of more aggressive tactics squares with his decision to retreat to Racedown and eventually Alfoxden, but his continuing radical commitment caused enough of a stir that spies monitored his activities before they knew of Thelwall's arrival (Roe, 1988, pp. 248–57).

While these three young men were clearly working along similar lines in the middle years of the decade, with varying degrees of exposure to the public eye, all three were also published poets and continued to write poetry during the years in question. Thelwall need not have deferred to Wordsworth or Coleridge on poetical questions, since he had published *The Rock of Modrec* (1792) and *The Peripatetic* (1793); in any case, he did not, since Coleridge's surviving letters to Thelwall show that the two were engaged in a sharp, if friendly, debate on literary topics from the beginning of their exchange in spring 1796.

It is thus inaccurate to divide the members of this circle from each other by profession or to imply that any figure dominated the rest. All three were committed radicals and poets, had participated in the emergent radical public sphere in mid-decade, and in the later months of 1796 were faced with the question of their appropriate place in the public scene. Even before Coleridge and Thelwall met, they were exchanging poems on the latter topic in which they attempted to persuade themselves to stick with public political activity despite the temptations of domestic life.[1] In the October 1796 issue of the *Monthly Magazine*, Coleridge published 'Reflections on entering into active life. A poem which affects not to be poetry', later entitled 'Reflections on

Having Left a Place of Retirement'. As the original subtitle suggests, this poem is an early instance of the 'conversation poem', presenting his 'reflections' in meditative blank verse. Here Coleridge takes a perspective nearly opposite to that common only a few months later, emphasizing his entry into the public arena. The poem frames retirement from the perspective of one 'having left' it, as if looking back upon it from the outside before actually leaving it. This perspective is introduced early in the poem, where Coleridge recounts how a citizen of Chatterton's 'Bristowa', contemplating his cottage, pronounced it 'a Blessed Place' (l. 17), a sentiment that Coleridge confirms. The fact he introduces his Arcadian state through the eyes of another hints that he can comprehend the status of retirement only when he sees himself being seen, only when he contemplates his condition from the vantage of the businessman on holiday (ll. 10–11). Retirement is always already mediated, never possessed; it is always something glimpsed from afar, even if one is the person being glimpsed. But once he takes that vantage, he declaims against the effeminacy of retirement, where he might 'dream away the entrusted hours / On rose-leaf beds' (ll. 46–7) or enjoy the pleasures of those sluggards 'Nursing in some delicious solitude / Their slothful loves' (ll. 58–9), vowing that he will take up a more virile practice 'and join head, heart, and hand, / Active and firm, to fight the bloodless fight / Of Science, Freedom, and the Truth in Christ' (ll. 60–62).[2] Still, in the final verse paragraph, he states, 'when after honourable toil / Rests the tir'd mind, and waking loves to dream, / My spirit shall revisit thee, dear Cot!' (ll. 63–5). In effect, he promises to be his own Bristol tourist, to draw upon the resources of nature or his memory of slothful love to help him face the good fight. Here retirement is rendered into a mental space; one can find refuge through one's daydreams. But to that extent, Coleridge relinquishes nothing much as he leaves this place, for, as he made clear earlier in the poem, such a spot is retired only when seen from afar. If it is already imaginary, its proper place is in the realm of projection; he can experience the delights of retirement while remaining in the public sphere. To this arrangement Coleridge adds a twist in the final lines, wishing 'that all had such! / It might be so – but the time is not yet. / Speed it, O Father! Let thy Kingdom come!' (ll. 69–72). Retirement prefigures that for which he is fighting; the idyllic scene might, in memory, enable political action, but it also constitutes its goal. It is simply unjust for him to experience its delights before they are available to all.

If Coleridge reconceives of retirement, he still keeps intact a fairly familiar sense of a radical public sphere. In contrast, given the charged circumstances of his public life, Thelwall had a much more vexed relation to the question of radical action. During his travels in 1796, he was personally attacked several times and his lectures disrupted by hostile townspeople throwing 'stones and brickbats at his audience' (Claeys, 1995, p. xxx). The difficult context of his action is reflected in a poem addressed to his wife, 'To Stella in the Country', written in December of that year (Thelwall, 1989). In the quatrains near the poem's end, he states that 'private bliss is lost in public woes', for 'Stern Duty bids to strike the bolder lyre' (p. 122). He uses remarkable terms to capture the effect of duty's call. Though the heart resists the sound, the groans of 'Man' still have their effect: 'The heart's torn fibres feel the call severe! – / The heart's best pleasures fly, with trembling wing'. The 'proudest joy' of the man who responds to this call will be 'a feverish, transient fire! / His fairest hope – a catalogue of woes'; he will scarcely slumber, envy and slander will afflict him, his friendships will be 'short-liv'd', 'And whom he shelters, load with heaviest wrong' (p. 123). To embrace such Duty is to choose an inhuman fate, and yet 'Man' calls; the sound of Duty's lyre is anti-poetic, grating – yet the 'heart's torn fibres' must respond. Such remarkable phrases hint that he experiences his heart as a source of pain, its feelings as a kind of mutilation; Duty's enjoyment, the 'feverish, transient fire', is a form of self-destructive disease. Thelwall does much here to demystify the moral masochism of his stance, yet he refuses to abandon it. In the final quatrain, he strives to imagine a less sadistic form of 'Imperious Duty', asking it to 'Strew, strew, at times, a rose among thy thorns; / Or steel each votive breast with stoic pride, / 'Till from the gloom refulgent Virtue dawns' (p. 123). But this final gesture does little more than salvage his political ethics from a biting critique. Where Coleridge conceives of retirement from the vantage of enforcing an ethical norm of male virtue upon himself, Thelwall turns his attention to the costs of obeying this norm, attacking the self-wounding required of the radical activist and by implication finding a human life only in 'private bliss' with Stella, only in retreat from political strife.

Thelwall's poem is something of a surprise. One might expect the leading 'Jacobin' public figure of the day to discuss the cause for which he fights and the forces arrayed against him. But as if to indicate that he can address those concerns elsewhere, in this poem he focuses on a novel subject for poetry: the difficult relation to political duty itself. Without mentioning the hostile crowds, Thelwall turns his wrath upon the compulsion to persevere in the face of great opposition. Perhaps because he is less of a public target, Coleridge can still enjoin himself to do his duty in a somewhat conventional way. It may be that only a speaker who repeatedly faces the brickbats can attack his own conscience so brutally and can resist attacking domestic life as merely effeminate. The result is that Thelwall gives the genre a new edge, allowing it to focus more explicitly on the competing obligations of public and private life.

By exposing the self-destructive dimensions of radical activism at the same time as he decides to persevere, Thelwall suggests that he is implicated in a violent public sphere as long as he remains politically active. Furthermore, he implies that his own emotions are now alien to him, objects of a fascinated horror. It seems as if his own conscience is a version of the violence directed against him – or, more precisely, that by intensifying his commitment in the face of such violence, he transforms commitment itself into something typically harsh and inhuman. In this way, his own generous impulses are transformed by the logic of mutual attack. The polarization of the public debate has transformed his own psyche; the division between the public and the self has begun to dissolve. Like the anti-war poems of Wordsworth, this text reveals that public strife injures people in the most intimate way possible, destroying their conviction of innocence and altering their relation to their own emotions.

During the next year, Thelwall was eventually forced to give up his lectures altogether, after having been harassed several more times and surviving the hostility of one mob in Derby by wielding a pistol and threatening to shoot any attacker (Claeys, 1995, pp. xxx–xxxi). At this juncture he decided to accept Coleridge's invitation of May 1796 to stay with him in the West Country (Coleridge, 1956, vol. 1, pp. 127, 131). Of course, the opportunity to meet each other in person would constitute a new stage in their friendship, but by mid-1797, such a meeting would also have other levels of significance. Both of their poems so far had envisioned an opposition between private and public life. But since so many British radicals were in retreat, perhaps they and others could find common refuge, sustain elements of the radical public sphere in a loose alignment of forces, renegotiate whatever significant differences remained among them (concerning religion or Godwinian philosophy), and join domestic lives in something neither strictly public nor private, a new kind of 'community'. The relation of Thelwall and Coleridge was representative in this regard: perhaps the relations of correspondence could become those of shared domestic lives or at least personal proximity. In moving to personal relations in this way, they would also create a new kind of network of living spaces in the West Country, bringing into play the existing links between Coleridge, the Wordsworths, Joseph Cottle and Thomas Poole, and visitors from London such as William Hazlitt and Charles Lamb.

The risks of embarking on such an experiment in everyday life were great. E. P. Thompson rightly states that Wordsworth and Coleridge must have known that spies would follow Thelwall, but they welcomed him anyway (1969, p. 160), perhaps because they knew they were already likely objects of local or government suspicion. They must have felt that the attempt was worth the risk, for by tactical skill they might be able to conceal Thelwall in the nearby hills, quiet suspicions, ignore spies and exploit local support long enough to brazen it out. After his visit in July 1797, Thelwall journeyed on to seek suitable places to settle, and Coleridge explored the Quantocks, the mountains near Nether Stowey, his home, for the same purpose (Holmes, 1989, pp. 158–9).

On 27 July, the anniversary of his birth and marriage, Thelwall composed 'Lines written at Bridgewater', a town not far from Nether Stowey, registering his response to the proposed community. By now he was falling under the influence of Coleridge's style, abandoning rhyme in favour of poetry 'which affects not to be poetry', indicating in his chosen form how he was willing to try out new modes of aesthetic and domestic practice. Certainly, he was charmed by his visit. The poem's tone rests on the edge between happy disbelief at the opportunity and doubt that it might not come to pass. It begins with the question as to whether he will still be subject to 'storms and persecutions' or whether his birthday–anniversary has brought a 'cheering prophecy of kindlier times' (p. 127). He would much rather 'hold converse' with Milton, Shakespeare and other bards 'Where Nature cherishes Poetic-Thought', far from the 'throng / Of cities, or of courts', than live in the 'hermit-like seclusion' that would await him apart from his friends (p. 128); ''twould be sweet ... / In philosophic amity to dwell', to tend their 'little garden plots' side by side, to debate 'Moral Truth', and to watch their infants, playing together, learn 'Wisdom's noblest lore / Fraternal kindliness' (pp. 129–30). The poem thus fuses the fantasies of poetic leisure, rustic labour, fraternity and homosocial attachment, imagining a social space where John and Samuel, 'Thy Sara, and my Susan', and perhaps William and Dorothy, would all innocently converse, reviving the 'Golden Age' itself (pp. 130–31). Yet because of the interrogatory syntax, the poem is almost wistful; the reference to the golden age is frankly mythological, bordering lines on the 'Wood nymph' and the 'Dryad' (p. 131). By this point retirement is a literary topos, perhaps a legitimate hyperbole in the wake of his visit, but one still laced with reservations. In the final verse paragraph, Thelwall expresses his profound wish to find the opposite of the stern duty of 'To Stella', referring to the 'domestic virtues' and its 'stingless extasies', 'gentlest Sleep' and 'envyless Obscurity', and finally marital bliss, all exact counterparts of the terms near the end of the earlier poem (p. 132). Thelwall's relief is palpable. At last he gives himself tentative permission to enjoy.

    Yet Thelwall remains subtly critical of his own ideal; he wishes, after all, for Sleep and Obscurity – for what he calls, in a related poem written soon after, the 'lap of Oblivion' ('On leaving the Bottoms of Glocestershire', p. 138). The reversal is too exact: he sacrifices duty so openly that he courts its retribution. To retreat might be to experience the loss of his virile identity in a kind of political death. He worries about the dangerously escapist dimension of the community ideal, exposing this particular version of the pantisocratic idea to the test of his own wishes. It seems for a moment that he endorses the charges of a critic like McGann, for 'Poetic-Thought' is the polar opposite of political engagement. But one cannot imagine him preferring a return to harsh Duty; even though he exposes the infantile quality of retreat, he convinces us that it is more humane than the alternative. His verse cuts through both domesticity and public virtue, making both options problematic. Were he to choose either now, he would do so seeing through its fictions. In the end he refuses the piety of a McGann-like critique, having exposed the harshness of its stoicism in the earlier poem, without fully embracing his longing for communal retirement.

The phrase 'Poetic-Thought' might still give one pause, insofar as it suggests, in context, that poetry is necessarily disengaged. But the poem itself undercuts such a claim. Even if he wishes to find refuge in a life of 'Poetic-Thought', his actual poetry is written from a vantage that includes full consciousness of the public scene. His poetry will never exemplify, only invoke, the myth of an Arcadian literariness. It will remain a sophisticated discussion of the relation between political and literary activity. What might seem to be a mystification turns out to be an element within a more compelling discourse which enables him to arbitrate between categories.

Despite the subtle undertones in this poem, Thelwall would prefer settling with his friends to living apart from them. But his fear that he would never get the chance was borne out by events. Coleridge wrote to him on 21 August to warn him that his return would probably lead to riots in the district: a claim that both E. P. Thompson (1969, p. 162) and Richard Holmes (1989, p. 159) find credible. In effect, the Stowey group admitted defeat. Thelwall's name was too infamous and the capacity of local zealots to incite riot against him too great for him to settle peacefully anywhere in the region. Furthermore, by September the Wordsworths were notified that their lease would not be renewed (Gill, 1989, p. 128), learning far in advance that they would have to reconsider their living arrangements the next summer. The members of the circle thus found themselves deprived of their chance not only to create an experimental community but also to live at peace in the countryside. Retirement was rapidly becoming a social impossibility.

For his part, Thelwall continued to search until he found a farm at Llyswen in rural Wales. Most of his correspondence from these years is lost, so one cannot know exactly the progress of his thinking during this period, but the full effects of his disappointment become clear in two poems written in October 1797, when he was in Derby preparing for the move to Wales. In the first, 'To the Infant Hampden. – Written during a sleepless night', he depicts himself as wrought with anxiety over his dispossessed condition and envious of his child's oblivion. '[S]leep on; / Sleep, and be happy', he tells his son; ''Tis the sole relief / This anxious mind can hope' that his three children 'As yet are blest' and that his wife 'is not quite / Hopeless, or joyless'. Hampden is 'As yet unconscious of The Patriot's name, / Or of a patriot's sorrows', including those of his father, who 'in his native land / Wanders an exile; and, of all that land, / Can find no spot his home'. Thelwall wishes that his son's 'dream of Life be ne'er disturb'd' with the visions of his father, 'Visions (Ah! that they were but such indeed!) / That shew this world a wilderness of wrongs – A waste of troubled waters', against whose 'pelting storms / Of cold unkindness' he is 'resistless', and in whose expanse his 'Ark ... Floats anchorless' (pp. 140–41).

The poem thus provides a partial answer to the question of the 'Lines written at Bridgewater': the 'storms and persecutions' have driven away all thoughts of a literary retreat. This poem ends with no consolation. The only hope is that the child will sleep on undisturbed, perhaps forever; to awake is to suffer. This relation to the child alters the conception of the masculine public sphere as it has operated so far in the retirement poems. Of course, only a son would be expected to enter the public sphere in adulthood. But rather than seeking relief from his troubles by contemplating his wife or domestic life generally, he considers a son ignorant of his fate but destined to become conscious. Unlike a wife, the son can thus be an oblivious counter-part to himself. The concept of private life is slipping into the figure of the sleeping child. Perhaps childhood itself is sleep, insofar as Hampden is unaware of the significance of his name; the two key terms, sleep and child-hood, may be redundant. Yet this equation implies a similar link between adulthood and sleeplessness, for the poem is written 'during a sleepless night', one that, represented in the 'dark' tempests of England's unkindness, seems to be endless. Any form of consciousness is already awareness of relentless persecution. One cannot escape the storms except in the sleep of the child. Thus Thelwall realizes that he will never truly find refuge, for he will always remain aware of the forces that are driving him into internal exile. His 'visions' of the storm are, unfortunately, true; the psychic and the politi-cal have become one. His mind has no means of resisting what he fears and can find rest only by contemplating the sleep of another. It is continuous with the social war being waged against him, so that even the interior space of thought, the region of the supposedly autonomous self, is occupied by 'vi-sions such as mar thy father's peace' (p. 141). Only the oblivious remain as a guarantee of a link to ordinary humanity. But their condition is inaccessible to him. Though he is at home, he finds no shelter; despite himself, he is still in the public world even there, forever denied domestic bliss. Whether in Derby or in Wales, the dwelling is merely an ark without an anchor and without the capacity to shelter him from the 'resistless' tempest. For him, there will be no refuge, only exile, only a ship drifting in an endless storm.

In the end, the poem represents the adult, rational self as almost disappear-ing between near-madness and death-like oblivion. It makes quite vivid the situation he articulates in another way in the prefatory memoir of *Poems chiefly written in retirement*, published in 1801, where all the Thelwall texts we are considering appear. In the memoir he attempts to treat the impossibil-ity of retirement as a political concern. There he neither retracts his radical opinions nor asserts them anew but claims his right to retain them in silence (Thelwall, 1989, p. xxxiii; Scrivener, 1990). He implies that the Tory regime, treating his political identity as a threat, seeks to erase his disloyal opinions. When the state not only deprives him of the right to speak freely, but also makes it impossible for him to choose where he might retreat from the public scene, it threatens his access to private life itself. As we have seen, 'To the Infant Hampden' dramatizes the condition of a mind under such a threat: the forlorn Jacobin is in an impossible position, at once haunted by the police and incapable of escaping their power. With the collapse of the radical public sphere and of any guarantee of his right to retreat into private life, the male political subject is left with nothing but the problem of his own traumatic condition and the futile search for relief. His only options are to politicize the fact of persecution and to write a new kind of poem, a 'Jacobin' crisis lyric that depicts the traumatic effects of persecution.

But perhaps such persecution has its own macabre appeal. The second lyric Thelwall wrote at Derby, 'Maria: A Fragment', offers a very different account of his traumatic experience. Addressed to his first-born, it describes how Thelwall, imprisoned during the Treason Trials, would eagerly await the visits of his wife and Maria. It revives the language of stern duty familiar from the poem 'To Stella', but with a startling difference: now duty's blandishments seem to be effective. Here the poet recounts how he would listen 'to the voice / Of patriots and of martyrs', who would tell him he suffered 'for Mankind', as did Hampden, Sidney and the Gracchi; at times, 'Warm'd by such thoughts, has the gaunt scaffold seem'd / A car of glorious triumph, banner'd round / With wreaths and well-earn'd trophies'. Such 'visions' are so 'inspiring' that they turn his 'bonds to trophies' and his 'solitude to high communion' (pp. 143–4). These voices promise him that death will not destroy him but will elevate him to the status of another Hampden; the suffering he shared with that martyr in 'To the Infant Hampden' here becomes his entitlement to a similar name in a radical pantheon of heroic masculinity. Martyrdom becomes a kind of inhuman joy, a version of Lacanian *jouissance* (Lacan, 1992). What was harsh anti-pleasure becomes a satisfaction beyond the pleasure principle; the force that colonized his mind is, in this poem, his own mind, much as the tempest in which he once tossed is now his own desire. Stern duty has come through for him, offering him not merely a rose ('To Stella', p. 123) but something much more enticing, a 'wreath' of glory. Furthermore, the thought of martyrdom enables him to 'laugh to scorn the threats of Power'; for a moment he is willing to put his life into the stakes in a game with a power that does not know how to respond to his challenge (Baudrillard, 1993, pp. 124–94). Thelwall admits to the secret satisfactions of persecution, stating that being one of the chief targets of the Pitt regime was a source of huge delight and a giddy sense of freedom. Suddenly, the terms of the retirement poems are reversed: what could possibly substitute for this delight? If the tempests of persecution are sources of emotional and political bliss, what could ever compete with them?

His daughter does: 'When thro' my grated dungeon I have gaz'd' to see Stella and Maria, 'ah! how high ... Swell'd the fond passion – for Thee, babe belov'd!' During the visits of his wife and child, 'fonder thoughts prevail'd, /

Soft'ning, but not abasing, the stern brow / Of Patriot-Emulation' (p. 144). In
prison, Thelwall evidently adopted the conception of male political virtue we
have seen already in Coleridge: while he allows himself to soften in the
presence of his wife and daughter, he does not wish to be 'abased' by the
comfort they bring him. He writes, 'there were *times* when fonder thoughts
prevail'd' (p. 144; emphasis added), hinting that he spent his remaining time
contemplating the harder pleasures of death and keeping his brow stern. The
tone of that line casts a pall over the joyful domesticity that follows. The fact
that his love for Maria must compete with other pleasures gives it a strange
quality, suggesting that love provides a refuge not from persecution but from
one's desire for something else entirely. The sight of Maria thus contains an
implicit rebuke to the would-be hero, reminding him of merely human charms
and of a femininity he wishes to repudiate.

Why would he write such a poem on this occasion? As he plans to move to
Wales, he remembers what brought him back from the longing for martyrdom. It is as if the move repeats that earlier gesture, as if retreat will release
him from the scaffold. But by removing his life from the stakes, he becomes
subject to 'Power' once again, relinquishing not only inhuman pleasure but
the freedom of heroic death. By choosing domestic love he returns to his
imprisoned condition, but at least he can peer through the grate, at the same
impossible distance from his daughter as from his son in 'To the Infant
Hampden'. In that case, the strange tone of these lines applies also to the
move to Llyswen: to retreat from heroic defiance is to relinquish the greater,
if inhuman, pleasure of radical public life. 'To the Infant Hampden' explains
that Llyswen will be exile, not retreat. 'Maria: A Fragment' goes further: it
will be exile from his own desire.

Some readers might regard the subject of 'Maria' as unremarkable. What
could be more commonplace than a martyr complex? But Thelwall depicts it
without apology, recounts it seriously, and states quite clearly that he did not
entirely renounce it on seeing his daughter. Thus, the poem accepts the desire
for martyrdom as a dimension of political life. It demonstrates that it is impossible to account for political activity entirely within the terms of post-
Enlightenment political philosophy, to understand it as the expression of reason, interest or opinion. One's response to the appeal of humankind must
always take place within the context of the subject's relation to gender, desire
and death. Whatever the ethical justification for political duty in relation to
others, one must also justify it in relation to one's own being. Overall, then, one
must take an ethical relation to the problem of political ethics itself (Lacan,
1992, pp. 179–90, 291–325). Duty calls; must we respond? Before such a
question, political and ethical philosophy founders. Thelwall's verse records
the crisis of the political subject: in 'Hampden', it nearly disappears into
tempest or oblivion, and in 'Maria', it reappears in the acknowledgment of the
conflict between *jouissance* and love. On some level, one's decision to accept

political duty depends less on the merits of the political cause than on one's willingness to defy the odds, to put one's life at stake. These poems suggest that those who force social antagonism, who identify themselves with the political divide and who willingly embody the place of potential violence must come to terms with their own fear of and desire for this violence.

Neither 'Hampden' nor 'Maria' is Thelwall's final statement on the problem of retirement, since these poems remain in tension with each other as well as with earlier texts, especially the 'Lines written at Bridgewater', where Thelwall shows contempt for 'honours emptier than the hollow voice / That rings in Echo's cave; and which, like that, / Exists but in the babbling of a world / Creating its own wonder' (p. 131). Such lines may show that after the Treason Trials of 1794 he disdains heroic fame. But his poetry consistently shows that he expected no refuge from the battles of his time, not even in Llyswen. Thus, he must not have been surprised when he faced hostility there from villagers fed by hostile rumour and anti-Jacobin propaganda, as if the mere proximity of a Jacobin were intolerable. Indeed, it seems he held up rather well: P. J. Corfield and Chris Evans quote government informants who state that he frequented a 'Society of Jacobins' and sustained a very active correspondence (1986, p. 236); they also provide a copy of a letter he sent to Thomas Hardy, the fellow survivor of the Treason Trials and linchpin of the London Corresponding Society (pp. 234–6). Evidently, he still attempted to belong to a community of correspondents, a counter-public sphere of covert activity, despite the frequency with which spies opened and destroyed his mail. This fact suggests that for Thelwall, retirement itself constituted a form of defiance, a way of expressing his refusal to accept the current terms of public debate. This interpretation is borne out by his decision to renounce even the level of resistance implicit in his Welsh sojourn. In 1801 he admitted political defeat, took up work as a 'teacher of lecturing' (pp. 238–9), and published the volume in which these poems and the important prefatory memoir appeared.

Not long after Thelwall the poet fell silent on these questions, Coleridge and Wordsworth wrote several poems in response. In the remaining space, I can do little more than indicate some ways in which those well-known poems attempt to expand upon or revise the terms of Thelwall's poems. Paul Magnuson argues that the first such response, 'Frost at Midnight', written in February 1798, bears a public meaning in the context of its publication with 'Fears in Solitude' and 'France: An Ode' in a small volume in 1798 (Magnuson, 1991). But in a recent article, Judith Thompson rightly argues that it responds to 'Hampden' and 'Maria' and thus, by implication, already has a political dimension (1997, pp. 427–8). Publishing it in the 1798 volume merely confirms its public status.

Although 'Frost at Midnight' is written in a supple blank verse not unlike that in 'Reflections', for the most part Coleridge focuses on the terms of

Thelwall's poems. Here, as in the poem to Hampden, we see a poet awake at night in his cottage, addressing an infant son. The uncanny quiescence at the beginning of the poem, and the midnight setting, both hint at an especially intense solitude that readily modulates into the memory of his isolation as a child at a charity school in London. Coleridge's use of memory here shows that on an embedded level he has explored the logic of Thelwall's poems further: if childhood is oblivion, can the adult find refuge through memory? Does something remain from childhood in the mind of the harassed adult? Such questions are consistent with the optimism of 'Reflections', which surmised that one could return to the place of retirement through memory alone. This time, however, his answer is not optimistic, for he discovers that the child is a young version of the adult and that memory confirms his present condition. The link between the present and remembered settings reinforces the impression that the poem's subject is, as in Thelwall, a kind of exile; but if for Thelwall childhood is oblivion and thus escape, for Coleridge the remembered child is still out of place. Furthermore, Judith Thompson points out that the child, like the Thelwall of 'Maria: A Fragment', yearns for a glimpse of his visitors, as if the charity-boy is imprisoned in the schoolroom (1997, pp. 441–4). The glimpse of the child is no longer a refuge for the adult; instead, he remembers peering through the dungeon grate as a child himself. But he also remembers that the child, already a counterpart to Thelwall, orients himself towards another version of *jouissance*; rather than anticipating the glories of death, he dreamed of the church bells that, he writes, 'stirred and haunted me / With a wild pleasure, falling on mine ear / Most like articulate sounds of things to come!' (pp. 32–3).

Having challenged Thelwall's myth of childhood, Coleridge now makes a crucial turn. Addressing his son for the first time, he imagines a future childhood in nature that will provide his son with a life he never had. The boy, Coleridge imagines, will commune with nature, understand its divine, 'eternal language' and partake of a certain 'secret ministery' [sic] (ll. 60, 72). Judith Thompson argues that the poem thus challenges Thelwall's atheism with a hopeful religious vision, as so many of Coleridge's letters do, not to carry out an 'ideological swerve' but to contest rationalist secularism with radical Unitarianism (1997, pp. 437, 448). This imagined future child gives Coleridge a response to the end of 'Hampden' (pp. 445–51): where Thelwall seems to be caught forever in the storm, finding no place where 'the tired foot / Of persecuted Virtue' can rest, Coleridge imagines at the end of the original version of this poem that all seasons will be sweet to the boy, who, on seeing the icicles' 'pendulous drops', will 'stretch and flutter from [his] mother's arms / As [he would] fly for very eagerness' (ll. 76, 79–80). Mythic childhood rescues one from the storm by converting it into a scene of delight. One need not find a place to rest, since one will always be ready to fly.

How credible is this solution to the impasse? The imaginary child is so blessed he scarcely seems human, for he will dwell in a space outside ordinary language or social relations. In effect, Coleridge resurrects the myth of the child's privilege, conferring a new kind of oblivion upon his son. As a result, the poem has a troubling undercurrent not present in Thelwall. If, indeed, the child's mind is wide open to the divine language, what will differentiate it from the storm? Introducing a saving difference from atheist despair, Coleridge creates a child who has too great an intimacy with the 'shapes and sounds intelligible' of the divine language (ll. 59–60) – sounds that uncannily resemble the 'articulate sounds' of the church bells. Nature becomes the scene not of a dreamed, but of a literal, *jouissance*. The child's mind is thus a counterpart to the adult mind of 'Hampden', similarly incapable of differentiating between itself and an envisioned tempest. Coleridge hints as much in a contemporaneous poem, 'The Rime of the Ancyent Marinere', the consciousness of whose eponymous hero is usurped by the forces of the universe. This poem, begun in November 1797, builds on key terms in the Thelwall poems of that October, such as a mind caught in the Deluge, an isolated hero peering through a dungeon grate, and a consciousness overwhelmed by paranoia and inhuman satisfaction. It appears that a mind truly 'haunted' by a natural language is indistinguishable from one colonized by political strife. In the conjoined terms of these two Coleridge texts of early 1798, the alternate state of consciousness to which the traumatized adult appeals for refuge may be another version of the same. Despite the appeal to Unitarian faith, Coleridge cannot break out of the impasse articulated so clearly by Thelwall; in fact, he extends it even further, reading even natural theology in terms of political trauma.

By linking the privileged child and the mad Mariner, Coleridge complicates Thelwall's version of political trauma. He hints that a world in which violence takes the place of debate and permeates private life, even the mind itself, is not easily distinguished from a world outside human experience where the political subject is in eclipse, for in the latter world the mind can also be haunted by an alien logic. Apparently, by sustaining the opposition between public and private – by reading the domestic as relief from public duties, or nature as a realm outside political discourse – one replicates the problem rather than solving it. Perhaps the very notion of refuge from distress deprives one of real relief. But in that case, what should one do? Should one find some other basis for at least a minimal distinction between the Deluge and the mind, thereby establishing anew the independence of the political subject? Or should one, on the contrary, repudiate such a distinction as a betrayal of history and insist on the duty to sustain and articulate trauma? Is it even possible to do the latter without on some level protecting oneself from the most brutal aspects of violence?

Coleridge's lived relation to the question of retirement changed in January 1798, the month before writing this poem, for he accepted a lifetime annuity

of £150 from the Wedgwood family which enabled him to decline an appoint-
ment as a Unitarian minister at Shrewsbury and released him from the ordinary
toil in which Thelwall was still engaged (Holmes, 1989, pp. 174–81). Knowing Thelwall would disapprove of his acceptance of such patronage, Coleridge
notified his friend of the annuity in an anxious and hasty manner, signalling
his guilt over their new difference in status (Thompson, 1997, pp. 432–3).
But this new status only made it clearer than before that his specific political
position – radical religious dissent – was being squeezed out of public discourse by the greater forces of loyalism and secularist radicalism. What made
him different from Thelwall also made him difficult to place in an ever more
polarized political scene. This discursive isolation is made vivid in 'Fears in
Solitude', composed, as the subtitle states, in April 1798, during the 'alarm'
over a possible French invasion. E. P. Thompson writes that 'March and
April, 1798, saw the greatest *levee* of the Volunteers in the whole decade'
(1969, p. 167). Every gentleman or professional, presumably including
Coleridge himself, was under pressure to enlist for such corps as that forming
to defend the coast adjacent to Stowey (p. 168). In effect, ordinary social
relations were now imagined in directly militarized terms, as if there were no
longer supposed to be any difference between a British citizen of a certain
standing and a warrior against France. By now, not only the public sphere but
also the ordinary social relations were to be grounded on the shared commitment to defend England against France and, by implication, against the likes
of Coleridge. The poem dramatizes these pressures in inconsistent ways, on
the one hand denouncing the thirst for war that Britain had recently displayed
and in contrast borrowing from loyalist rhetoric to rouse England's troops to
battle. As Magnuson argues, Coleridge attempts to be both 'a friend of liberty
and a loyal patriot', teetering between two rhetorics and two audiences (1991,
p. 7). The strangeness of his stance may be partly intentional, for the political
incoherence of the poem attests to his dissatisfaction with the very terms he is
forced to use. Neither radicalism nor loyalism can do justice to the non-secular
radical stance he wishes to take. At one point he seems to attack the public
sphere itself, that 'vain, speech-mouthing, speech-reporting Guild, / One
Benefit-Club for mutual flattery' (ll. 57–8), not to mention the institutions of
patronage (ll. 59–63). He presumably excepts himself from this attack. Yet
his disdain for the domain of public debate signals that he does not wish to
join it. The title is thus quite deliberate: he speaks to the public, but he speaks
in and from solitude, as if to dramatize the uniqueness of his political position. Even if during these months Daniel Stuart at the *Morning Post* was
willing to commission 'poetry and articles' from him (Holmes, 1989, p. 175),
he decides to challenge each of his audiences and to take up a space they no
longer recognize as a significant part of the political terrain.
    The response to Thelwall in 'Frost at Midnight' is thus symptomatic of
Coleridge's eventual response to public discourse. In effect, he locates him-

self apart from involuntary exile and the public sphere alike, choosing a third option: self-imposed exile in Germany. Since for Coleridge Germany represents the cultural project of religious, philosophical or philological innovation, a possibility foreclosed in the belligerent nations, he departs from the debate not into silence but into another conversation entirely. Thus, it is no great step from 'Frost at Midnight' and 'Fears in Solitude' to Germany itself. While the journey abroad is not entirely voluntary, caused as it is by the foreclosure of alternative political positions in England, it contrasts starkly with Thelwall's retreat to Llyswen. The annuity allows Coleridge to conceive of exile in a more fruitful way, to imagine it not as near-defeat but as the possibility of finding another as yet unsuspected stance, even if he will not as yet be able to capitalize on such a stance in Britain itself.

With very little money and even less interest in German culture, the Wordsworths consented to accompany Coleridge abroad, even though, as would soon become apparent, they conceived of the trip very differently. Before departure the principal parties made several journeys, including an August visit with Coleridge to Thelwall at Llyswen, as well as the famous walking tour of the Wye Valley near there. Johnston points out that one stimulus for the latter trip was Thelwall's essay, 'The Phenomena of the Wye, during the Winter of 1797–98', published in the May issue of the *Monthly Magazine* (1998, p. 589). During this journey, Wordsworth composed 'Lines written a few miles above Tintern Abbey on revisiting the banks of the Wye during a tour, July 13, 1798' (Wordsworth, 1984), at long last his response to the poems of his friends on the problem of retirement and political duty, whose title already alludes to 'Lines written at Bridgewater, in Somersetshire, on the 27th of July, 1797; during a long excursion, in quest of a peaceful retreat'. In recent years, critics have opened up unsuspected political dimensions of this text, but what remain especially relevant are the overtones of the retirement poems for a poet retracing another poet's path in another July, travelling in the Wye Valley not far from Llyswen as he prepares for his departure from England.

This poem is replete with echoes of the texts so far discussed. There are several strong verbal echoes: the repeated 'once again' of the poem's beginning resembles the same repeated phrase, used for farewell rather than greeting, in 'On leaving the Bottoms of Glocestershire' (Thelwall, 1989, p. 138), and the tentativeness of 'If this be but a vain belief' echoes doubtful moments in 'Bridgewater', where Thelwall wonders 'if the Year / Thou usherest in, has aught, perchance, in store / To realize this vision' (p. 132). But the poem also responds on an explicit thematic level. From 'Reflections', it appropriates the idea of retirement as a place in the mind, though not to strive for in political action. Like 'Lines written at Bridgewater', it disdains the life of towns and cities, celebrating the joys of nature, perhaps voicing Wordsworth's similar joy at renouncing the strife of the London political scene of 1795 (Johnston,

1998, p. 12). Taken together, these echoes suggest that Wordsworth, like Thelwall, wishes to be free of the burdens of public life but, like Coleridge, searches for refuge in memory. Renouncing both public life and a literal retreat, he will take comfort in his own mind. The echo of 'Bridgewater', which imagines retreat into a literary community, blends with allusions to 'Frost at Midnight', where the child communes with nature, as if poetic community may be found in the mind's own responsiveness to nature. In a challenge to Coleridge, Wordsworth regards the unthinking joys of the child as inferior to adult pleasures; setting aside the solution of 'Frost at Midnight', he proposes instead that one finds best communion if one hears in nature 'The still, sad music of humanity, / Nor harsh nor grating, though of ample power / To chasten and subdue' (ll. 91–3). The sound of humanity's appeal, Wordsworth implies, is not nearly so harsh as in 'To Stella': trauma relieves a person of the conditions of Coleridgean childhood but need not lacerate one's heart. Yet the child's sleep somehow survives in adulthood, enabling one to become 'a living soul' (l. 47).

A key allusion in the final lines is also telling. In 'Maria', Thelwall remembers the intensity of his joy upon seeing his daughter: 'Then – ah! then', when he gazed through the 'grated dungeon' to see his 'only babe' and his 'best beloved! – ah! how high' did his passion swell for Maria and 'for Her, more dear / To my connubial heart, that she had giv'n / Birth to thy infant sweetness' (p. 144). In a similar vein, William reassures Dorothy that when her mind is matured, 'Oh! then, / If solitude, or fear, or pain, or grief' should afflict her, 'with what healing thoughts' will she remember him and his 'exhortations' (ll. 143–7). And if they are separated, she will remember that he, 'so long / A worshipper of Nature', came there 'Unwearied in that service: rather say / With warmer love, oh! with far deeper zeal / Of holier love'– and that these woods, cliffs and landscape 'were to me / More dear, both for themselves, and for thy sake' (ll. 152–6, 159–60). The strong resemblance between these joyful exclamations of love suggest that Wordsworth regards nature as his true beloved, and that it is dearer to him for Dorothy's sake, much as Stella is dearer for giving birth to Maria. Gender enters this poem through an address to nature and to his sister, a sister imagined in no domestic space but in the analogous mental space of his earlier self (ll. 120–22), the Coleridgean child (ll. 135–8), his mature self (l. 139) and a self that will remember him.

To some extent these lines confirm a familiar hierarchy of male and female while displacing it into a narrative of mental development. But by imagining that Dorothy will, in her troubles, take comfort from his love for nature, he places her in the metaphorical prison and makes himself her Maria. It is as if Dorothy, embodying nature, relieves him of his sorrows and that he, in love with nature, does the same for her: nature is the requisite third party, an element that may be shuffled at will between human categories. But nature serves this role only because it is not immediately available to either of them; it is represented, articulated, remembered by each, obviously having become subject to language and social relations. Thus, Wordsworth challenges the terms of the previous poems, seeking refuge not in the child's oblivion or in an unmediated nature, but in the mutual responsiveness of adults. On one level, this position suggests that one can withstand trauma not by seeking refuge but by attempting to explore the significance of historical violence for oneself and others – perhaps in poems like this or in those to which it alludes. But on another level, the fact this exchange is structured around nature suggests that the poem evades a direct approach to violence, conducting its discussion indirectly through the allusions to various dates, biographical events and the lyrics of others. The poem at once complicates previous discussions and masks the implications of its insights, as if exploring a possible new mode without wishing to make its import explicit.

Within weeks the three travellers were in Germany. There Coleridge embraced new experiences and new traditions, learning the language, relishing an unusual perspective on the European scene. But on the theme of retirement he fell silent as a poet. Of the 1797 poetic community, only Wordsworth remained. And for him, Germany scarcely existed. A cultural impasse, not writer's block, engendered *The Prelude*: a crisis in the discourses of British radicalism which, for the moment, he exactly embodied. Stuck in a freezing Goslar for the winter with Dorothy, separated from Coleridge, more stranded even than Thelwall in Llyswen, cut off not merely from England but from a credible political discourse, bored by the possibility of writing heroic verse (perhaps not unlike Thelwall's abortive *The Hope of Albion*, published in *Poems*, 1801), little remained to him but to make good on the astonishing claims of 'Tintern Abbey' and thereby to take up more seriously than ever the questions of refuge, historical trauma and vocation. Why write *The Recluse* if he has it in his power to be the recluse, to explain how he can find refuge from history in himself or in his relations to his friends?

Soon he is embarked upon the *Two-Part Prelude* (Wordsworth, 1979), whose opening lines often allude to 'Frost at Midnight' (Magnuson, 1988, pp. 187–9) and through that text, to the poems by Thelwall. Nature now provides its secret ministry through 'characters / Of danger and desire' (I, 194–5), through 'sanctifying by such discipline / Both pain and fear' (I, 139–40). The child receives his privileged status in episodes of high tension, through anxious visitations and troubled pleasures, through thefts and encounters with drowned men and haunted gibbets, through accidents too numerous to tell: through trauma transfigured into bliss. Elsewhere I have argued that this text continually reworks earlier statements on war, trauma and cultural dismemberment, including the Salisbury Plain poems and the 'Rime' (Collings, 1994, pp. 129–56); if it seems to inaugurate the millennialist romanticism Abrams describes, in fact it continually evokes the experience of historical trauma that he, writing in 'Germany', associates both with revolutionary France and the Pitt regime. Simon Bainbridge, taking issue with Alan Liu's new-historicist argument, has recently argued that the Simplon Pass episode's allusions to the Napoleonic crossing of the Alps may be 'delicate and subtle', but they 'are also conscious, considered and deliberate' (1995, p. 57). The allusions to terror, war and murder in this early text are equally deliberate. They might even include elements of Thelwall's recent experience. In the prefatory memoir, Thelwall writes that he was hunted down by loyalist thugs and that his Welsh neighbours accused him of being a conjurer (1989, pp. xxxiii, xxxvii); as we have seen, in 'Hampden' he also seemed lost in an endless midnight storm. Wordsworth, no doubt having heard these tales during his visit to Thelwall in August 1798, reworks them into signs of privilege. The child steals from nature so that he will be hunted down; in the final spot of time, the child and the poet conjure up a deeply satisfying tempest at a crossroads and at midnight (Bewell, 1989, pp. 182–3). Blending Thelwall's ordeals with the Mariner's paranoia, the blessed condition of the Coleridgean child and the entranced state of the protagonists of his own anti-war poetry of mid-decade, Wordsworth celebrates them all as providing access to imaginative power.

With these outrageous reversals of Thelwall's experience, not to mention that of Coleridge and himself, Wordsworth clearly abandons the attempt to find a saving difference between trauma and the self, instead reading intolerable crisis positively and embracing the accusations of sinister intent and occult power as signs of a superior vocation. If the world broke apart, it did so to reveal another world. The destruction of the public sphere through military, ideological and social war melted down received forms of public agency into something new and strange, an agency not anticipated in the terms of Enlightenment political philosophy, one that lives permanently and explicitly in relation to *jouissance*. But it does so only at the cost of obscuring what is intolerable in trauma and generalizing extravagantly upon the specific political reference of this new agency. Thelwall revealed how any deep political commitment must address the question of taking obscene pleasure in the prospect of martyrdom; Wordsworth, following on the logic of his anti-war poems and Coleridge's 'Frost' and 'Rime', finds *jouissance* everywhere, in childhood and in nature. Apparently, once one celebrates the accusation or considers harsh duty a form of bliss, one becomes capable of imagining all the relevant problems in a new way: at least potentially, total war promises to transfigure the political world.

Yet this shift is not quite successful, for in the thirteen-book *Prelude* completed in 1805, Wordsworth disinters the coded references to revolutionary violence, addressing it openly in books 10 and 12, in passages on the September Massacres and the Terror. These scenes remain so traumatic he cannot integrate them into the overall logic of his poem, except primarily as something to be overcome – even though those moments which heal him (the spots of time) are elaborate reworkings of the same crisis (Collings, 1994, pp. 207–36, 139–56). Through this resistance to trauma, he points to the limits of the political stance proffered in the *Two-Part Prelude* and reveals both that a specifically political trauma lurks at the heart of his experience and that his vocation is built upon the evasion of its most painful aspects.

Taken together, the crises lyrics of these poets show that they could not finally be free of the trauma visited upon them and their fellow travellers. Once political life becomes warfare, there can be no refuge. In this context, McGann's critique seems well beside the point; rather than judging poets by how seriously they engage material history, one can instead follow how they account for their relation to the site of political antagonism and, by extension, to their own *jouissance*. One can apply such a norm only in the full knowledge that what it commands is impossible, for 'at a certain level, fantasms cannot bear the revelation of speech' (Lacan, 1992, p. 80). Even the attempt to reveal the fantasm directly and intolerably can become its own convention, contributing through its very aggression to a style that aestheticizes the trauma. Some form of ideology is thus inevitable in these matters – ideology conceived of as the attempt to block out the site of social antagonism (Žižek, 1989). Few poets of the eighteenth or nineteenth centuries meet the standard set by Thelwall. But even he fails to recognize the full implications of his writing or to see the value of his de-idealization of political virtue, for he does not insist upon his insights in the prefatory memoir or in further poems of the same sort. Coleridge at once represents trauma in such poems as the 'Rime' and keeps such poems safely apart from others more obviously about his condition, thus establishing a saving difference between himself and the inhuman. Wordsworth extravagantly enlarges upon trauma and yet evades it, thereby veiling its most unassimilable elements.

Despite such evasions, these crisis poems unmistakably begin the process of rethinking political experience. What survives of revolutionary violence, the traumas of war, the judicial and mob violence of the Pitt era, and of social antagonism generally, cannot be told in the terms of any single political position, for it looms at the limits of political agency itself. These poets teach us that at those limits we find no secret principle of history but rather the question of how the political subject will live history in relation to fear, desire and death. Political experience at its limits asks even more intractable questions about one's relation to *jouissance* and to love.

Notes

1. For evidence that Thelwall and Coleridge exchanged their poems or notified each other of publication, see Coleridge, 1956, vol. 1, pp. 205, 259, 277–9, 285–6, 307, 351 (including remarks on 'To the Infant Hampden'). The nature of this

exchange and the fact of Coleridge's long-standing intimacy with Wordsworth make it extremely probable that Wordsworth was also familiar with the key Thelwall texts discussed here. Quotations from Thelwall's poetry and prose are taken from his *Poems chiefly written in retirement* (1989) and will be cited by page number. Quotations from Coleridge's poetry are taken from his *Poetical Works* (1969) and will be cited by line number.

2. Coleridge's sonnet to Thelwall uses the same terms to praise his friend's virile courage and to condemn his own effeminacy (Coleridge, 1969, p. 588).

Bibliography

Abrams, M. H. (1971), *Natural Supernaturalism: Tradition and Revolution in Romantic Literature*, New York and London: Norton.

Bainbridge, S. (1995), *Napoleon and English Romanticism*, Cambridge: Cambridge University Press.

Baudrillard, J. (1993), *Symbolic Exchange and Death*, trans. Hamilton Grant, I., London: Sage Publications.

Belchem, J. (1985), *'Orator' Hunt: Henry Hunt and English Working-Class Radicalism*, Oxford: Clarendon Press.

Bewell, A. (1989), *Wordsworth and the Enlightenment: Nature, Man, and Society in the Experimental Poetry*, New Haven: Yale University Press.

Claeys, G. (ed.) (1995), *The Politics of English Jacobinism: Writings of John Thelwall*, University Park: Pennsylvania State University Press.

Coleridge, S. T. (1956), ed, Griggs, E. L., *Collected Letters of Samuel Taylor Coleridge*, 6 vols, Oxford: Clarendon Press.

————. (1969), ed. Coleridge, E. H., *Poetical Works*, Oxford: Clarendon Press.

Collings, D. (1994), *Wordsworthian Errancies: The Poetics of Cultural Dismemberment*, Baltimore: Johns Hopkins University Press.

Corfield, P. J. and Evans, C. (1986), 'John Thelwall in Wales: New Documentary Evidence', *Bulletin of the Institute of Historical Research*, 59 (140).

Favret, M. A. (1994), 'Coming Home: The Public Spaces of Romantic War', *Studies in Romanticism*, 33 (4).

Gill, S. (1989), *William Wordsworth: A Life*, Oxford: Clarendon Press.

Goodwin, A. (1979), *The Friends of Liberty: The English Democratic Movement in the Age of the French Revolution*, Cambridge, Mass.: Harvard University Press.

Hampshire-Monk, I, (1991), 'John Thelwall and the Eighteenth-century Radical Response to Political Economy', *Historical Journal*, 34 (1).

Holmes, R. (1989), *Coleridge: Early Visions*, New York: Viking.

Johnston, K. R. (1998), *The Hidden Wordsworth: Poet, Lover, Rebel, Spy*, New York: Norton.

Lacan, J. (1992), *The Ethics of Psychoanalysis 1959–1960*, The Seminar of

Jacques Lacan, book VII, ed. Miller, J. A., trans. Porter, D., New York: Norton.

Magnuson, P. (1988), *Coleridge and Wordsworth: A Lyrical Dialogue*, Princeton: Princeton University Press.

————. (1991), 'The Politics of "Frost at Midnight"', *Wordsworth Circle*, 22 (1).

McGann, J. J. (1983), *The Romantic Ideology: A Critical Investigation*, Chicago: University of Chicago Press.

Roe, N. (1988), *Wordsworth and Coleridge: The Radical Years*, Oxford: Clarendon Press.

Scarry, E. (1985), *The Body in Pain: The Making and Un-Making of the World*, Oxford: Oxford University Press.

Scrivener, M. (1990), 'The Rhetoric and Context of John Thelwall's "Memoir"', in Rosso, G. A. and Watkins, D. P. (eds), *Spirits of Fire: English Romantic Writers and Contemporary Historical Methods*, Rutherford, NJ: Fairleigh Dickinson University Press, pp. 112–30.

Thelwall, J. (1989), *Poems chiefly written in retirement*, Oxford: Woodstock Books.

Thompson, E. P. (1969), 'Disenchantment or Default? A Lay Sermon' in O'Brien, C. C. and Vanech, W. D. (eds), *Power and Consciousness*, London: University of London Press, pp. 149–81.

Thompson, J. (1997), 'An Autumnal Blast, a Killing Frost: Coleridge's Poetic Conversation with John Thelwall', *Studies in Romanticism*, 36 (3).

Wordsworth, W. (1979), ed. Wordsworth, J., Abrams, M. H. and Gill, S., *The Prelude: 1799, 1805, 1850*, New York: Norton.

————. (1984), ed. Gill, S., *The Oxford Authors: William Wordsworth*, Oxford and New York: Oxford University Press.

Žižek, S. (1989), *The Sublime Object of Ideology*, London and New York: Verso.

CHAPTER FIVE

Duty and mutiny: the aesthetics of loyalty and the representation of the British sailor c. 1789–1800

Geoff Quilley

In 1798 James Stanier Clarke published a set of sermons given on board the Channel fleet ship the *Impetueux*, where he had served as sea chaplain since 1796 (Clarke, 1798; Taylor, 1978, pp. 210–11). As well as being part of a naval population whose political and social composition had been transformed by the effects of the 1795 Quota Acts, the crew to whom they were addressed had participated directly in the mutiny at Spithead in April 1797, and manned a ship which by 1799 had gained the reputation of being one of the most mutinous vessels in the navy (Price, 1990, p. 84).[1] The sermons address the general themes of obedience and duty; and with their prompt publication following the thanksgiving for naval victories preached on 19 December 1797 (also included in the volume), they are clearly a response to the extreme events of 1797 – the crisis of the mutinies, followed by the crucial victory at the Battle of Camperdown – as well as to the continued fears over invasion from France and the uncertain loyalty of the lower deck. I shall deal with Clarke's sermons in detail later. For now I want to claim that they constitute part of a remarkable shift in attitude towards the ordinary sailor. Their suasive character implicitly acknowledges that the stereotype of Jack Tar as the unthinkingly loyal 'son of Britannia', which had been the predominant character attributed to the sailor during the eighteenth century, could no longer be sustained in the light of recent events. Instead, his loyalty was to be won by sophisticated and reasoned argument.[2] Tacitly acknowledged too, however, is the presence of a large constituency of the navy whom reason might lead to republicanism rather than constitutional monarchy; and the presence of many, particularly Irishmen, whose loyalty might not, anyway, be naturally towards England.

Their publication thus marks an acute realization of the pivotal role of the sailor for the constitution and significance of British national identity, and alludes to several highly-loaded ideological values about his status in late eighteenth-century Britain. Throughout the book Clarke makes explicit the relation, conventionally understood, between the social structure on board ship, and that of the nation: the ship-of-war is also the ship of state in microcosm. For a nation as self-consciously reliant on naval power as Britain, particularly at this time, the analogy assumed a peculiarly powerful significance, integrating the practical military, economic and political needs of the state with the cultural construction of national identity.

What may be termed the 'mythology' of the maritime nation had been articulated with increasing depth and complexity over the course of the century. Simply put, this asserted the providentially-sanctioned destiny of Britain – the 'sceptred isle' – a political union after the 1707 Act of Union, to achieve military and commercial glory as a maritime nation.[3] The ideological circle was completed by the idea that the civic and individual liberty created by commercial wealth would be enacted under the special balance of the English constitution; and, further, under the unique institution of the Anglican church: which brought the project of the nation back within the orbit of divine determination.

Central to this construction of the nation was, of course, navigation, which depended upon the sailor. His persona could implicitly, therefore, be assigned a great deal of ideological and political weight. But he was a peculiarly problematic figure in eighteenth-century life, more so during the French Wars. Clarke infers the two conventional but polarized conceptions of his identity. As the dutiful servant of the Crown, he is like the good citizen, in his proper place and contributing his share, so that 'the vessel is conducted through the waves in safety' (Clarke, 1798, p. 71). The corollary of this, which in the context of the recent mutinies did not need to be stated, was that the ship and nation would founder if, like the mutineers, those whose proper place was to obey, had aspirations above their condition. The archetypal sailor addressed by Clarke is a figure veering between extremes of patriotism and treachery, obedience and subversiveness.

His situation was encapsulated by the advice of a late eighteenth-century mariner to a new recruit: 'There is no justice or injustice on board ship, my lad. There are only two things: duty and mutiny – mind that. All that you are ordered to do is duty. All that you refuse to do is mutiny' (Weibust, 1969, p. 372; Rediker, 1987, pp. 211, 244–5). It is the unstable character of this binary construction of his identity which I shall examine in this essay, as it finds expression in the visual representation of the sailor, and its critical moment in the contested cultural climate of the 1790s. The polarized representation of the tar was well rehearsed in eighteenth-century culture generally, and I shall argue that the changes noticeable in his visualization during the 1790s should be seen not so much as a complete reformulation of his identity, from a *tabula rasa* appropriate to the demands of a revolutionary era, rather as the aesthetic emergence, prompted by the unprecedented ideological character of the French Revolutionary War, of a dialectical opposition already resident in the established articulation of the sailor's cultural persona. It will be necessary, therefore, to consider something of the earlier period of the mid-eighteenth

century to put into relief the representational innovations surrounding the
sailor in the 1790s. Similarly, his representation was not confined to graphic,
painted or sculpted images and, while I shall be concentrating on prints and
paintings in particular, the ways in which they responded to other forms of
culture, above all theatrical performance, was essential in projecting the
sailor as a popular, pervasive national stereotype. Like the ship, the consistent
features of his personality, displayed alike in high and low forms of art,
literature and music, and across regions, could register as a latent but potent
ideological confirmation of a unified national identity and an essential British
character, transcending local regional or class differences. The larger cultural, political and representational contexts within which the sailor figured,
both as active labourer and as a predominantly fictive cultural icon, cannot be
overlooked if his significance, both in eighteenth-century Britain as a whole
and in the 1790s particularly, is to be understood. Essential to this understanding also is the awareness that the former role, that of active labourer, is
very rarely displayed in the picturing of the tar, in favour of the view of him
as 'Britannia's steady champion and filial friend'.[4] Such displacement carries
its own ideological weight, and functions importantly as another, though
negative, context in the determination of the aesthetic construction of the
sailor, as a form of representational absence, which has a particular salience
for the sailor's distinctive social circumstances and status.

If the ideological significance of the ship operated simultaneously at allegorical and functional levels, that is as the symbol of the nation – the ship of
state – and the material provider of the state's economic prosperity, the
persona of the sailor was articulated similarly. In his ideal evocation, apparent particularly at time of war, he was the 'pillar of the nation', the 'heart of
oak', and a national hero. By contrast, his more vulgar stereotype was that of
an oversexed drunkard, blasphemer, reveller and brawler. And this conforms
more closely with his social and political actuality. Seamen were notoriously
irreligious, anti-authoritarian, filthy-tongued, drunken, riotous and propertyless
(Rediker, 1987, pp. 162–86, 244–53, 297–8).

The greater paradox of the sailor's social identity, however, was that in his
professional capacity as a productive labourer, he was of necessity removed
from society. In this sense, his cultural identity was located at some level in
the imaginary. The idea of representational absence already mentioned has a
dual sense: it refers to both the absence of the sailor from the conventional
iconography of the eighteenth-century labouring poor, his being as a labourer
out of sight; and also to the ambiguity that, when he is represented, it is
conventionally ashore, revelling, and with the tacit possibility of being absent
without leave from his work.

The sailor's 'otherness' was rooted in social actuality. While sailors were a
familiar sight to landed society, this was only as much as

the inhabitants of modern European cities are familiar with tourists. They recognised their curious clothes and eccentric behaviour, they laughed at their oddities, they profited from their ignorance – but they did not understand seamen, and they knew nothing whatever of the world from which they came. Superficially familiar, the seaman remained to his contemporaries profoundly strange. They knew him only on land, out of his element.

(Rodger, 1988, p. 15)

This 'familiar strangeness' had two major consequences as regards the subject of this essay. First, it provoked an ideological distancing in the social attitude to seamen, typified by Defoe's early eighteenth-century description of their antisocial nature:

'Tis their way to be violent in all their motions. They swear violently, drink punch violently, spend their money when they have it violently ... in short, they are violent fellows, and ought to be encourag'd to go to sea, for Old Harry can't govern them on shoar.

(Earle, 1998, p. 13)

There was, therefore, a certain ideological incommensurability about the sailor, which necessitated his exclusion from society in order to be accommodated within it. His social persona fits precisely Michel Foucault's definition of the 'other': 'that which, for a given culture, is at once interior and foreign, therefore to be excluded (so as to exorcize the interior danger) but by being shut away (in order to reduce its otherness)' (1970, p. xxiv).

Second, owing to the sailor's ideological exclusion, his necessary interiorization – that is, in Foucault's terms, the function of reducing his otherness – relied heavily on representation: he was 'shut away' in theatre, novels and images. This was particularly true of the theatre, where nautical productions were a growing and increasingly spectacular part of the repertoire during the French Wars, but where sailors ashore also formed a significant and distinctive component of the audience watching the naval plays, ballads and afterpieces. The seagoing spectators were thereby engaged in a joint social performance with their stage counterparts of mutually self-validating and ideologically sustaining representation (Russell, 1995, pp. 95–115). But if, as Gillian Russell has argued, the theatre could replicate the social structures and spaces of the ship,[5] a similar pattern was apparent across other cultural forms. Shipboard hierarchy was reproduced pictorially. The numerous maritime portraits by Reynolds, Hoppner, Beechey and others are, needless to say, all of officers. Though overwhelmingly setting the subject either in battle or against the backdrop of the ocean, they rarely, if ever, include any reference to the men under his command, in the way that, for example, a portrait of a country gentleman might include his servant, or even his dog.[6] This may be a form of aesthetic reproduction of social stratification typical of eighteenth-century art, but it has a more acute and specific political significance in the context of the maritime.

For, as Marcus Rediker has written, there were two fundamental confronta-
tions in seafaring culture: that between man and the natural forces of the sea,
and

> the showdown between man and man, the class confrontation over the
> issues of power, authority, work and discipline. This encounter pro-
> duced ... a subculture or 'oppositional culture' shared by common
> seamen, with a distinctive set of attitudes, values, and practices. Mari-
> time culture, then, was fractured.
>
> (Rediker, 1987, pp. 154–5)

Such a fracture was replicated in the invisibility of the workforce in maritime portraiture. Likewise, in the seemingly documentary literature of
published journals and voyage narratives, he is generally only redeemed from
invisibility in cases of dispute or litigation (pp. 312–16). There is, therefore,
little or no self-generated aesthetic representation of the ordinary seaman in
the eighteenth century. Yet, in contrast to the dearth of reference to the sailor
in his actual social circumstances, his fictive character is a constant presence
in the novels, plays and music of the period. And in this guise, as has been
well documented, his character conforms to certain recurrent stereotypes. He
is variously the untameable brute, to be beaten into submission; the rough
diamond, gross but quick-witted and true; the dull but loyal servant of the
crown, laying down his life for the nation; the sensualist, boozing and whor-
ing his way to his next passage, living for the moment; or the faithful Jack
seeking wealth to claim his true love back home (Robinson, 1909; Watson,
1931; Bratton, 1991; Glenn, 1989). As we shall see, more than one, or even
all, of these often contradictory traits may be ascribed to a single character.
What is notable is how corporeal they are, asserting a material physicality for
the seaman which is in stark contrast, as I have suggested, to his labouring
identity.

The political economy of the sailor comprised the transformation of the
physical body into a unit of labour currency, an economic value like the cargo
it heaved and shipped. Almost proverbially, the seaman's tools were 'but a
pair of good Hands, and a Stout Heart' (Slush, 1709, p. 16). And the economic identity of the seaman, whether military or mercantile, was a
disappearance of the body into a 'pair of good Hands', transferable between
ships and widely differing manual tasks, for which the sailor was rewarded
with a monetary wage; a disappearance which was accentuated for landed
society by the unavoidable projection of seamen's work into the realm of the
imaginary. This could be affirmed even at a metaphorical level, in the popular
conception of the jolly Jack Tar. The common idea, first given literary currency by Garrick during the Seven Years War, of the sailor as 'heart of oak',
does not simply envisage him as a figure seamlessly integrated into the
organization and purpose of the ship, but notionally transforms his very body,
the supposed seat of the soul, into the material of the ship. Of course the

metaphor operates on a complex level, the oak being a symbol of the nation as well as the fabric of ship-building. This only compounds it further: that the identity of the sailor, in this jingoistic image of him, as a loyal servant of the state, is one in which he is both figuratively and symbolically subsumed into the composition of the ship.

Similarly, the sailor's notorious sexual appetite, which on the face of it offers the most extreme assertion of his physicality, opposed to its effacement into a commodity of labour, is, conversely, contextualized almost without exception within the moneyed exchange of prostitution. In *The Sailor's Pleasure* (figure 5.1), published by Carington Bowles, a print which could stand for countless similar images, and one to which I shall return, the foreground juxtaposition of the coins with the letters to his 'Doxies' makes plain the nature of his pleasure and how it is to be derived. It may not be going too far to notice a visual equivalence between the currency and the sailor's body in the way the bag with its money pouring out echoes the sleeve and hand holding it. (Not to mention the suggestively onanistic overtones in the angle of the wrist and hand causing the contents of the bag to spill fulsomely over the table.) However many sublayered readings one wants to make of the image, there is a sexual currency transaction implied here, as well as what might be termed a currency consummation.

Other images are more ambiguous. I want to dwell at length on Francis Wheatley's *The Sailor's Return* (figure 5.2) because of the ways in which it problematizes the difficult identities of the sailor at this period, particularly through the comparisons offered by its companion piece *The Soldier's Return* (figure 5.3). These 1786 paintings were among the first of Wheatley's fancy pictures to be engraved, remaining popular throughout the 1790s and 1800s, a fact itself suggestive of the marketability of this conventional subject; and it is the 1787 mezzotint by Ward which I choose to examine here, with its richer semantic play between image and the text of the caption, and its implicitly wider and more heterogeneous potential spectatorship. The comparison with its companion reveals far more than a superficial contrast of subject, and indeed helps to illuminate the representational problems surrounding the sailor.

Far from being a view of him in his element at sea, he is shown at the moment of return of the culturally-stripped and unfixed space of a garret, where his beloved tends her dying mother at her bedside.[7] Only his uniform denotes his vocation, as in a declamatory gesture he proffers his hat full of gold. The hat, angled in full view of the spectator, forms the crux or fulcrum of their mutual theatrical communication of gesture, and offers several contradictory layers of meaning. On the one hand, via the hat and its contents, his return signifies a relief from poverty for the girl, with security and a new life in marriage. Yet she rebuffs his offer, demanding priority for her final moments with her dying mother, against which the

The SAILOR'S PLEASURE,

When Storms and Tempests all are o'er,   *Then for his Doxies all he'll send;*
And Jack receives his Cash on Shore;   *What's dearly earn'd he'll freely spend.*

Printed for CARINGTON BOWLES, Map & Printseller at N.º 69 in St Pauls Church Yard, LONDON.

5.1   Anon., *The Sailor's Pleasure*, n.d., mezzotint, 314 × 250.

offer of money comprises an undignified intrusion of material interests into a moment of intense spirituality. The rejected hat and money therefore serve to highlight her virtue in subordinating material interests to her 'filial

5.2 W. Ward after Francis Wheatley, *The Sailor's Return* (1787), mezzotint, 500 × 345.

duty'. On the other hand, there are no furnishings or accoutrements in the room, save the basket hanging from the beam, suggesting that she ekes out a living as a street hawker, an identification bringing into question 'virtue'

5.3 W. Ward after Francis Wheatley, *The Soldier's Return* (1787), mezzotint, 500 × 345.

which the caption ascribes to her.[8] The established association of the sailor with sex and prostitution offers the dominant narrative a destabilizing subtext, in which the central hat full of money, as the axis of the protagonists' relationship, assumes a discrete but unmistakeable sexual significance; particularly when it is remembered that 'hat' was a slang term for 'a woman's privities: because frequently felt' (*Dictionary of the Vulgar Tongue*, 1994). The placement of money in the hat, offered to a street-seller by a sailor, and its compositional centrality (as the single defining moment of contact between them), are all too suggestive of the commerce of prostitution to be ignored. Given, moreover, their low-class environment, and the fact of who they are, such an inference may legitimately be projected onto the protagonists, even if it was not one which the more genteel viewers of the picture would have claimed for themselves. Yet again, the virtuous surface narrative counters its darker subtext, in her gesture of rebuff: that she rejects his offer may suggest a morally redemptive potential, that, after all, 'Virtue & Love shall reward his Constancy & Faith' – despite her poverty and the reputation of street-sellers, she is not that sort of girl. The ambivalences could be pursued through comparison with other images dealing with the abundant iconographies of 'the sailor's departure' and 'the sailor's return'.[9] The important point is that the oxymoronic structure of the print, where narrative and counter-narrative, image and text, cancel each other, leaves the signification of the image of the sailor unfixed and unstable. For it is to be wondered how the constant and faithful tar may displace his conventional visualization as oversexed spendthrift. The smiling tar of *The Sailor's Pleasure* (figure 5.1) holds his cornucopia-like bag overflowing with coins firmly between a large bowl of punch, his tobacco and pipe, and in the foreground for the viewer's consideration three billets-doux. Here there is no ambiguity between image and caption:

> When Storms and Tempests all are o'er
> And Jack receives his Cash on Shore,
> Then for his Doxies all he'll send –
> What's dearly earn'd he'll freely spend.

Conversely, the ambiguity of Wheatley's image is grounded in the rhetoric of denial, in the woman's rejection of his money.

If cash, as I have suggested, may be taken as metonymic of his physical labour in a system of political economy, the body transformed into sign, the picture thus endlessly defers his 'reincarnation', his re-presentation as a bodily presence into landed society, poised as he is between entry and non-entry, between promiscuity and fidelity. While it is true that pictures were produced in profusion of the 'sailor's return', often as illustrations to Dibdin's ballads on the same theme, as the loyal spouse returns safe to the bosom of his family, it is noticeable, in a print such as *Jack's Fidelity* (figure 5.4), of

5.4   Anon., *Jack's Fidelity* (1796), mezzotint, 354 × 253.

1796, that his fidelity is achieved through Jack's giving up the sea, forming a semantic closure around his identity:

And so now to sea I shall venture no more,
For you know, being rich I've no call.
So I'll bring up young tars, do my duty ashore
And live and die constant to Poll.

Reclaimed from the unstable realm of the imaginary, he is made visible by being placed as far from the sea as possible, in the comforting familiarity of the country cot, clasping the hand of a paragon of rustic maternity, with his faithful hound asleep at his feet, a restrained amount of tobacco and liquor on the table, and the marriage bed beyond. Yet the extensive verse also makes clear that his is a new Jack, reformed from the youthful philanderer with 'a wife at each port'; and that his constancy has been maintained despite the various charms and temptations of the world's exotic women, 'tawny, lilly, and black', from an Indian squaw to 'one near Sumatra ... As fond as a witch in a play', who appears as a Circe-like foil to his Odyssean resolve to return to his English Penelope. The exotic otherness of the sailor's life thus simultaneously acts as a parable for the relation of the roving tar to his home, and is demystified by being used as a foil to emphasize the English virtues of his Poll. His potential for sexual libertinism, with its worryingly subversive transgression of moral codes, and dilution of national character through miscegenation, is again defused and instead transformed into the expression of patriotic devotion to the homeland, once more personified as the paragon of feminine virtue, a surrogate for Britannia; and is redirected to the nationally beneficial end of bringing up 'young tars', one of whom nestles plumply in his mother's arms. It is significant, perhaps, that she is centrally placed in the composition and given the brightest tonality. At the date of publication, with the instability caused in the navy's ranks by the effects of the Quota Acts, and with the recent events of the *Bounty* mutiny still present in public discourse, a mutiny which was commonly characterized as the abandonment of the British ship in favour of the exotic sexual freedom of Tahiti, the print may be seen as a rather overstrained assertion of the sailor's loyalty, and of the charms of English femininity.

Similarly, while Wheatley's tar hints unmistakeably at the sailor's proverbial sexual promiscuity, the caption asserts a moral idealism, by which we are to understand his bringing money from overseas to a humble and industrious home synecdochally, as an analogue for the navy's economic relation to the homeland. Once again there is an equivalence between currency and body: he appears to offer himself as his money, and this offering of himself and his wages or prize money to his true love replicates his 'Constancy & Faith' to Britannia, for when he is, as here, at once son and champion. And for his loyalty he receives both Britannia's and his beloved's 'Virtue & Love'. Yet, there is no similar formal closure, whereby Wheatley's tar may assume the domestic stability of 'Jack'. In being rebuffed he remains both at sea and at home, half entered and half turned away, both within and without, yet neither.

The image therefore oscillates between two irreconcilable registers, and confers upon the sailor a worryingly unfixed and unstable identity. Its instability becomes even more marked when compared with the welter of secure and anchored identities projected in the companion print.

By a heavy contrast, the soldier's return is to a conspicuously wealthy environment, displayed in the fine clothes, fashionable furniture and goods, and the presence of a well-fed dog. It is a patriarchal rather than a matriarchal scene, in which the seated father joins the hands of the young couple in blessing. (In *The Sailor's Return* the recumbent presence of the dying mother provokes a sundering rather than a uniting of hands.) Unlike the sailor's moll, the girl here is demure and undemonstrative, casting her eyes downward and away from the dominant stares of the two men. Her body is contained and immobilized, held by the waist and the hand and wrist, with her other arm hidden from view. Prominently displayed is her sewing basket, with its assurance that her work is virtuously domestic and recreational (she is not financially dependent upon it), the tome of the white cloth in the basket exactly matching that of her dress. Despite the assurance of the caption, that besides 'honour', 'beauty' and 'love', 'wealth' is also to be the soldier's reward, there is no display of money in the form of currency here, nor does the soldier introduce cash into the house. The manliness evident in his upright dominance of the scene is understood, of itself, to warrant the wealth and beauty of the daughter. This scene of courteous propriety, saccharine as it may be, serves to underline the problematics of the representation of the sailor. Most noticeable, the association in *The Soldier's Return* of masculine control with the tasteful display of inferred wealth, and with a paternalism in which the social relations of power are conventionally ordered, alerts us to the transgressive disruptions of its counterpart, where the sailor's entry, set against a backdrop of maternal moribundity, is towards a woman who dominantly repels his advances, and where the only wealth amongst conspicuous poverty is his hatful of coins. The nexus of values here is of feminization, cash and death.

The transgressive potential of *The Sailor's Return*, in which the sailor appears to alternate between the incommensurable poles of his social identity, is reinforced by the feminization of the scene, and of the sailor within it. His gentle features and attitude of retreating sensibility, as well as his subservience to the woman's gesture, contrast both with the figure of his soldier counterpart, and with the nature of the work by which he is presumed to have earned his money. It points once again to the theatricality of the scene discernible in the exaggerated gestures, and suggests how closely such pictures as this reciprocate and are mediated by the stage representation of the tar, rather than offering a redaction of some perceived reality of sailors' circumstances. For Wheatley's feminization of the sailor parallels the common theatrical practice of women playing the part of the tar.[10] As Gillian Russell states:

the stage sailor was not uncomplicatedly masculine, as might be expected. His martial vigour is combined with a 'feminine' capacity for
monogamy, in contrast to the sailor's reputation for promiscuity, a girl
in every port, and the more taboo view of the ship as concealing rampant
homosexuality. The tar is often represented either as a boy or as promis-
ing adolescent ... In 1791 the actress Dorothy Jordan was depicted as
the sailor Little Pickle in Isaac Bickerstaffe's farce *The Spoil'd Child* in
a way that suggests that on this occasion martial cross-dressing was not
being used to draw attention to the female body but instead to create an
image of androgyny – the adolescent sailor as 'masculine–feminine' ...
To some extent, the feminization of the sailor is linked to the persistent
emphasis on him as passive and unthinking. If the heroicization of the
tar represented a legitimation of plebeian patriotism, to characterize the
sailor as a creature of feeling rather than intellect, like a woman, was
one way of ensuring that the legitimation would not go too far.

(1995, pp. 102–3)

In addition, Wheatley's portrayal of a theatrical, feminized tar doubly re-
moves him from his actual political circumstances as a maritime labourer, a
removal even further enforced by the transformation of his appearance from
the rough, scarred and weather-beaten visage with its 'deep ... hue of tarpau-
lin' which was the inevitable consequence of life at sea (Rediker, 1987, pp.
11–12).[11] It therefore misrepresents the tar in virtually every respect, but self-
reflexively points to its own aesthetic dilemma, induced by the sailor's unfixed
social status, in the referral of his (mis)representation to an already ambiguous theatrical mediation.

Such a removal clearly has political implications, while simultaneously neu-
tralizing the historical actuality of the seaman's political expressiveness which,
as Rediker and others have shown, was extensive and energetic (Rediker, 1987;
Lemisch, 1968; Stevenson, 1992, pp. 80–81, 89–90, 155–7, 180). But the
issues of fidelity versus promiscuity, homeliness versus otherness, which I have
argued, apropos of Wheatley's print, characterized the construction of the
sailor's subjective identity, became openly annexed in the ideological contexts
of the 1790s to his military and nationalistic role in the war against France. The
issue of the seaman's uncertain loyalty related no longer just to Moll or Polly in
their confined domestic sphere, but to Britannia herself, prompted by mutinous
protest against lack of pay and intolerable conditions, and by a severe manning
problem which necessitated the impressment of numerous landsmen, including
many Irishmen and other potential political dissidents.[12] As N. A. M. Rodger
has argued, by 1800 the navy required some 125,000 men (as compared with a
total of almost 85,000 men and officers at the height of the Seven Years War),
an increased population which created a dilution of English seamen among
foreigners and Irishmen, reversed the ratio of skilled to unskilled labour, and
increased the proportion of convicted criminals among the lower-deck population (1992, pp. 29–30). The already questionable reputation of the sailor was
thus further tarnished and destabilized.

Even though the ideological correlations between lower-deck culture in the form of the sailor's proletarianization and the principles of the French revolutionary government could have been ignored for most of the 1790s, in 1797 they converged in a cataclysmic event which presaged disaster of national proportions, and likewise implicated every individual subject of the state. In the spring of 1797 the navy mutinied, first at Spithead, and subsequently at the Nore. The extent to which connections between maritime culture and revolutionary mentality went unrecognized is indicated by this event appearing to have come as a complete surprise to the establishment, and to a nation in 'total isolation against the might of France and her continental allies' (Wells, 1983, p. 84). One of the most extraordinary aspects of the first mutiny at Spithead, as noted in a letter from Admiral Lord Bridport to Evan Nepean, Secretary of the Admiralty on 16 April 1797, was that 'not an officer in the whole Channel fleet appears to have had a suspicion of anything of the kind having been in agitation ... the extraordinary part of the business is in the secrecy with which it was conducted' (qtd Wells, 1983, p. 85).

The calamitous nature of these events made them of general interest. Between May and June, Joseph Farington recorded the mutiny as a subject for discussion on no less than sixteen separate occasions. On 8 May it was clearly an overriding concern at the Royal Academy: 'Academy I went to. – met Dance there. much alarm abt. Mutiny of Sailors at Portsmouth' (1978– 84, vol. 3, p. 835).[13] David Bindman has suggested that the apocalyptic and Miltonic imagery of radical sympathizing artists such as Blake, Fuseli, Banks, Romney, Barry, Sharp, Smirke and even Girtin, may be seen as an oblique commentary upon the events and ideologies of the Revolution, to the extent that Fuseli's Milton Gallery (1790–1801) 'must reflect in some way the artist's changing responses to the unfolding tragedy of the Revolution, though in what way is not immediately clear' (1989, p. 87). It is equally plausible that the momentousness of the mutinies should have had some effect upon the aesthetic understanding of the sea and the sailor.

Importantly, the extraordinarily efficient organization of the mutiny overturned the conventional image of the lower-deck sailor as either a robotic 'heart of oak', or a barely controllable, illiterate savage. The drawing up of petitions among the fleet was run according to democratic principles, with two representatives elected from each ship, and deriving precedents not from the British Parliament, but 'from the United States Congress, the French Assembly, the Irish underground, and the forbidden British reform societies ... The mutiny – with its skilful planning, determination and discipline – wrecked the jolly jack tar mystique. It was hard for most officers to believe in the new man who had come unexpectedly on deck' (Dugan, 1966, p. 90). Certainly, the rhetorical sureness and skill of the seamen's addresses to the nation refute the usual paternalistic image of the seaman:

Shall we, who amid the rage of the tempest and the war or jarring elements, undaunted climb the unsteady cordage and totter on the top-mast's dreadful height, suffer ourselves to be treated worse than the dogs of London streets? Shall we, who in battle's sanguinary rage, confound, terrify and subdue your proudest foe, guard your coasts from invasion, your children from slaughter, and your lands from pillage – be the footballs and shuttlecocks of a set of tyrants who derives from us alone their honours, their titles and their fortunes? No, the Age of Reason has at length resolved.

(Dugan, 1966, pp. 278–9)

This is patrician rhetoric in the mouth of the lower deck, and demands a corresponding respect, particularly in the reference to the 'Age of Reason' with its Painite overtones. The mutiny, then, helped to establish the idea that the seaman was endowed with a potential for sophisticated political thought and organization, and for noble language and action. What remained the vital subject of contention was the cause for which such language and action was to be enlisted. This contest was fought on an aesthetic ground also.

The visual rhetoric of the few prints dealing directly with the mutiny is instructive. The supposed linkage between revolutionary politics and the mutiny is made explicitly by Isaac Cruikshank's *The Delegates in Council or Beggars on Horseback* published 9 June 1797 (figure 5.5), an attempt to expose the mutineers as the mere stooges of the radical Foxite opposition, thus to deny them any sophisticated political awareness or motivation. So (in direct contrast to the genteel profile at the extreme left of Admiral Buckner, the principal negotiator on behalf of the Admiralty and the government) the delegates (one of whom, it is worth noting, is black) are portrayed as stereotypically savage members of the mob: grotesques clearly reminiscent of the caricatures of the revolutionary *sans-culottes*.[14] In the background the icon of Britannia is overturned, as a commentary on the mutineers' progress, and literally inverting the conventional male–female relations emphasized in *The Sailor's Return* or *Jack's Fidelity*. The composition is itself an inversion of religious iconographic types, here recalling the format of the Last Supper, or of the Marriage at Cana (suggested particularly by the right-hand figure of Thelwall filling a glass from a grog can). The subliminal message is clear: that the mutiny is a contravention of divine truths and a God-given worldly order. Hidden from Admiral Buckner, but exposed to the viewer, there lurks beneath the table the unholy, secret (and implicitly illegal) 'combination' of Lauderdale, Horne Tooke, Stanhope, Grey, Fox and Sheridan, whose con-spiratorial and knowledgeable smiles admit 'Aye, Aye, we are at the bottom of it', and contrast sharply with the thuggish grimaces of the delegates above who, therefore, assume the character of republican henchmen: twelve diabolical apostles.

Against such denunciations there survive just one or two pro-mutineer prints, but one of these (figure 5.6) is highly significant in its heroic and

5.5 Isaac Cruikshank, *The Delegates in Council or Beggars on Horseback* (9 June 1797), engraving, 253 × 349.

RICHARD PARKER,
President of the Committee of Delegates, tendering the List of Grievances, to Vice-Admiral Buckner, on Board the Sandwich at the Nore.

Found Guilty by a Court Martial June 26. 1797. Executed June 30 on Board the Sandwich.

Publish'd July 8. 1797 by J. Thompson, N° 110 St. Martins Lane, & Evans, N° 42 Long Lane West Smithfield, London.

5.6   Anon., *Richard Parker, President of Delegates tendering the List of Grievances, to Vice-Admiral Buckner on Board the Sandwich at the Nore* (1797), mezzotint, 353 × 253.

noble portrayal of Richard Parker, the president of the delegates' committee at the Nore: he is disposed in a manner hitherto reserved for full-length portraits of military officers, connoting values of poise, dignity, strength and command. The alert expressions of the background figures point up the contrast between Parker's declamatory, almost tragic attitude, and the comparative awkwardness of Bucknor.[15]

The depth and extent of establishment political anxiety emerge clearly from Cruikshank's imagery and its contrast with the heroic pictorialization of the common seaman, Parker. Perhaps unsurprisingly, the cultural references to the mutinies are extremely sparse. Andrew Franklin's musical entertainment *A Trip to the Nore*, first performed at Drury Lane on 9 November 1797, constitutes an astonishing denial of any mutinous activity, not to say the near-downfall of the country. It displaces such anxieties by celebrating instead the proposed visit of the King to the Nore to view the fleet of Admiral Duncan, just returned with prizes from his victory at the Battle of Camperdown, to conclude 'with a View of the British Fleet, and the Dutch Prizes' (Hogan, 1968, vol. 3, p. 2019). The only trace of insecurity is found in O'Thunder's exaggerated assertion, 'I'm an Irishman and a British sailor' (Franklin, 1797, p. 14). In London alone there were numerous other performances of one-act entertainments and afterpieces on the same celebratory theme.[16] These culminated in a performance at Covent Garden on 19 December of John O'Keeffe's musical farce *Britain's Brave Tars!!; or, All for St. Paul's* 'written with allusion to Their Majesties' attendance at St. Paul's' on the same day to participate in the capital's open theatre of celebration, the thanksgiving for naval victories, for which the preparation of the cathedral was commissioned from the leading architects James Wyatt and George Dance (Hogan, 1968, vol. 3, p. 2019; Colley, 1984, p. 100). It is perhaps significant that Covent Garden's spectacle of lower-deck loyalty was a farce, as the unprecedented royal decision to include 250 ordinary sailors and marines in the event at St Paul's was a contentious one. It both drew attention to the fact that what was being celebrated was victory not only over France and its allies but, just as importantly, over the mutinous sailors themselves, a point made when 'the red flag of the naval mutineers and the white flag of surrender were briefly flown from a house on Ludgate Hill, recalling the government's repression of naval discontent and the disregard of seamen's grievances seven months earlier' (Jordan and Rogers, 1989, p, 213). At the same time its accommodation of a disreputable lower-class element smacked too strongly of the levelling popular pageants of revolutionary France, to the evident distaste of the *Morning Chronicle*, which dismissed the event as a 'Frenchified farce' (Colley, 1984, pp. 109–10). The lower deck were still identifiable as a class with the crowd, whose popular loyalism could not be invoked 'without unleashing a spontaneous process of riot whose political destinations were uncertain'. The naval thanksgiving was further 'soured by the discordant demands for peace and antiministerial rancor at the increasing tax burden ordinary citizens were expected to carry at a time of poor harvests and spiraling prices' (Jordan and Rogers, 1989, pp. 212–13). Nonetheless, the same newspaper (17 October 1797) could cite the heroism of the tar by way of criticism of the government's conduct of the war:

> However we may deplore the calamity, or condemn the impolicy of the war itself, it is with pride and pleasure that we witness the exploits of our defenders on our natural element, and that we see our Country saved against the incapacity of our Government by the courage of our Tars.
> (Jordan and Rogers, 1989, p. 214)

While the identity of the tar remained decidedly ambiguous, therefore, it was becoming increasingly visible as the focus for a range of issues surrounding the vexed question of national loyalty. Furthermore, there was increasing consensus in the wake of the mutinies about the seaman's capacity for virtue, both as a figure able to make rational decisions concerning his loyalty, and as the saviour of the nation (his virtue consisting, of course, in deciding to be loyal). Increasingly, too, this visibility took the form of aesthetic representation. While the government proposed in 1795 to erect statues in St Paul's 'commemorating the nation's naval and military officer-heroes', it was only after 1797 that the project, along with the parallel one of the proposed construction of a Naval Pillar, took hold (Yarrington, 1988, pp. 61–78, 338–46). Similarly, as Jordan and Rogers argue, the changing political events at the time of and after the mutinies were an important factor in enabling the enormous popularity and subsequent hagiography of Nelson, also manifested substantially in visual form (1989, pp. 214–22). In a parallel development, the issue of the seaman's loyalty (and, by extension, of loyalty in general) was constructed as an aesthetic discourse.

I want now to return to Clarke's *Naval Sermons* to explore this further. Sermon 4 (out of a total of nine), 'The Necessity and Advantages of Obedience', may be taken as paradigmatic of the extent of the problem posed by the questionable loyalty of the audience to whom it was addressed.

It opens by restating the well-established truism of commercial ideology: that human beings are naturally social, and that the individual receives and communicates strength through her or his participation in society. But the beneficent social state can only be maintained by the individual's strict adherence to the essential laws and principles which govern it. Such a construction of the law may itself be seen as a form of the aesthetic, to the extent that, like the work of art, it is its own justification, revealing itself in its intrinsically beautiful, ordered and moral state only to the sensible bourgeois subject with the proper qualifications of taste and virtue to perceive it (Eagleton, 1990, pp. 19–28; Everett, 1994). Britain, of course, has the best constituted society, 'where, in every part appears a gradual, regular, wise subordination' (Clarke, 1798, p. 66), quite opposed to the disastrous social composition of France, which is presented as the apocalyptic agent of divine wrath, 'the most bitter and severe scourge, which heaven, in its anger, ever employed to chastise the earth' (p. 69). And since the war, conducted on such a cosmic scale, has the sea as both its ideological and its actual theatre, the ship itself becomes the paradigm of the ideal social state of Britishness:

> A Ship, in which so much of your life is past [sic], is a just emblem of the Social State; or in other words, of a political government. Here every one has his appointed station. The various gradations of command and obedience are clearly marked: and it is a truth, as evident to your understandings, as the meridian sun is to your sight: that by a joint co-operation of all in their respective departments; of those who command, and of those who obey; the vessel is conducted through the waves in safety, appears to defy the tempest; and often returns, rich in victory and in honour.
>
> (Clarke, 1798, pp. 70–71)

The necessity for obedience is predicated as a natural fact, as plain as the midday sun. Significant also is the way that such naturalization of social ideology is embedded in the visual. Thus the law of social obedience, exemplified in the social microcosm of the ship, is described by Clarke as an aesthetic one. It is, indeed, sublime: the proving ground for the sailor's loyalty is the sight of the sea's sublimity. The imagination, the irreducible basis for religious faith, is stimulated by the contemplation of nature's wonder and variety, most especially 'this abyss of waters, rolling in the greatness of its strength' which provokes 'the sublimest sentiments of devotion' (pp. 27–30).

The sailor's loyalty is interpellated by both the sublime and the beautiful, in the form of the ship made from the native English oak which, 'having towered amid the forest, falls to arise with new glory, the naval bulwark of our country' (pp. 32–3), constructing loyalty around the conventional aesthetic discourse of art as the refinement of nature:

> Ye, who live amid the vicissitudes of contending elements, whose representation alone fills the common beholder, though in safety, with dismay, pass your lives in a continual survey of the most sublime object of nature, which is the ocean; and in conducting the most wonderful work of art, which is the ship that bears you through it.[17]
>
> (p. 35)

For Clarke, by a heavily overcoded tautology, the sea is the manifest proof of God's existence, with all that implies in terms of the construction of national identity, and the war against French atheism. The logical corollary is that mutiny must be a sin against nature and God; therefore, against the nation and its preordained maritime destiny.

The problem, of course, with Clarke's patriotic invocation of the sublime sea was that it flew in the face of the recent realities of lower-deck culture.

His solipsistic argument leads him to bewilderment: 'It is a natural subject of astonishment, that those *who go down to the sea in ships* are ever otherwise than religious and devout characters: as *they see the works of the Lord, and his wonders in the deep'*. Clarke's difficulties in reconciling this actuality with the ideological requirements of the sailors and the sea, force him, by way of resolution, to project an identity for the seamen which is quite new, and entirely at odds with the recent reality of their mutinous, democratic demands, and with the conventional pejorative characterization of the lower deck.

> No class of men, taken as a body, has ever shown a greater respect for religion, when properly presented to their attention; and however the vices of a few individuals may have drawn unjust aspersions on their profession; the religious disposition, and that attention to propriety of demeanour, which of late years has appeared among you, and been so much cherished by your respective commanders; will not fail, if thus continued and supported, to withdraw the only shade, which malice or ignorance has often cast over THE NOBLE CHARACTER OF A BRITISH SEAMAN.
>
> (pp. 36–37)

Significantly, given the centrality of St Paul's Cathedral as the site both of proposed commemorative naval sculpture and of the highly-publicized thanksgiving, the master narrative through which Clarke appeals to this unlikely residual religious disposition among seamen is that of the shipwreck of St Paul, using it to allude directly to the mutiny and its national import, via his guiding text, 'Except these abide in the ship, ye cannot be saved!' (Acts 27.31): St Paul, uniquely informed by God, must assure the crew of the foundering ship, through inducing their unquestioning faith, that unless they all remain on board, all will be lost. A reliance on God in this state of extremity is therefore a 'duty', a form of Kantian moral law, beyond the power of mere human reason to understand its necessity (p. 140; see Eagleton, 1990, pp. 78–86).

Through a subjective experience of an aesthetic, sensible kind – in Clarke's terms, it is still the sublime sea which must, ultimately, move the hearts of the seamen – will their loyalty be revealed to them. In practical effect, this will lead them to understand and fully appreciate the necessity of obedience to, and 'a sincere love and respect for', their officers:

> Submission unto our Governors, unto them who are in authority over us, is a doctrine, which the apostle St. Paul, whose conduct you have so much reason to admire, continually inculcates; 'that with well doing, we may put to silence the ignorance of foolish men.' In its various forms and effects, it may be justly styled the grand link of Social Life. To obey and command, are the leading features in your profession ...
> You are all immediately the servants of your King and Country: the just performance of your duties, will consequently have a considerable

and lasting effect, on the happiness of the community at large. If this
important and noble service, should ever appear ungrateful; if a too
warm and active imagination should eagerly grasp at some advantage,
which promises attainment, in a situation different from that, where you
are at present placed; still have the resolution to abide in the ship! The
prospect, which seems so flattering, may be only a snare, to seduce you
from Duty. Arise! pursue again with zeal the commands of your Superi-
ors, and the dream will cease.

(pp. 145–7)

By an ideological sleight-of-hand, the subject's loyalty is held to be a natural
consequence of his subordinate position, and his position proper to his loyalty. The sleight-of-hand comes about through referring the construction of
individual national identity to the image of the sacralized sea.

This sacralization, effected particularly in the implication of the figure or
icon of St Paul, is paralleled by the concomitant aesthetic elevation of the
maritime conspicuous in the monuments to naval heroes erected in St Paul's
and Westminster after 1798. For if the military isolation of Britain, combined
with the mutiny, both rendered its relation with the sea a suspect one, and
also necessitated an upward re-estimation of the tar, this was itself counter-
balanced by the naval victories in 1797 and 1798 at Camperdown and the
Nile, which appeared to reaffirm the divine mission of the nation. Clarke
again, in his thanksgiving sermon of 17 December 1797, says as much. While
victory at Camperdown was ultimately due to national faith in God, it was
also brought about by the bravery of ordinary seamen. This once more en-
tailed a revision of the conventional view of the common tar, highlighting his
heroic instead of his dissolute nature:

Called up repeatedly during the night, when the lowering vapour, and
the howling blast, would agitate the most decided resolution; with a
presence of mind, that baffles all description, the hardy Mariner points
out the track, where preservation may be expected. Feverish and languid
from want of rest; from occupation that allows not of the least cessation;
surrounded by a treacherous element; amid thirst and hunger! weariness
and pain! – the instant that the tumult of battle commences, all is cool,
steady resolution: While every sense of danger is lost in a sense of Duty,
and the real Horror of the scene is absorbed in the animating hope of
National Glory.

(pp. 214–15)

Here the tar has been accorded the virtuous qualities of the hero. And his
elevation to the level of national martyr, to be celebrated at the altar of the
sea, finds its visual counterpart in monuments such as Bacon's to Captain
Edward Cooke, in Westminster Abbey, of 1806, where the figure of the sailor
takes on the role of a latter-day saint receiving the body of Christ from the
Cross (Physick, 1969, pp. 176–7).[18] Bacon's design is remarkable not just in
the prominent place given to the common sailor, but in the way the overall
design, with its clearly defined and separated registers, echoes the articula-

tion of the Renaissance or Baroque altarpiece. Below the principal scene is a secondary tier with a roundel relief of the naval action in which Cooke died. This operates in the manner of a descriptive 'predella', offset against the idealized heroic action shown above. This device also, of course, allows the elevation of the sailor without disrupting his proper position of subordination to his superior officer.

The same mode of idealization of naval action occurs in contemporary painting, for instance in the sublime, Deluge-like effects of *Loutherbourg's Battle of Camperdown* (London, Tate Gallery). But it is more noticeable in his later *The cutting out of the French Corvette 'La Chevrette' by English sailors, with portraits of the officers engaged, 21st July 1801* (figure 5.7). Unlike Loutherbourg's earlier large-scale canvases of naval battles, there is less reliance here on precise anecdotal, descriptive detail of rigging, figureheads, or the positions of ships relative to one another, and temporal accuracy. Instead, he 'shows here no concern for the battle array of the vessels, but forces a segment of the action into the foreground. The bravery of man-to-man combat supersedes the patriotic conflict of nation versus nation' (Joppien, 1978, no. 71). The marginalization of the descriptive detail traditional to Dutch-derived marine painting, accentuates the heroic aesthetic language and grand painterly style which such a subject could now command. The particular is suppressed in favour of the universal, expressed, as Joppien indicates, through the depiction of the battle as a series of man-to-man, gladiatorial contests whereby, far from superseding the 'conflict of nation versus nation', the individual's struggle, in Clarke's terms, is referred to a higher general plane in which 'every sense of danger is lost in a sense of Duty, and the real Horror of the scene is absorbed in the animating hope of National Glory'. This sense of the heroic is enforced in the painting by the poses of the principal figures, being clearly taken from classical statuary: the figure in white at the lower centre imitates the Borghese Gladiator, the standing uniformed figure to his left recalls the Horse Tamers, while the two figures at the foot of the bowsprit resemble the Borghese Gladiator (again, though from a different angle), and Laocoon (Haskell and Penny, 1981, pp. 136–40, 221–4, 243–7). Likewise, the disposition of the figures around the bowsprit and figurehead is again suggestive of a deposition.[19] It appears that Loutherbourg did not go to Plymouth, where the vessels were subsequently taken, to study their details; so the composition relies to a greater extent than usual in such battle scenes on the imagination: that is, in accord with the academic prescriptions of history painting.

The problematic identity of the tar has been resolved into the sacralization of the sea, through contemplation of which the self is revealed as a patriotic subject[20] and thus paradoxically, in one sense, not as a self at all, since the spur to duty connoted by the sublime sea and battle displaces the individual, physical, everyday sufferings of life at sea, in favour of the greater collective

5.7 J. Rogers after Philippe-Jacques de Loutherbourg, *The Cutting out of the French Corvette 'La Chevrette' by English sailors, with portraits of the officers engaged, 21st July 1801* (1802), steel engraving, 316 × 480.

ideal of 'national glory', just as the harmonious, integrated composition of Loutherbourg's picture subordinates, through its aesthetic procedure, each individual element or figure to the formal demands of the overall design.

In this sense, it is not going too far to view Loutherbourg's picture, and in particular the compositional structure of the print that was taken after it, as a type of secular altarpiece, a devotional image to the national altar of the sea, in which the cartouche appears again as a form of predella, and the symmetrical placement of the lateral onlookers recalls the votive figures of the Renaissance altarpiece, while their freestanding *grisalle* depth (emphasized by their gentle chiaroscuro and casting of shadows) and their discrepant scale against the bodies in the main picture draw attention to the latter's status as an icon. Like a religious altarpiece, this offers itself as a vehicle for the revelation and redemption of the subject through the acquisition of faith:

> On that Altar, which our forefathers reared to Liberty, the flame of patriotism arises! Around it, let every age and rank assemble: the Nobles, and the Rulers, and the Elders of the People, and take that oath, which the Genius of Britain proffers:– WE SWEAR, THAT WE WILL REMEMBER THE LORD! WE WILL FIGHT FOR OUR BRETHREN, OUR SONS, OUR DAUGHTERS, OUR WIVES, AND OUR HOUSES! AND WILL FIRMLY UNITE, IN THE PRESERVATION AND DEFENCE OF HER, WHO DWELLETH, WITH SO MUCH TERRIBLENESS, IN THE CLEFTS OF THE ROCKS; WHOSE RAMPART, AND WHOSE WALL, – IS FROM THE SEA!
>
> (Clarke, 1798, pp. 171–2)

Notes

1. The events of the 1797 mutinies are dealt with in detail in Gill, 1912; Dugan, 1966 and Lloyd, 1963. For the impact of the Quota Acts upon the composition of the navy, see Wells, 1983, especially pp. 79–109.
2. Although there were women among the shipboard population, including the lower deck and on warships, the ship and the navy generally were overwhelmingly homosocial environments, and in the following discussion I shall refer to the sailor as male, even though his representation could be ambiguous, as I shall discuss below. This should not be taken as a disregard for the historical presence of women at sea.
3. Witness, for example, Lord Bolingbroke's mid-century analysis of national identity, a view which became virtually axiomatic during the second half of the century:

> The situation of Great Britain, the character of her people, and the nature of her government, fit her for trade and commerce. Her climate and her soil make them necessary to her well being ... As trade and commerce enrich, so they fortify our country. The sea is our barrier, ships are our fortresses, and the mariners, that trade and commerce alone can furnish, are the garrisons to defend them.
> Bolingbroke, 1967, vol. 2, p. 414.

The importance of the visual image of the sea and navigation for the development of British national identity is discussed in Quilley, 1998a and Quilley,
1998b.

4. As he was labelled in the 1778 frontispiece to Jonas Hanway's *Rules of the
Maritime School at Chelsea*.

5. 'the pit they [sailors] call the hold; the gallery, up aloft, or the maintop landing;
the boxes, the cabin, and the stage, the quarterdeck': Bernard, 1830, vol. 2, p.
129, quoted in Russell, 1995, p. 98.

6. An obvious example is Reynolds's celebrated portrait of Commodore Keppel
(1753, Greenwich, National Maritime Museum). While contemporary critical
notices of the painting made much of the recent circumstances of shipwreck of
the *Maidstone*, of which Keppel had been in command, and related the composition of the portrait to the Commodore's deliverance, the pictorial emphasis is
firmly centred on the singular masculine, heroic figure, not the leader of a
community of seamen, each labouring to bring the ship safe to port. There is no
indication of the fate of the crew, nor any hint that their fate should be of any
aesthetic or ethical concern.

7. Surely not yet his wife, as he has only now returned from sea with sufficient
money to be able to propose marriage. Alternatively, the caption makes it plain
that she is not his sister, which would be the other possible, and iconographically
conventional, relationship between them.

8. An identification which fits with the conventional treatment of this iconography. Compare, for example, Mosley's print from the 1750s: C. Mosley, *The
Sailor's Return* (London, National Maritime Museum). On the dubious reputation of female street-sellers, see Barker-Benfield, 1995, p. 55.

9. Consider, for example, the blatant sexual duplicity which forms the subject of
Rowlandson's pornographic satire *Departure of the Husband* (c. 1815–20, British Museum), where the wife waves her white kerchief at a window, to the
departing ships visible through it, in a display of fidelity, while astride a priapic
young tar concealed from the view of the husband out to sea.

10. Wheatley does the same in other pictures, for example the attributed canvas of
The Sailor's Return in Bournemouth City Art Gallery. See Quilley, 1998b,
chapter 6.

11. Tom Bowling, for example, in Smollett's *Roderick Random* is described as
'somewhat bandy-legged, with a neck like a bull, and a face which (you might
easily perceive) had withstood the most obstinate assaults of the weather'
(Smollett, 1979, p. 8).

12. David Bindman discusses a 1794 print relating to the battle of the Glorious
First of June which makes clear reference to mutinous activity in the navy
(Bindman cat. no. 182 and p. 65). For the issues of impressment and United
Irishmen in the navy, see Wells, 1983.

13. The other occasions in May and June when Farington mentions the mutiny are
15, 20, 26, 27, 30, 31 May; 2, 4, 6, 8, 9, 10, 11, 14, 27 June.

14. Compare the facial profiles, for example, in Gillray's *Un Petit Souper a la
Parisienne – or – A Family of Sans-Culottes refreshing after the fatigues of the
day*, engraving, 1792.

15. Parker's 'tragic' character may be explained by the fact that the print was
published after his court-martial and execution. Chris Jones has noted, also, the
tragic theatrical effect of Parker's 'Dying Declaration' upon his audience, reportedly moving his judges to tears (1993, pp. 17–18).

16. Hogan lists three separate pieces at Drury Lane and Covent Garden, whose first

performances were on 11, 16 and 18 October. Given that the battle only took place on 11 October, the response of the theatres in staging such spectacles was remarkably swift (1968, vol. 3, pp. 2011–12).

17.   A useful and interesting contemporary alternative view of the oak as an ideological symbol, and once again suggesting the instability of symbols of the nation and of loyalty in the 1790s, is Coleridge's poem 'The Raven' (1797). For discussion of the poem see Ruddick, 1993.

18.   The same relationship of sailor to dead officer is recapitulated in the abundant imagery relating to the death of Nelson, but in particular, Benjamin West's celebrated picture *The Death of Lord Nelson* (1806, Liverpool, Walker Art Gallery).

19.   Particularly Rubens's *Descent from the Cross* (1611–14, Antwerp Cathedral).

20.   I have argued elsewhere a similar case for Turner's views of the sea at this period, by comparison with the poetic description of the sea in the work of William Lisle Bowles: Quilley, 1998a, pp. 148–9.

Bibliography

Barker-Benfield, G. J. (1992), *The Culture of Sensibility: Sex and Society in Eighteenth-Century Britain*, Chicago and London: University of Chicago Press.

Bernard, J. (1830), *Retrospections of the Stage*, 2 vols, London: H. Colburn and R. Bentley.

Bindman, D. (1989), *The Shadow of the Guillotine: Britain and the French Revolution*, London: British Museum.

Bolingbroke, H. St. John, Viscount Lord (1967), *The Ideal of a Patriot King in The Works of Lord Bolingbroke, in Four Volumes*, London: Cass.

Bratton, J. S. (1991), 'British heroism and the structure of melodrama', in Bratton, J. S. et al., *Acts of Supremacy: The British Empire and the Stage, 1790–1930*, Manchester: Manchester University Press, pp. 18–61.

Clarke, J. S. (1798), *Naval Sermons, preached on board His Majesty's Ship 'The Impetueux' in the Western Squadron, during its Services off Brest: to which is added a Thanksgiving Sermon for Naval Victories: preached at Park-Street Chapel, Grosvenor-Square, Dec. 19. M,DCC,XCVII*, London: T. Payne, B. White.

Colley, L. (1984), 'The Apotheosis of George III: Loyalty, Royalty and the British Nation 1760–1820', *Past and Present*, 102 (February).

Dugan, J. (1966), *The Great Mutiny*, London: Deutsch.

Eagleton, T. (1990), *The Ideology of the Aesthetic*, Oxford: Blackwell.

Earle, P. (1998), *Sailors: English Merchant Seamen 1650–1775*, London: Methuen.

Everett, N. (1994), *The Tory View of Landscape*, New Haven and London: Yale University Press.

Farington, J. (1978–84), ed. Garlick, K. and MacIntyre, A., *The Diary of*

Joseph Farington, 16 vols, New Haven and London: Yale University Press.

Foucault, M. (1970), *The Order of Things: An Archaeology of the Human Sciences*, London: Tavistock Publications.

Franklin, A. (1797), *A Trip to the Nore, A musical Entertainment, in One Act. As performed by their Majesties Servants at the Theatre-Royal, Drury-Lane*, London.

Gill, C. (1912), *The Naval Mutinies of 1797*, Manchester: Manchester University Press.

Glenn, G. D. (1989), 'Nautical "Docudrama" in the Age of the Kembles', in Fisher, J. L. and Watt, S. (eds), *When They Weren't Doing Shakespeare: Essays on Nineteenth-Century British and American Theatre*, Athens, Ga. and London: pp. 137–51.

Haskell, F. and Penny, N. (1981), *Taste and the Antique: The Lure of Classical Sculpture 1500–1900*, New Haven and London: Yale University Press.

Hogan, C. B. (ed.), (1968), *The London Stage 1660–1800*, part 5: *1776–1800*, 3 vols, Carbondale: Illinois University Press.

Jones, C. (1993), *Radical Sensibility: Literature and Ideas in the 1790s*, London and New York: Routledge.

Joppien, R. (1978), *Philippe-Jacques de Loutherbourg, RA 1740–1812*, London: Greater London Council.

Jordan, G. and Rogers, N. (1989), 'Admirals as Heroes: Patriotism and Liberty in Hanoverian England', *Journal of British Studies*, 28 (2).

Lemisch, J. (1968), 'Jack Tar in the Streets: Merchant Seamen in the Politics of Revolutionary America', *William and Mary Quarterly*, 25 (July).

Lloyd, C. (1963), *St. Vincent and Camperdown*, London: Navy Records Society.

Physick, J. (1969), *Designs for English Sculpture 1680–1860*, London: Victoria and Albert Museum.

Price, A. (1990), *The Eyes of the Fleet: A Popular History of Frigates and Frigate Captains 1793–1815*, London: Hutchinson.

Quilley, G. (1998a), '"All Ocean is Her Own": The Image of the Sea and the Identity of the Maritime Nation in Eighteenth-Century British Art', in Cubitt, G. (ed.), *Imagining Nations*, Manchester: Manchester University Press, pp. 132–52.

———. (1998b), 'The Imagery of Travel in British Painting, c. 1740–1800: With Particular Reference to Nautical and Maritime Imagery', University of Warwick: unpublished PhD dissertation.

Rediker, M. (1987), *Between the Devil and the Deep Blue Sea: Merchant Seamen, Pirates, and the Anglo-American Maritime World, 1700–1750*, Cambridge: Cambridge University Press.

Robinson, C. N. (1909) *The British Tar in Fact and Fiction*, London: Navy Records Society.

Rodger, N. A. M. (1988), *The Wooden World: An Anatomy of the Georgian Navy*, London: Fontana Press.

————. (1992), 'Shipboard Life in the Georgian Navy, 1750–1800: The Decline of the Old Order?', in Fischer, L. R., Hamre, H., Holm, P. and Bruijn, J. R. (eds), *The North Sea: Twelve Essays on the Social History of Maritime Labour*, Stavanger, pp. 29–40.

Ruddick, W. (1993), 'Liberty Trees and Loyal Oaks: Emblematic Presences in Some English poems of the French Revolutionary Period', in Yarrington, A. and Everest, K. (eds), *Reflections of Revolution: Images of Romanticism*, London and New York: Routledge, pp. 59–67.

Russell, G. (1995), *The Theatres of War: Performance, Politics and Society, 1793–1815*, Oxford: Oxford University Press.

Slush, B. (1709), *The Navy Royal: Or, A Sea-Cook Turn'd Projector*, London.

Smollett, T. (1979) ed. Boucé, P.-G., *The Adventures of Roderick Random*, Oxford: Oxford University Press.

Stevenson, J. (1992), *Popular Disturbances in England, 1700–1832*, London and New York: Longman.

Taylor, G. (1978), *The Sea Chaplains: A History of the Chaplains of the Royal Navy*, Oxford: Oxford Illustrated Press.

The 1811 Dictionary of the Vulgar Tongue: Buckish Slang, University Wit and Pickpocket Eloquence, facsimile reprint: London, 1994.

Watson, H. F. (1931), *The Sailor in English Fiction and Drama 1550–1800*, New York: Columbia University Press.

Weibust, K. (1969), *Deep Sea Sailors: A Study in Maritime Ethnology*, Stockholm: Nordiska Museet.

Wells, R. (1983), *Insurrection: The British Experience 1795–1803*, Gloucester: Alan Sutton.

Yarrington, A. W. (1988), *Commemoration of the Hero 1800–1864: Monuments to the British Victors of the Napoleonic Wars*, New York and London: Garland.

Invasion! Coleridge, the defence of Britain and the cultivation of the public's fear

Mark Rawlinson

On 23 February 1797, a Roman Catholic Irish American landed on the North Pembrokeshire coast with the *légion noire*, a force recruited amongst ex-convicts. Tate's precipitous surrender, before the reluctant local Volunteers or Lord Cawdor's more aggressive Cardigan Militia could be formed up for action, had caused as much confusion as his landing:

> Fourteen hundred men, with arms in their hands, could unquestionably have done something; but, from their conduct, it appeared clear that they had been landed for no other purpose than that of being made prisoner. Under this consideration, we could not help sounding an alarm to the country.
>
> (*Complete History*, 1801 p. 83)

This unnamed parliamentarian understandably fudged the connection between fear or apprehension and a call to arms, and between fantasy and pragmatism, senses of alarm which, as shall become apparent, reveal the representational and ideological ambivalence of invasion threats as they are articulated in the threatened territory. In addition to assessing the nature of the imaginative work involved in being alarmed, this essay will consider the wider implications of cultural preparations for a war that does not occur. The excess of representation over actuality in this instance confounds the paradigm of war's under-representation, and with it our confidence that events at the core of the state's military activity, the wounding and killing of persons, always go missing when, conspiratorially or not, they are mediated to society at large.

The site of this last French invasion is commemorated by the Ordnance Survey (Landranger series, sheet 157), though since the Second World War the landing beach has been closed off by the defensive instruments elaborated in a later episode of island peril (Walters, 1994). A non-event from a military point of view, this baffling expedition (an expulsion from the enemy's territory as much as an attempted conquest of Britain) is now an annotation of space, a cultural inscription in the text of heritage signifying the quasi-providential meanings of physical geography. From the first dissemination of intelligence from the Welsh coast, the landing's significance in the cultural mobilization of a psychological front far outweighed its physical and strategic consequences as a contest of arms.

While the existence of a threat seemed incontrovertible (and not only because the need for one was an inescapable component of national self-identification), its meaning was subject to much speculation. The idea that the logistics of cross-Channel assault were a cover for the policing of the French state is elaborated in a caricature of Napoleon's blood-lust by James Gillray, published during a later episode of invasion alarm in November 1803. Hoisted onto his lieutenant's shoulder to watch the destruction of his gunboat flotilla through a telescope rolled up from 'Talleyrand's plan for invading Great Britain', the consul congratulates himself: 'We've worked up Johnny Bull into a fine passion! – my good fortune never leaves me! – I shall now get rid of a hundred Thousand French Cut Throats whom I was so afraid of!' (Gillray, 1968, plate 282).[1] In the longer term, the tactical and strategic imponderables of the Fishguard landing (an element in the Directory's plan for a three-pronged assault on Cork and Newcastle as well as Wales, where it was hoped to foment a popular rising against the common English enemy) have lent themselves to folkloric simplification and national myth-making: 'Welsh country women in their red petticoats and tall hats were taken by the French for red-coated soldiers coming up as reinforcements' (Stuart Jones, 1950, pp. 21–3; Vaughan-Thomas, 1969, p. 46; see also Colley, 1992, pp. 256–7 and Walters, 1994).

Reconstructing the production of alarm (both apprehension and readiness) in that era is all the more problematic because we are dealing not with logistical events alone, but also with imaginary scenarios, and because these resonate with both earlier and later invasion threats. The Scottish genealogist James Fraser wrote that history 'is indeed that telescope by which we see into distant ages and take up the actiones of our forefathers with as much evidence as the newes of the last gazette' (1905, p. 18). But the history of what we might call imaginative telescopy, the way people in Napoleonic Britain made the distant stuff of French military preparations appear nearer and larger, is troubled by the condensation of specific but similar moments in the cultivation of fear and military unity, reaching back beyond the Normans to Caesar, and forward to the blood- and sweat-stained beaches of Churchill's parliamentary rhetoric. Telescoping (in the figurative sense which draws on the action of sliding the tubes of an optical instrument into each other) is a usage of more recent times indicating an uncertainty about temporal discriminations or an imaginative forgetting.

Something of this kind is going on in *Losing Nelson*, when Barry Unsworth has the Nelson-biographer protagonist assert that his hero's victory at Copenhagen in 1801 averted a danger not equalled until 1941. An Englishman like Charles Cleasby, born in the 1950s, especially one who interprets the world through hagiographic rituals, might not know that by this date Hitler had, Napoleon-like, abandoned his plan to invade Britain for what would be a decisive assault on the Soviet Union (Unsworth, 1999, p. 133). Similarly, Jeanette Williamson in *The Passion* notes General Lazar Hoche's landing in Ireland in 1799, two years after his death in the history books, though unlike Cleasby, she is confident that stories, rather than determinate historical facts, are all we have.[2] In this cock-and-bull incarnation, Hoche's contribution to cross-Channel surveillance is the employment of a defrocked Irish priest 'whose left eye could put the best telescope to shame' (Winterson, 1988, p. 21), while every schoolboy once knew that monocular Nelson achieved his Baltic victory by ignoring Sir Hyde Parker's signal of recall: '"I have a right to be blind sometimes." He raised his spy-glass to his right [i.e. wrong] eye, and announced, "I really do not see the signal"' (Oman, 1967, p. 391).

The telescope enlarges but it also narrows the field of vision. It might stand, for the purposes of this investigation, as a figure for certain discursive repertoires, notably exaggeration and selection, bringing some things closer and keeping some out of sight.

> We have seen a flotilla of four frigates go and cast upon the coast of Wales the scum of the banditti of France, without their having been able to find out the end of that hideous expedition, which carried dread even into the capital itself, because the telescope of the fear of the one party, and desire of the other, magnified their object.
>
>   (Dumourier, 1798, p. 5)

In the years between the first and second coalitions the telescope of fear was a crucial element in a project of verbal and visual propaganda that, on closer inspection, raises significant questions about participation in the culture of garrison Britain between 1795 and 1805, and more generally about the imagination and war.

Alarm's telescope also points us to issues concerning the conditions under which war may be said to be visible.

> How did war appear to the English public of the romantic period? In the years between 1793 and 1815, when England was almost constantly at war with France, publicity raised a paper shield – a shield of newspaper reports, pamphlets, songs and poems – against the destructive violence of war. In simply empirical terms, the displacement of fighting onto foreign lands and waters meant that the immediate activity of war, 'the activity of reciprocal injuring,' remained for the most part outside the visual experience of the English population.
>
>   (Favret, 1994, p. 539)

The precise relationship between the self-evident absence of military operations from England and the workings of the 'paper shield' which occludes the nature of operations elsewhere is clarified somewhat by a subsequent thesis, namely that war widows 'undermine the fiction motivating the war effort:

that it will keep violence from coming home' (p. 547). But violence may be brought home in a number of ways, and for a number of reasons: the cultural production of alarm was predicated on just such a translation of war from afar. Scenarios involving paper armies of Frenchmen laying waste to south-east England are a major cultural production of these years. Such imaginings invite us to reassess the terms in which bringing war home is held to be just a process of euphemistic redescription of war for domestic consumption. A sense of vulnerability to war's material consequences is instrumental in the production of assent to perpetrating them.

In 'The English Mail Coach', his meditation on a revolution in the cultural synchronization of the nation, Thomas De Quincey, alighting paper in hand in 'some little town', tells the anxious mother of a dragoon not the news that has sped with him, that her son's regiment lay 'stretched, by a large majority, upon one bloody aceldama', but how 'these dear children of England, officers and privates, had leaped their horses over all obstacles as gaily as hunters to the morning's chase' (De Quincey, 1897, vol. 13, pp. 299–300). However, as when Marlow scripts Kurtz's dying words as a last endearment at last brought home to his fiancée, the text that represents culture's verbal shields is not itself merely an instrument in a conspiracy of silence, it bespeaks the 'fascination of the abomination' (Conrad, 1988, p. 10). De Quincey's heavily coded 'aceldama' does not, admittedly, have the same visual force as Favret's reconstruction of the scene as a '*bloody* trench' (my emphasis), a complement determined by the hegemonically 'visible' fortifications of the Western Front of 1914–18. However, in naming a place of slaughter after the field purchased with Judas Iscariot's blood-money, De Quincey's invocation of what his 'forebearance' kept hidden suggests that a geographical opposition between foreign fields and native hearths, direct sense experience and its substitution by official culture's sanitizing witness, could narrow our field of vision. It is because that geographical boundary is the symbolic site of imaginative transgressions, namely the projection of enemy incursions and of the convergence of domestic political radicalism with the example of republican France, that we should not prejudge the function of martial representations in terms of their correspondence to the idea of the self-evident content of military activity.

Distrust of the public and private propaganda that prevents war coming home perceptually and cognitively remains an important critical stance in the conversations of political subjects. But its currency, in academic circles whose own boundaries are defined in part by the subscription to a hermeneutics of suspicion, should not lead us to dismiss as mere delusions those discourses that lend a rational purposiveness to war efforts designed to prevent war, in the persons of the soldiery of a belligerent state, coming into the homes of citizens. However, the outline of British military history encourages just that. The idea that war is a cultural absence because not experienced here, only elsewhere, is widespread in twentieth-century British art and criticism, good luck read perversely as a national epistemological misfortune in not having been occupied. It is one thing to note how 'insulation' from war might limit the capacity of a culture to imagine the consequences of war, another entirely to suppose that *Einfühlung*, empathy, is conditional on an identity of experience with victims of wars (see Jonathan Glover, 1999, p. xi; Berlin, 1997, p. 108; Nussbaum, 1995, *passim*). From Robert Graves's and Siegfried Sassoon's verbal assaults on a bellicose but allegedly ignorant civilian population to the changing patterns of Second World War remembrance, which voice an 'obscure guilt within British culture about its own isolation from the real horrors of the war' (Piette, 1995, p. 1), insular immunity from conflict has been repeatedly invoked as an irremediable lack. This reflex rests on an ultimately reductive assumption about war, namely that its empirical truth is beyond the reach of, or occluded by, values. It is also a response to the power of the manifold fantasies about war which characterize civil life. However, from the perspective of representational form and content, the domestication of war as wish-fulfilment turns out not to be categorically distinguishable from the emancipatory propaganda of liberal and progressive critiques of war, in particular the visual and verbal signs that are deemed to bring war home because they are adequate to war's empirical content, the broken bodies of persons. The heuristic grid of soldier versus civilian, home and overseas, is ethically compelling in proportion to its power to distract us from historical and cultural specificities, the local contexts in which military violence acquires meanings we could promote or contest.

When veteran nurse and anti-strategic-bombing campaigner Vera Brittain wrote that in the London blitz 'mothers in their homes, run risks comparable to those of the fighting soldier in the first Great War', the opposition between soldier and civilian obviously survived her assessment of its erasure by technology (Brittain, 1940, p. 117). This reflects not only the persistence (in ethical discourse, though not in the military strategies of the industrial state) of distinctions going back to St Augustine, but also of the seductions of the fantasy of visiting the truth of war on civilians who might be deemed responsible for the slaughter of citizen soldiers. Siegfried Sassoon's bloodthirsty articulation of his protest against the prosecution of the Great War in the poem 'Blighters', in which a tank is unleashed on a jingoist music hall audience, anticipates a number of pre-1940 fantasies, most notably those of Orwell and Betjeman, in which bombers bring home the truth of war (or of modernity) to pacified civilians. Images which target those at home with the weapons aimed by and inflicted on the troops are homologous with, though not precisely analogous to, the imaginative disasters of invasion alarm, and the manifold cultural forms in which war is brought home, counterfactually, in the administration of the war efforts of Georgian England. The visual and verbal depiction of war is not solely directed at passive consumers: such images have '*created*, as well as represented, combat performance' (Bourke, 1999, p. 28). Preserving a distinction between form and function is important if we are to pursue the complicated reciprocity between paper war and war experienced.

In privileging the empirical over the cultural and imaginative, Favret's assumptions become obstacles to comprehending the signification of war in Napoleonic Britain even as she calls attention to 'aphasia about war in current romantic studies'. It is significant that this troping of literary criticism's blindness to war rests on a loss of speech due to somatic injury, rather than on the figural or literal mutism which the twentieth century has associated with the repression of the traumas of war experience (see for instance Benjamin, 1973, p. 84 and Barker, 1991, 1993, 1995). This choice brings to light a residual dualism which obscures reciprocal practices in wartime; namely that the body is idealised and values or symbols are embodied, even to dying or killing for them. Herein lies another justification for exploring the way fear's telescope brought war home via verbal and visual projections of conditional injury and occupation. To say that wars require the active participation of peoples in reproducing a symbolization of violence which facilitates military conduct is not the same thing as to suppose that as a result of disseminating critical consciousness of the function of discourse in achieving consent to violence, war would cease to function politically, socially or psychologically. Military practice in Napoleonic Britain, conditional or otherwise, seems to rely on the capacity of large fractions of the population to simultaneously imagine the horrors of war and to direct those imaginings to the production of assent to military conduct.

Imagined conflict, a rubric under which we must include both redescriptions of injuring that has occurred as well as counter-factual and alarmist projections, cannot be relegated to a position of instrumental inauthenticity or mendaciousness without some loss of purchase on the symbolic economies which shape behaviour and belief in both public and private spheres of agency in time of war. The accessibility of a plethora of British print culture from this period which is explicitly directed at the production and dissemination of invasion alarm makes literary critics' silence about war all the more significant. A clue to this puzzle is to be found in the ironic tone of the cultural criticism in *Napoleon and the Invasion of England* (1908), which includes a substantial survey of the cultural vehicles of an invasion fear that, by the summer of 1803, 'began to intrude into every kind of ephemeral literature' (Wheeler and Broadley, 1908, vol. 2, p. 294). Published four years after the revived entente cordiale with France (which would help bring Britain into the First World War), Wheeler and Broadley's archive is contemporary with notable developments in the genre of future-war fiction like Erskine Childers's *The Riddle of the Sands* (1903), William Le Queux's *The Invasion of 1910* (1906) and H. G. Wells's *The War in the Air* (1908) which located the threat in German militarism. Even if the 'geography of "invasion literature"' remained constant in its concentration in the south-east of England, the French had finally been relegated in the imagination of invasion (Moretti, 1998, p. 139).

The Prussian occupation of Paris in 1871 reoriented not only the geopolitics but also the forms of invasion fictions. The appearance of Sir George Chesney's *The Battle of Dorking* (1871) defined 'a new type of purposive fiction in which the whole aim was either to terrify the reader by a clear and merciless demonstration of the consequences to be expected from a country's [defensive] shortcomings, or to prove the rightness of national policy by describing the course of a victorious war in the near future'. From then on, 'Chesney's story showed Europe how to manipulate the new literature of anxiety and belligerent nationalism' (Clarke, 1992, pp. 32, 38). But a literature of anxiety had existed in Britain before the counter-factual imagination was parcelled up into exportable narrative and ideological conventions. Discourse about war in Napoleonic Britain is not an absence in Romantic studies alone. It does not register sufficiently in the prehistory of twentieth-century novelistic, radiophonic and cinematic imaginary wars in their relationship to policy and modes of popular consent to military ideologies. While homologies between early nineteenth-century mass mobilization and British society in the two world wars continue to sustain myths of the popular basis of national security, from the perspective of cultural history the linkage is a buried one.

In the light of a shifting balance of power, and the increasing rhetorical sophistication and affective power of future-war fiction, England's imaginary Great Terror of 1803–1805 appeared, in 1908, to be a parochial travesty of republican France's civil bloodbath. Wheeler and Broadley's amused commentaries on the crassness of the output of '"invasion" publisher[s]' register not only the knowledge that invasion did not come (puncturing the alarmists' bellicose postures) but also that it will not come from France (1908, vol. 2, p. 258). When, little more than thirty years on, after Hitler's strategic defeat in the Battle of Britain, Churchill asked, 'What is it that has turned invasion into the invasion scare?', the answer was vigilance, not that the threat was a phantom (Langdon-Davies, 1940, p. 8). In both of its relevant senses, alarm was the sign of a strategically crucial readiness, not of unrealized bogeys. But Napoleonic scares became doubly distanced from the realm of 'empirical' war by the non-occurrence of occupation and by their association with the 'wrong war', that is their lack of articulation with the Germano-British (and American) conflicts which have dominated thinking about military experience and its representation in twentieth-century artistic and critical culture.

While Britain was not, like continental Europe, a war zone, invasion was threaded through its history and origins, as attested by frequently reprinted works like David Hume's *The History of England, from the invasion of Julius Caesar to the Revolution in 1688* (8 vols, 1763–78) and Oliver Goldsmith's

The History of England from the invasion of Julius Caesar to the death of George II (1774, with a 13th edition by 1805). The French wars lent urgency to the rehearsal of the narrative of successive descents on the archipelago, and to the contemplation of an unhappy ending to the story. The *Complete History of the Invasions of England including most memorable Battles and Sea Fights from Julius Caesar, down to the French landing in Wales in 1796* [sic] (1801), which annexed reports of the 'Calamities of France' to an encyclopaedic record of two dozen attempted and realised invasions, was designed for the 'instruction of the lower classes'. The circulation of this collection (with its terrible inferences from the 'present awful crisis') was advertised as a patriotic duty of 'wealthy proprietors'; there was money to be made in suggesting how fortunes might be lost to Republican hordes.

Propagandist histories of relations with an enemy across the Channel appeared throughout the nineteenth century. Sir Edmund Creasey (a military historian who influenced a genre of redescriptive war writing with his *Fifteen Decisive Battles of the World*) directed his alarm about the impact of steam power on naval tactics into the writing of *The Invasions and Projected Invasions of England from the Saxon Times* (1852). The opening of Suez and the beginning of the construction of the St Gotthard tunnel provided impetus not only for the association of a Channel Tunnel Company in 1872 but also for the publication of Captain H. M. Hozier's *The Invasions of England: A History of the Past, with Lessons for the Future* (1876), well ahead of a stream of alarmist fictions concerned with nefarious French penetrations through the proposed tunnel written after 1882. The burden of both books was that insular impregnability was a matter of luck, not might or judgement: 'we have been very frequently indebted to the favouring influences of variable elements' (Creasey, 1852, p. 263). *Vain Boastings of Frenchmen The Same in 1386 as in 1798* (1798), despite the patriotic confidence of its title, admitted as much in recalling a French descent on Ricardian England, an attempt ended only when the invasion fleet was scattered on the wind about the Thames estuary.

The pattern of this providential history is at once a source of patriotism and of defeatism. Once a people becomes unaccustomed to the threat of invasion, or to 'the idea that our country might ever be made a theatre of war', the possibility becomes 'chimerical', but invoking it risks 'the wild terror which may be nurtured by an alarmist' (Hozier, 1876, vol. 1, p. v). Alarm is as ambivalent as war itself. 'He that runs may read!' reads the title-page of the *Complete History*: the motto reflects the populist address of the volume (though not contemporary literacy) and the ideal that an alarm is productive of resistance, not flight. But it also speaks to the assimilation of aggression to culture, and to a capacity to discover a fascination, even pleasure, in the representation of events that, in normal circumstances, we would flee from.[3]

Solitary manoeuvres: 'resisting the temptations / To skyline operations'[4]

Coleridge's 'Fears in Solitude' invites us to ask how imaginary war, in the form of alarm and alarmism, bears on the relationship between the represen-tation of war's empirical and somatic actuality and the ideologies which vouchsafe the prosecution of war in the face of both egocentric and altruistic care for the safety of the body. That this text seems at once to stand above the scrum of ephemeral invasion literature, and to be part of it (Coleridge in-scribed an autograph manuscript with the description, 'a sort of middle thing between Poetry and Oratory', 1957, p. 257) recommends it all the more as an instance of the production of invasion alarm and as an occasion for thinking through the imaginary and symbolic components of conflict. In the month of its composition, the surviving committee members of the London Corre-sponding Society were arrested as they debated whether they should or should not join the Volunteers to resist the despotism of the French republic (Thompson, 1968, p. 188).

Favret has remarked that 'war structures and sustains the landscape that cloaks it' from the view of Romantic criticism (p. 539). In respect of Coleridge's poem, this proves even more fruitful if taken literally, rather than in the figurative sense implied. The terrain of 'Fears' is topographically and axiologically configured in relation to injuring events. Imaginary wounds align the temporally fluid episode of meditation, movement and reconnais-sance in the poem with counter-factual projections disseminated widely in contemporary print culture. Published in 1798 with 'France an Ode' – occa-sioned by the invasion of Switzerland (Bonnard, 1940, p. 2) – the poem was excerpted in the *Morning Post* half a year after the Treaty of Amiens in October 1802 (hostilities were resumed six months later) and reprinted in the *Friend* in 1809 in a defence of the author as 'a loyal Subject' (Coleridge 1969, vol. 1, p. 23). These bibliographical facts give a clue to the poem's instability as a document of alarm, signifying patriotism and anxiety, belli-cosity and revulsion. But it remains to locate the fundamental tensions which sustain this ambivalence. I would argue that it is not simply a question of whether one is disposed to read the poem as protest or provocation. For in the social practices and psychological dynamics of invasion alarm there exists a structural linkage of being wounded and wounding, of shrinking from and commending violence.

We might read the ruin of 'calmness' in the opening lines of 'Fears' as the overmastering of nature's 'sweet influences' by the far-reaching effects of public discourses of alarm on the individual psyche. The poem will appear to dispel its fears by invoking again, as it does at the outset, 'nature's quietness' (l. 239) as the occasion of the 'thoughts that yearn for human kind' (though these are the thoughts, in another military context, that have earlier disturbed the soul). How is this revaluation achieved, and does it consist solely of a

jingoist telescoping, whereby the horrors of war are excluded from the range
of the visible or visualisable? Rhetorically and at the level of the poem's
outer locomotory narrative, joyous, as opposed to apprehensive, 'solitary
musings' are restored by the fiat of a micro-climatic disturbance. Anxiety is
quelled by calling upon providential meteorological defences: immunity lies
not in the navy's vaunted walls of oak, but winds – which shiver all timbers –
temporarily favourable to the defenders ('Peace long preserved by fleets and
perilous seas').

> May my fears,
> My filial fears, be vain! and may the vaunts
> And menace of the vengeful enemy
> Pass like the gust, that roared and died away
> In the distant tree: which heard, and only heard
> In this low dell, bowed not the delicate grass.
>   (ll. 197–202)

The roar that is 'heard, and only heard', and which leaves no mark on the
dell, is a figure which reinterprets the 'uproar' which the poet earlier imagined in the surrounding hills, an uproar of conflict which is not only unheard
but whose confirming manifestations (in John Whiting's period comedy *A
Penny for a Song* resistance is to be mustered by posters marked 'INVA-
SION') would be in any case invisible because of the limits that the depression
places on the field of vision. It is not just the possibility of, or even the
national fiction of, invasion that has broken the spell of solitude, but the
poet's capacity to perceive military conflict imaginatively, peopling the region which is perceptually out of range with injurors and injured, so that

> he must think
> What uproar and what strife may now be stirring
> This way or that way o'er these silent hills –
> Invasion, and the thunder and the shout,
> And all the crash of onset; fear and rage,
> And undetermined conflict – even now,
> Even now, perchance, and in his native isle:
> Carnage and groans beneath this blessed sun!
>   (ll. 33–40)

The vision of a land untrod by invaders (the 'unbowed grass' of the dell
proffered as an image of national security) is in tension with these awful
inferences. The mind that has filled silence with sounds of battle regroups by
naturalizing that noise as a passing gust (cancelling the alarm). But does this
make the imagined army of invaders as redundant as their threat is fleeting?
Rather than asserting that the poem is either an anti-war polemic or a docile
rehearsal of a general call to arms, we might attend to its deployment of the
content of alarm, in particular the way in which apprehensively imagining the
scourge of war is articulated with imagining going to war. Readiness to fight,

a state of alarm, is in part produced by alarm at the prospect of fighting, a connection affirmed in contemporary citations of historic invasion threats (each of which raises the spectre of defeat in order to procure the conditions which will exclude that possibility).

Noting the absence of a tradition of anti-war poetry from which First World War poets 'could draw sustenance', Jon Silkin writes that Coleridge was not so much answering his objections to war, as 'responding to two pressures: those of his political ideals and those of patriotism' (Silkin, 1979, p. 23). These pressures coincide with the strategic necessity of disseminating fearful images of war to generate patriotism. Coleridge's poem is a micro-cosm of the representational economy of Britain in the period of the French Wars. Apprehension could 'scarcely be carried beyond the extent of the real danger' (Fox, 1794, p. 7). In 1803, 'Publicola' told the people of England that invasion was to be averted 'by feeling the full extent of your danger' (Klingberg and Hustvedt, 1944, p. 33).

But it may be that the way 'Fears' speaks to twentieth-century ideologies of war, as much as its congruence with contemporary patriotic discourses, leads to a conviction that it represents a betrayal of critical consciousness. The rhetorical power of Coleridge's treatment of the redescriptive conven-tions that make war palatable at the breakfast table provides modern literature of war experience with a paradigm of the 'insensitivity ... incarnated in the *civilian*' (Silkin, 1979, p. 21). But this anticipation of a later moral consensus about 'feckless discussion of war' means, 'oddly enough', that he supplies the terms of his own indictment for domesticating violence, recasting war 'as defence of women ... not the killing of other men' (Favret, 1994, pp. 542–3).

The idea that insularity, 'impressing an idea of security, has emboldened us to adopt a peculiar language and conduct' in relation to war was a common-place in an era when war might be brought home at any moment, and therefore had to be brought home to mobilize resistance (Fox, 1794, p. 9). Security depended, then, on teaching Coleridge's 'poor wretch' to fear the force of arms on British soil. In this context, the wretch as 'fluent phraseman, absolute / And technical in victories and defeats' was a strategic obligation, 'invasion being very properly the topic of general conversation' (*Complete History*, 1801, p. ix). The same verbal and graphic resources that represent combat which is geographically remote, in contexts in which its constituent events lack moral resonance, are deployed to generate consciousness of hu-man vulnerability to its violence.

Coleridge's critique of martial small-talk bears on the substitution of signs for deeds:

> Terms which we trundle smoothly o'er our tongues
> Like mere abstractions, empty sounds to which
> We join no feeling and attach no form!
> As if the soldier died without a wound;

As if the fibres of this godlike frame
Were gored without a pang; as if the wretch,
Who fell in battle, doing bloody deeds,
Passed off to Heaven, translated and not killed ...
                            (ll. 114–21)[5]

The insubstantial soldiery are, however, kin to the imaginary forces Coleridge arrays about the Quantocks, as are 'empty sounds' (lacking emotional or somatic connection) to the unheard sounds pregnant with corporeal suffering. These representations are not, that is, simply the inverse of each other, the latter a disquieting return of the content of war which is repressed by the abstractions of public propaganda and private fantasies of sanitised violence.

The poem's most strained forensic juncture lays responsibility for the emergency with newspaper-gorged tattlers who have swelled 'the war-whoop': 'Therefore, evil days / Are coming on us' (ll. 122–3). Coleridge urges a connection between insensitivity and policy that is publically unacknowledged: the failure to attach forms to bellicose noises is the source of a delusory immunity from a tyranny which will plague its makers 'Like a cloud that travels on, / Steamed up from Cairo's swamps of pestilence' (ll. 47–8). But lack of an imaginative capacity to give martial conduct painful embodiment is at one and the same time the cause of violence coming home ('mandates for the certain death / Of thousands and ten thousands' returned to sender), and of an unreadiness to resist it violently. Apprehending the horrors of war lends itself both to opposition to war and violent opposition to an enemy. It is not so much that Coleridge's poem turns on its head (though in its projection of a victory already won it seems to do just that) as that what it imagines can face two ways. 'Good' representations of war do not have an intrinsic power to stem the violence that other representations appear to foster: Coleridge's critique of verbal conduct receives its due gloss in Walter Benjamin's conclusion that mankind's 'self-alienation has reached such a degree that it can experience its own destruction as an aesthetic pleasure of the first order' (1973, p. 244). But the poem's worrying intellectual apostasy is more complex than a dutiful surrender to the claims on mind and body of political hegemony, as if it incarnated a revision of the Hammonds' remark that 'The history of England at this time ... reads like a history of civil war' by the emphasis in Linda Colley's work on the invention of patriotism: an 'active commitment to Great Britain' that had to be learned (Thompson, 1968, p. 215; Colley, 1992, p. 295). Opposition to 'mad idolatry' of authority's images makes the undeceived 'enemies / Even of their country' (ll. 172–5). This is a scandalous accusation whose implications are threaded through the topographical movements of 'Fears'.

The 'soft and silent spot' to which Coleridge bids farewell in the poem's coda has acted as a telescope of fear, concealing a landscape to which he has mentally ushered foreign troops and on which he has deployed them in an

unseen scene of carnage. Ascent is a literal reinforcement of the wished-for
gust which drives the enemy back to sea:

> recalled
> From bodings that have well-nigh wearied me,
> I find myself upon the brow, and pause
> Startled! And after lonely sojourning
> In such a quiet and surrounded nook,
> This burst of prospect, here the shadowy main,
> Dim-tinted, there the mighty majesty
> Of that huge amphitheatre of rich
> And elmy fields, seems like society –
> Conversing with the mind, and giving it
> A livelier impulse and a dance of thought!
>
> (ll. 210–20)

Gaining the tactical advantage of elevation to survey the field of projected
slaughter (combat recalled in another form by that elmy amphitheatre),
Coleridge's reintegrating viewpoint coincides with the perspective of the
invader:

> And now, belovéd Stowey! I behold
> The church-tower, and, methinks, the four large elms
> Clustering, which mark the mansion of my friend;
> And close behind them, hidden from my view,
> Is my own lowly cottage, where my babe
> And my babe's mother dwell in peace!
>
> (ll. 221–6)

Mapped onto the terrain of future war, home and the 'quickened footsteps'
that speed the poet's descent to human society confound the fantasy of a
French descent on England by revoking the space in which such forces might
be deployed. Sublimity ('undetermined conflict') is repressed, not expressed,
by a topographical vista which becomes a counterpart of imagined defensive
preparations:

> If any military man will look to the large map of Essex, on a scale of
> two inches to a mile, sold by Mr. Faden, opposite Northumberland
> House, Strand, they will easily perceive that the position may be much
> shortened between these two towns … this makes the town doubly
> strong … shortens the position of the troops behind it, and requires
> fewer numbers to defend it.
>
> (Hanger, 1970, p. 23)

Texts like Hanger's, and John Burney's *Plan of Defence against Invasion*
(1797) must imagine disaster to commend theoretical designs against it. As in
'Fears', the ideals of national resistance to invasion are dependent on con-
ceiving the results of such an incursion. Unoccupied Stowey, with the family
cottage still precariously 'hidden from my view', is bound up with the prospect of its denizens falling into enemy hands, and suffering the rapine and

undisciplined violence which, anticipating the Gallic descent, broadsiders and pamphleteers unleashed on the reading public: 'In the whole village there was neither maiden, wife nor widow who was not forcibly and repeatedly dishonoured' (*Warning to Britons*, 1798, p. 29).

The referential instability of the imagination of invasion alarm

Alarmist documents acknowledge the absence of war because they must stand in for the experience of war: they bring us no closer to its content conceived empirically than De Quincey's gay hunters. But the question of the functions of war's visibility (and the representational detours in which that visibility inheres) is reordered if we learn to register how our readings of the symbolic economies of wartime cultures are shaped by an ethical imperative to see war as possessing 'some brute facticity made of sterner and solider stuff than signs', a paradox given that 'war is relentless in taking for its own interior content the interior content of the wounded and the open human body' (Clark, 1984, p. 6; Scarry, 1985, p. 81). War imagined has an efficacy of a different order and degree to war experienced.

Coleridge's apostasy, taken together with the ways in which 'Fears' substitutes its author for the enemy, brings to light further ambiguities which structure the imagining of war in Britain at this period. As was apparent to contemporaries, these imaginings were neither idle pastimes nor simply recruiting stunts:

> The opposition to Government, revolutionary spirit, discontents of numerous workmen without work or victuals, the falling of commerce, the distrust which the stoppage of payment and partial bankruptcies will produce in mercantile transactions, the embarrassment of the Bank, the activity of the French in fomenting discord in the three kingdoms, the necessity of keeping up a numerous army to put the coasts above insult, the dearness of this expense, the danger of arming the whole nation in the midst of the discord and innovation which agitates it: this combination of real calamities is sufficient to depress the resources and courage of the nation, which derives all its strength from its riches and commerce, though the French should not even employ more decisive measures against it
>
> (Dumourier, 1798, p. 5)

If the prospect of invasion is a calamity (fear and readiness disrupt a social order favourable to commerce whether the threat materialises or not), then the dissemination of alarm must be controlled and its production becomes a matter of national security. The enemy's power (actual or potential) over the mental and social life of Britons, as again in the years running up to the London Blitz, makes civil culture a battleground between the symbolic resources of contesting states in what Scarry has called a 'reality duel'(1985,

p. 130). In the empirical absence of physical combat between people killing
and dying for those states, psychological warfare is not merely a bloodless
substitute but a crucial competition in manoeuvring ideas and information.[6]
In an era that anticipates the mass mobilizations of men, *matériel* and propaganda of the twentieth century, the complexity and fugitive character of
central control over the ideas and symbols which facilitate the administration
of a war effort has fully emerged. The problem of the ambivalence of such
messages was apparent, as was the way in which 'cultural weapons' could
undergo a process of switching, either returned to sender or running out of
control to generate unforeseen counter-meanings. There is more to this cultural dimension of warfare than the brandishing of boastful icons.

Dumourier, with his nice appreciation of the psychological aspects of war,
is himself emblematic of a passage across military and ideological fronts that
must complicate any contention about the separation of home and abroad in
the period. A soldier in exile from revolutionary France – 'in its pride and
ignorance, this Convention orders the conquest and disorganization of the
whole Universe' – Dumourier settled in England – 'the only country that can
eventually SAVE MINE' – in 1803, working in an informal capacity for the
British government (Dumourier, 1793, p. 5; Holland-Rose and Broadley,
1909, p. xiv). An expert in the 'make-believe' of invasion (having planned the
capture of the Isle of Wight when Commandant at Cherbourg in the 1770s),
he was living proof of the historical precariousness of British shores while
living off the problem of precautions.

That threatened invasion visits the consequences of overseas control over
sovereign territory in the same moment that alarm is propagated for national
interests is a structural consequence of warfare which is echoed in a variety
of representations of Napoleonic Britain. The verse of Charles Dibdin, 'the
real laureate of the Great Terror', articulates these paradoxes with unwitting
force:

> The French are all coming, so they declare
> Of their floats and balloons all the papers advise us
> They've to swim through the ocean, and ride on the air,
> In some foggy evening to land and surprize us,
> Their army's to come and plant liberty's Tree
> Call'd the army of England, what matchless presumption!
>   (Wheeler and Broadley, 1908, vol. 2, pp. 293, 288)

This is the army that Coleridge imagines laying waste to Somerset, unaware
that it was bound that summer for Egypt as the Army of the Orient, and that
'Cairo's swamps of pestilence' would mutate in later broadsides into a per-
sonification of its commander, Napoleon, as the 'Poisoner of Jaffa', murderer
of his own wounded (Klingberg and Hustvedt, 1944, p. 67). It has been
suggested that Wordsworth's 'Salisbury Plain', by invoking Celtic human
sacrifice at Stonehenge as a context for the miseries of modern warfare, is

identifying contemporary states through their sponsorship of suffering – 'Britain *was* France' (Liu, 1989, p. 193). The threat of invasion impressed upon commentators the apparent necessity of this convergence, and it did so in terms the political and military implications of which brought into play distinctly unconventional representations of war.

The commonplace opposition between France's indomitable Continental armies and the comparably insuperable might of the British navy was over-determined by myths of geographical security. 'The Snug Little Island', a song premiered at Sadler's Wells in April 1797 – and which became 'almost a second national anthem' – fused walls of oak and coastal frontiers:

> Daddy Neptune one day to Freedom did say,
> If ever I live upon dry land,
> The spot I should hit on would be little Britain,
> Says Freedom, 'why that's my own island!'
> Oh its a snug little island!
> A right little, tight little island,
> Search the globe round, none can be found
> So happy as this little island.
>
> (Longmate, 1991, pp. 247–8)

But the prospect of landings modified a differential grounded in the myth of naval Britain: 'We begin now, though rather late, plainly to see (France having become an armed nation) that the safety of our country depends on a strong military force *by land*, and becoming an *armed nation* ourselves, and not to place our sole reliance on fleets, which imprudently we formerly trusted too much' (Hanger, 1970, p. 74). Napoleon's Army of England meant there would be an army in England; the question was not just whose army, but what its politics would be. 'To beat the French, the British had been required to imitate the French, and the challenge this presented to its old order was potentially corrosive' (Colley, 1992, p. 318).

The centralization of the home defence initiative with the Defence of the Realm Act of 1798 and ensuing legislation, together with the uneven yet unprecedented enthusiasm for volunteering, witnessed both the efficacy of invasion culture and its potentially subversive political implications. The telescope of alarm generated both anxiety and pleasure:

> Surrounded by loud and exhilarating noises, equipped with brand new uniforms and unfamiliar pikes and muskets, bombarded with tales of French oppression and atrocities in other lands and constantly told that only they could prevent similar evils from befalling their own shores, their own home town or village, some labouring men, it is clear, saw in volunteering a window onto a broader and more vivid existence.
>
> (Colley, 1992, p. 308)

The psychological content of this scenario of bellicose euphoria is speculative (and again the homology with the twentieth century's iconography of mass delusion, in particular urban European crowds in August 1914, is striking, and clearly struck Linda Colley). Nevertheless, the demographics of enthusiasm remain open to radical as well as to suspicious readings, as evidence of the precariousness of power in an armed nation and of ideological domination and manufactured enthusiasm. That participants in the Second World War constructed parallels between their situation and that of Napoleonic Britain, particularly in the context of 'socialist' consequences of their war effort, helps keep these non-contradictory but conflicting meanings before us. The 'People's War' of 1940–45 was itself a contested symbol of popular agency and mass-media propaganda. Citing a half million Englishmen mobilized by the Levee en Masse Act of 1803, Home Guard historian Charles Graves noted 'preparations to combat invasion were much the same as those of 1940' (a connection apparently reinforced by the observation that some of Eden's Local Defence Volunteers were armed with pikes liberated from HMS *Victory* (Graves, 1943, pp. 9–10)). Orwell's remarks in 1941 about 'near a million British working men [who] now have rifles in their bedrooms and don't in the least wish to give them up' dramatically overstate the political unpredictability of mass-mobilized patriotism (Orwell, 1970, vol. 2, pp. 181–2). Coleridge, writing in 1800, had also drawn conclusions about the potentially transformative effects of the state's turning to its subjects for its security: 'Every state, in which all the inhabitants without distinction of property are roused to the exertion of a public spirit, is for the time a Jacobin state' (cited in Colley, 1992, p. 312).

But the anxieties attending mass mobilization were real, fed on the same images of undisciplined rapine, plunder and enslavement employed to generate alarm at invasion by a (French) nation-in-arms (Klingberg and Hustvedt, 1944, pp. 64, 106, 199). The cut-throat in uniform could be an indigene. Colley draws on government censuses of active patriotism to modify a picture of Napoleonic Britain dominated by the visibility to scholars of evidence for popular protest and, with the example of Gillray, contemporary culture's 'inability to come to terms with plebeian patriotism' (1992, pp. 283–4). Rates at which Britons volunteered, and the terms on which they were prepared to serve (at home or posted to other parts of the country) correlated with region and community. The highest levels of recruitment occurred in urban and industrializing areas. Colley notes that the conclusion that militarization was aided by economic and social modernization has been slow to impress itself on British historians wedded to identifications of town and protest, countryside and docile duty (1992, p. 298). These prejudices are evident in the culture of invasion itself. In his elaborate scheme of defensive preparations against a landing in Essex, George Hanger meets Cobbett's criticism of the military effectiveness of volunteers with arguments that do not disguise his resistance to a popular force. Hanger's corps would consist of men practised in fowling (he who can hit partridge or lark can kill a Frenchman), who are

superior in physique to 'the impoverished half-fed labouring countryman, or
the lower order of mechanics, enlisted at Birmingham, Manchester or Shef-
field' and, because they aspire 'to a character in life', superior in courage too
(Hanger, 1970, pp. 147–9). Hanger's very tactics are grounded in property,
relying on defensive positions provided by field enclosures. His conservative
anti-urbanism (made explicit in his criticism of the demographics of the '*levy
en masse*') is the antithesis of Southey's faith in the war effort as a force for
social transformation: 'if they arm the people as is talked of', he wrote to
John May in July 1803, 'I think I can foresee much good to arise out of the
present evil – a system more favourable to the morals and security and
liberties of the country than that of militias and standing armies' (Wheeler
and Broadley, 1908, vol. 2, pp. 345–6).

But while Hanger is essentially defending a social order, his tactical imagination, fed on the fantasy of war as transcendent sport, leads him to create no
less radical scenarios via the pressure that war places on the *patria* to imitate
its enemies. As a primer in irregular warfare, *Reflections on the Menaced
Invasion* meets the charge that volunteers lack proper discipline, the mark of
standing forces, by identifying the defence of the country with the tactics of
the colonists who embarrassed its own military in the American War of
Independence. The revisionary perspective goes even further than this. As
Napoleon's military failure in Egypt 'gave birth to the entire modern experience of the Orient' (Said, 1991, p. 87), Hanger was recalling the frontier
struggles of his idealized colonists against Native Americans, and complicat-
ing the relations of British (and French) imperial projects to indigenous
peoples, enemies of Europeans but sometime mercenary allies: 'if I com-
manded a corps of light troops to-morrow I would *make them imitate the
Indians in action in every thing except scalping*' (Hanger, 1970, p. 171). This
reconfiguration resonates with the more knowing ironies of David Halberstam's
Vietnam novel *One Very Hot Day*, when an audience of American advisors,
cheering Gregory Peck in *The Guns of Navarone* (1961), realise that the hero
behind enemy lines is acting in the role of the Viet Cong (Rawlinson, 1990, p.
180). The tension between reaction and innovation in Hanger's defensive
thinking is one amongst many signs of the way war brought home does more
than feed fantasies of violence, though that component is crucial in reinforc-
ing more pragmatic intentions.

Much contemporary invasion culture was conceived to resolve the contradictions created by imaginative and social mobilization, and to mask the
uneveness of their impact, but these tensions break through nevertheless.
Wordsworth's 'Lines on the Expected Invasion' (written 1803 but unpublished until 1842; 1981, p. 246), is a reduction of the debate over social
conformity in 'Fears in Solitude' to the confines of the sonnet form, invoking
dissent as an occasion for imagining universal consent whereby alarm is a
source of unity. The peculiarity of this poem is that it seems to bare a

conspiracy to employ war as an instrument of social cohesion: 'save this honoured Land from every Lord / But British reason and the British Sword' (ll. 19–20).[7] Wordsworth does not urge that the fact of mobilization reveals a deep structure of national unity occluded by more superficial stratifications, rather he enunciates a call to bury the hatchet and come to a parley in the 'strife' of internal affairs, to 'have one soul, and perish to a man' in defence of national sovereignty. If that sovereignty rests indeed on the rule of the 'British Sword' in Britain, the poem, in its reference to the Civil War, generates uncertainty about who that sword will be used against in a scenario of a national future that contains potentially both a Waterloo and a Peterloo.

'Anticipation', a sonnet which by contrast entered the public domain of Napoleonic Britain (reappearing in 1804 in the *Anti-Gallican*), is a less ambiguous prophecy, though a representatively ambivalent image of war's pleasures and pains. As in 'Fears', the labour of killing is transubstantiated into providential weather:

> Shout, for a mighty Victory is won!
> On British ground the Invaders are laid low;
> The breath of Heaven has drifted them like snow,
> And left them lying in the silent sun,
> Never to rise again! – the work is done.
>
> (ll. 1–5)

The elision of struggle is also achieved by cancelling repressed uncertainties inherent in the soldier's change of status, from civilian to potential killer or corpse: the pageant of recruitment is a rehearsal for the victory parade – 'drums beat and trumpets blow' (l. 7). But Wordsworth has to work harder and harder to maintain both the sublimity and the domesticity of this fiction:

> Divine must be
> That triumph, when the very worst, the pain
> And even the prospect of our brethren slain,
> Hath something in it which the heart enjoys
> (ll. 10–13)

Coleridge's 'soften[ing]' topographical prospect of home displaced scenes of carnage (both defeat and victory), whereas Wordsworth's temporal and conditional prospect dispels fears ('the very worst') and pain itself by proposing pleasure in slaughter. It is not, ultimately, that killing is suppressed in either of these poems, rather that human misery is situated as a means rather than the end of war. But not even on the battlefield, despite Clausewitzian strictures concerning its defining character in war as the place of reciprocal injuring, are physical actions lifted clear of the signifying activities which are always at work to make them something more than, and of course less than, brutal assaults on the flesh of persons.

The national fictions of the state as well as those of what Jay Winter has called private-enterprise propaganda may have been stubborn, but the telescopic play of physical and temporal distance and proximity made them labile too (Winter, 1991, p. 155). Bringing the past closer to shape the future undid boundaries and essences. The rediscovery of the Bayeux tapestry during the preparations of a second Army of England in 1803 (the one that would become the Army of Austerlitz) led to the successful exhibition in Paris of a depiction of English history woven in Kent (Samuel, 1994, p. 32). Napoleon's propaganda stunt drew from the pamphleteer 'Tyrtaeus Junior' the suggestion that the Armada tapestry in the Lords be counter-exhibited (Wheeler and Broadley, 1908, vol. 2, p. 300). What Wordsworth had in mind the men of Kent should exhibit was 'the countenance / Of your fierce war' and 'the glittering lance', and that these, in another figure of telescopic bringing home, should act as an invitation to the French. 'To The Men of Kent' (written 1803 and published in 1807) yokes historical restitution and geographical unification. Contemporaneously, Charles Dibden was attempting to draw all the county militias and local volunteers into a national front against an invasion force (his febrile invention failed him and the inventory is incomplete): 'In *Kent*, they'd soon send them *hopping*, / In *Bedfordshire* send them to sleep' (Wheeler and Broadley, 1908, vol. 2, p. 293). Wordsworth, by contrast, founds unity on images of defeat and regional inequity: if Kent's 'Soil ... doth advance / Her haughty brow against the coast of France' (ll. 2–3), its sons are the ones who will have to bear the brunt of the offensive. Little may it help them that they won a 'gallant wreath' against the Normans:

> No parleying now. In Britain is one breath;
> We are all with you now from shore to shore;–
> Ye men of Kent, 'tis victory or death!
> (ll. 12–14)

That 'one breath' – no longer a providential wind (the 'breath of Heaven' of 'Anticipation') – is the spirit of the body politic, but more mundane senses assert themselves. What is behind the men of Kent is the sharp inhalation of alarm, and talk, like this dedication of others' flesh to destruction. Yet again, the poem surprises because it takes so little care over covering the tracks of its partiality, in this case a myth of nationhood promoted in the face of the unequal chances of which hearths war is brought home to.

The more sophisticated contemporary appraisals of Napoleon's *matériel*, transport and tactics located the danger in Kent and Sussex (the location of extensive works completed by 1806, including a line of Martello towers and the Royal Military Canal which turned Romney Marsh, all too accessible to the Boulogne flotilla, 'into an island detached from the rest of England'), in the Thames estuary, and along the coast of East Anglia, where further towers of an upgraded design were constructed (Richard Glover, 1973, p. 122). The example of Paul Jones's attack on Whitehaven in 1778, together with more recent French landings in Wales and Ireland, kept vivid, however, the threat

to the whole coastline. It is out of such perceptions, rather than the apprecia-
tions of strategists, that the geography of Napoleonic Britain has been created:

> The part of England in which Hardy grew up was haunted by memories
> of Napoleon. The Dorset coast had been the one primarily threatened by
> invasion in 1805; and the menace was a vivid memory to Hardy's
> parents. Traditions of the time, recounted memories of the contempo-
> rary Home Guard, out-house doors still riddled with the bullets aimed at
> them for practice: these things had provoked Hardy's imagination since
> childhood.
>
> (Reed, 1943, p. 137)

It is *The Trumpet Major*, rather than *The Dynasts*, that reimagines most
forcefully the imagination of alarm (and this tells us something about the
triumph of the novel as the prime genre of future-wars). But as Henry Reed's
wartime refraction of the tradition constituted by the memory of those
imaginings suggests, it has taken on a cultural life of its own, reproduced
whenever homologous fears and events impress themselves on consciousness.

'heard from afar / Ancestral voices prophesying war'[8]

Today, official euphemism concerning war's destructiveness is counterbal-
anced by a presentist tendency to insist on the enormity of, and absence of
precedent for, 'our' wars. This involves drawing demographic and statistical
rather than moral distinctions, in a manner which is not so much a consequence of technological and bureaucratic erosions of ethical constraints on
killing as a mode of collusion with them. 'Our' wars are the wars with
reference to which, in its remembrance, contemporary culture negotiates
contradictions and traumas in national life, and selectively reproduces the
legacies of past crises. In consequence, they are also the wars which, to adapt
Zarathustra's bellicose response to the redeeming Christian idea of the good
cause of the just war, are the good wars 'that hallow every cause' (Nietzsche
cited in Glover, 1999, p. 15). Even the Great War, after the cultural work of
literary remembrance, has taken on the paradoxical function of hallowing
peace. The war against Hitler was, early on, interpreted as an episode of
emancipatory modernity (the 'People's War' of mass participation in forging
a new world and the Atlantic Charter which led to the founding of the United
Nations organization). The utopian and strategic dimensions of this symbolization of conflict were intimately linked with the media of mass
communication. Anthony Eden summoned the Local Defence Volunteers
with the aid of the British Broadcasting Corporation on 14 May 1940, four
days after the German attack in the west and while the Luftwaffe bombed
Rotterdam: 'Never before has it been possible for a Secretary of State for War

to enter the homes of millions and invite them to fight the King's Battles' (Graves, 1943, p. 9).

In this context it is easy to overlook the modernity of earlier periods of warfare. As technology has facilitated remote and indiscriminate killing, a technological sublime has helped determine the forms and reference of revulsion from warfare. In a curious way, non-Western conflicts in our century are morally remote in proportion to their apparent distance from the hegemonic conception of modern war as a by-product of a military–industrial complex. War films modernize war's *matériel*, making contemporary footage of Nazi German horse-drawn artillery in Poland seem an anachronistic slippage into Tolstoyan imagery of the retreat from Moscow. Western ways of war are dissociated from the spectres of irrational uncivilised aggression, and even its intellectual rationalization in modern nationalisms, by our fear and admiration of the apparatus of high-tech killing. It is not material interest alone that accounts for the different cultural experiences in the West of campaigns in the Falklands and the Gulf, and of events in Yugoslavia and Rwanda. The cultivation of fear in Napoleonic Britain may have been relatively low tech – both in propagandistic and aesthetic terms – but it represented a significant development in the use of print to try to bring about a war effort that was morally and 'emotionally co-ordinated' (Calder-Marshall, 1941, p. 238).

The evidence of the imagination of alarm in Napoleonic Britain suggests that we might need to rethink some of the paradigms of war and culture which retain a crucial bearing on the maintainance of reflexive ethical discourse about military killing. Notable vehicles of modern war literature's characteristic ironies, in particular the trope of war's theatricality, had already been set in motion a century earlier. The extension to warfare of histrionic figures for social experience has as much to do with kinds of visibility conferred on complex physical and psychological events by the simplifying space of the stage or the frame of the proscenium, as with the ironic charge of likenesses between soldiering and modes of theatrical make-believe such as dressing up, the assumption of roles and scripted agency: 'France, indeed, may be considered as one great theatre, where they perform no other piece, on that marauding and bloody stage, than Gay's Beggar's Opera, as translated by Beaumarchais, and *philosophically* adapted to the genius of France, by Abbé Seyeyes's alterations, and those of Tom Paine' (*Complete History*, 1801, p. xv). In the context of invasion threats, metaphors drawn from the business of staging a fictive action were ready to hand for the mockery of military preparations. Broadsides posed as playbills to deflate a threat which was itself sustained by imaginative labour. The rehearsal for a farce in one act called '*The Invasion of England*' is obviously not the real thing: 'It is probable that it will *not* be played in this COUNTRY, but will certainly never be *acted* in TOWN' (Klingberg and Hustvedt, 1944, p. 94). Theatrical tropes urged the illusory nature of enemy power at the same time that theatrical performance encouraged acting on the as yet unrealized threat, as exemplified by the patriotic prologue and a military interlude, 'All Volunteers', written into the Haymarket Theatre's 1803 *Henry V* (Wheeler and Broadley, 1908, vol. 2, pp. 261–4).

In twentieth-century Britain, as Fussell's landmark reading (1975, pp. 191–230) and scores of writers from 1939 to 1945 demonstrate, troping war as theatre has at once highlighted and assuaged the moral contradictions and disasters of military conflict. By designating war as a vicious game in which persons temporarily assume roles proscribed by reason, killing is made simultaneously less serious, and more serious than any military ethos will allow. That the military's upper echelon, with its own 'theatres of war', has co-opted dramaturgic language adds to the productive but also treacherous semantic fluidity of this field of imagery. War's unreality (civil life cannot prepare you for its strangeness) is brought under fleeting ironic control by lending to its routines the less discomforting unreality of theatre: if life before donning the costume of soldiering is real, 'military life must be a pretense' (Fussell, 1975, p. 191).

But what makes '"theater" and modern war seem so compatible' is not just a need on the part of combatants for mechanisms of 'psychic escape', the participant becoming a spectator, the 'real' self observing the implausible acts of the military 'character' he has been conscripted into (Fussell, 1975, pp. 191–2). War is itself never less than the combination of physical acts and their symbolic meaning, and translations between the somatic and the ideal which permitted Clausewitz to call war 'another kind of writing and language for political thoughts' (Clausewitz, 1986, p. 402). But when the absence of the experience of war 'in a country not invaded since 1745' is connected to the claim that 'the majority of the population experienced war as theatre', we need to take stock. This mode of analysis, even as it brings to light the degree to which war is assimilated to everyday, and even polite, culture, risks reifying both an over- and underestimation of war, respectively as brute facticity occluded by bellicose representations and performance ('manoeuvres and sham fights, the display, colour and music of a parade') and as a species of fiction, 'the successful general was one who could be simultaneously director and interpreter of the "theatre of war", reading the signs of battle and moving his men accordingly' (Russell, 1995, pp. 17, 20).

The integral relationship between war preparations and imagined war in Napoleonic Britain reveals that the cultural dimension of warfare has more complex functions than, alternatively, denying or testifying to the violent means and ends of military policy. Images of war's brutality sponsor violence as well as disturbing the peace with reminders of violence's enormity, sometimes simultaneously. To suggest that war in Napoleonic Britain was just theatrical, and to put this down to the fact that war remained, for the nation at home, a distant and scary threat but no more, begs the question of how war imagined, not experienced, makes possible both bellicose and ethical thinking.

Balzac, whose Paris is a battlefield on which takes place a 'Red Indian kind of war: unforeseen attacks, ambushes, betrayals', compared his artistic project in *La Comédie Humaine* with the conquests of Napoleon (Balzac, 1980, p. 66; Prendergast, 1978, p. 181). It was in this megalomaniac invention that the nineteenth-century French critic Sainte-Beuve located Balzac's artlessness:

> He is a little like generals who force the most minor defences only by prodigiously spilling the blood of his troops (it is merely ink that Balzac spills) and in sacrificing vast numbers of people.
> (C. A. Sainte-Beuve, cited in Balzac, 1998, p. 224)

Spilling ink and spilling blood were yoked together by both policy and necessity in Napoleonic Britain, but not only in metaphorical and metonymic substitutions through which the realities of war were cloaked by palliative landscapes. It is not, in the last analysis, the absence of war experience which can be held to fully determine the dissemination of bellicose fantasies and facile chatter about military violence. In the period under consideration, bringing war home for patriotic purposes, and keeping it distant in the interests of the ideological underpinning of the aggressive state, converged in an imagination of alarm. The cultural products of this projective consciousness, far from resolving the relationship of aggression to fears for the vulnerability of persons, reveal how the representation of war is marked by a fundamental moral ambivalence. This, in turn, has as much to do with the dependence of military strategy and tactics on signs of violence as with the otherness of war experience, or its fortunate absence from the fields of Essex and Kent, from the Quantock Hills, and from the coast of Wessex.

Notes

1. 'It was supposed by some that he looked forward with no feelings of regret to the immense loss of life which must attend on his attempt to effect a landing upon the British shores, as a relief to him, by checking the military spirit which he had excited to such a pitch that he could no longer manage it himself' (Wright and Evans, 1968, p. 229).
2. General Humbert landed with a force of 900 regulars in County Mayo in August 1798.
3. Thus 'the so-called artistic representation of naked bodily pain ... contains ... the potentiality of wringing pleasure from it', Theodor Adorno quoted in Langer (1975), p. 1.
4. W. H. Auden, 1977, p. 28.
5. Elaine Scarry's inspirational work on the verbal alchemy which translates injury in torture and war into power might, without condescension, be considered a long and elegant footnote to these lines.

6. In the CIA's definition, psychological warfare is 'The planned use by a nation of propaganda and activities other than combat which communicate ideas and information intended to influence the opinions, attitudes, emotions and behavior of foreign groups in ways that will support the achievement of national aims' (Saunders, 1999, p. 4).
7. A conspiracy that modern criticism sees everywhere. For instance, Clive Emsley, perhaps with performances of Shakespeare's *Henry V* in London in 1803 in mind, observes that the loyalty of the populace depended on external threat (Emsley, 1979, p. 115).
8. Coleridge, 1957, p. 298.

Bibliography

Auden, W. H. (1977), ed, Mendelson, E., *The English Auden: Poems, Essays and Dramatic Writings 1927–1939*, London: Faber.
Balzac, H. (1980), trans. Hunt, H. J., *The History of the Thirteen*, Harmondsworth: Penguin Books.
Balzac, H. (1998), trans. Raphael, B., *Père Goriot*, New York: Norton.
Barker, P. (1991), *Regeneration*, London: Viking.
————. (1993), *The Eye in the Door*, London: Viking.
————. (1995), *The Ghost Road*, London: Viking.
Benjamin, W. (1973), trans. Zohn, H., *Illuminations*, London: Fontana.
Berlin, I. (1997), ed. Hardy H., *Against the Current: Essays in the History of Ideas*, London: Pimlico.
Bonnard, G. (1940), 'The Invasion of Switzerland and English Public Opinion (January to April 1798): The Background to S. T. Coleridge's *France: An Ode*', *English Studies* (Amsterdam), 22 (1).
Bourke, J. (1999), *An Intimate History of Killing: Face-to-Face Killing in Twentieth Century Warfare*, London: Granta.
Brittain, V. (1940), *England's Hour*, London: Macmillan.
Burney, Capt. J. (1797), *Plan of Defence against Invasion*, London.
Calder-Marshall, A., et al. (1941), 'Why Not War Writers? A Manifesto', *Horizon*, 4 (22), October.
Clark, T. J. (1984), *The Painting of Modern Life: Paris in the Art of Manet and His Followers*, London: Thames and Hudson.
Clarke, I. F. (1992), *Voices Prophesying War: Future Wars 1763–3749*, 2nd edn, Oxford: Oxford University Press.
Clausewitz, C. von (1986), trans. Graham, Col. J. J., ed. Rapoport, A., *On War*, Harmondsworth: Penguin Books.
Coleridge, S. T. (1957), ed. Coleridge, E. H., *The Poetical Works of Samuel Taylor Coleridge*, Oxford: Oxford University Press.
————. (1969), ed. Rooke, B. E., *The Friend*, 2 vols, in *The Collected Works of Samuel Taylor Coleridge*, vol. 4, London: Routledge and Kegan Paul; Princeton: Princeton University Press.

Colley, L. (1992), *Britons: Forging the Nation 1707–1837*, New Haven and London: Yale University Press.

Complete History of the Invasions of England including the memorable Battles and Sea Fights from Julius Caesar, down to the French landing in Wales in 1796 (1801), London.

Conrad, J. (1988), ed. Kimborough, W., *Heart of Darkness*, 3rd edn, New York: Norton.

Creasey, E. S. (1852*), The Invasions and Projected Invasions of England from the Saxon Times*, London: Richard Bentley.

De Quincey, T. (1897), ed. Masson, D., *The Collected Writings of Thomas De Quincey*, 14 vols, London: A. and C. Black.

Dumourier, General (1793), *A Letter from Gen. Dumourier to the French Nation*, London.

————. (1798), *Thoughts on the French Invasion of England*, London.

Emsley, C. (1979), *British Society and the French Wars 1793–1815*, London: Macmillan.

Favret, M. A. (1994), 'Coming Home: The Public Spaces of Romantic War', *Studies in Romanticism*, 33 (4).

Fox, W. (1794), *Thoughts on the Impending Invasion of England*, London.

Fraser, Master J. (1905), ed. Mackay, W., *Chronicles of the Frasers: The Wardlaw Manuscript Entitled 'Polichronicon seu Policratica Temporum,' or, the True Genealogy of the Frasers*, Edinburgh: Constable, for the Scottish Historical Society.

Fussell, P. (1975), *The Great War and Modern Memory*, Oxford: Oxford University Press.

Gillray, J. (1968), *The Works of James Gillray*, New York and London: Benjamin Blom.

Glover, J. (1999), *Humanity: A Moral History of the Twentieth Century*, London: Jonathan Cape.

Glover, R. (1973), *Britain at Bay: Defence against Napoleon 1803–1814*, London: George Allen and Unwin.

Graves, C. (1943), *The Home Guard of Britain*, London: Hutchinson.

Hanger, Col. G. (1970), *Reflections on the Menaced Invasion, And the Means of Protecting the Capital by Preventing the Enemy Landing in any Part Contiguous to it* (including 'Extracts from a Book published by Colonel Hanger, in the Year 1795, intituled, Military Reflections on the Attack and Defence of the City of London'), London: E. and W. Books.

Holland-Rose, J. and A. M. Broadley (1909), *Dumouriez and the Defence of England Against Napoleon*, London: John Lane, Bodley Head.

Hozier, Capt H. M. (1876), *The Invasions of England: A History of the Past, with Lessons for the Future*, 2 vols, London: Macmillan.

Klingberg, F. J. and Hustvedt, S. B. (eds) (1944), *The Warning Drum: The*

British Home Front Faces Napoleon: Broadsides of 1803, Berkeley and Los Angeles: University of California Press.

Langdon-Davies, J. (1940), *The Home Guard Training Manual*, London: John Murray and Pilot Press.

Langer, L. L. (1975), *The Holocaust and the Literary Imagination*, New Haven: Yale University Press.

Liu, A. (1989), *Wordsworth: The Sense of History*, Stanford: Stanford University Press.

Longmate, N. (1991), *Island Fortress: The Defence of Great Britain 1602–1945*, London: Hutchinson.

Moretti, F. (1998), *Atlas of the European Novel 1800–1900*, London: Verso.

Nussbaum, M. (1995), *Poetic Justice: The Literary Imagination and Public Life*, Boston: Beacon Books.

Oman, C. (1967), *Nelson*, London: History Book Club, first published 1947.

Orwell, G. (1970), eds Orwell, S. and Angus, I., *The Collected Essays, Journalism and Letters of George Orwell*, 4 vols, Harmondsworth: Penguin Books.

Piette, A. (1995), *Imagination at War*, London: Macmillan.

Prendergast, C. (1978), *Balzac: Fiction and Melodrama*, London: Arnold.

Rawlinson, M. (1990), 'War Stories', *Essays in Criticism*, 40 (2).

Reed, H. (1943), 'The Making of *The Dynasts*', *Penguin New Writing*, 10, September.

Russell, G. (1995), *The Theatre of War: Performance, Politics and Society 1793–1815*, Oxford: Oxford University Press.

Said, E. (1991), *Orientalism*, Harmondsworth: Penguin Books.

Samuel, R. (1994), *Theatres of Memory: Past and Present in Contemporary Culture*, London: Verso.

Saunders, F. S. (1999), *Who Paid the Piper? The CIA and the Cultural Cold War*, London: Granta.

Scarry, E. (1985), *The Body in Pain: The Making and Unmaking of the World*, New York: Oxford University Press.

Silkin, J. (1979), *The Penguin Book of First World War Poetry*, Harmondsworth: Penguin Books.

Stuart Jones, E. H. (1950), *The Last Invasion of Britain*, Cardiff: University of Wales Press.

Thompson, E. P. (1968), *The Making of the English Working Class*, Harmondsworth: Penguin Books.

Unsworth, B. (1999), *Losing Nelson*, London: Hamish Hamilton.

Vaughan-Thomas, W. and Llewellyn, A. (1969), *The Shell Guide to Wales*, London: Michael Joseph.

Walters, S. (1994), *Last Invasion of Britain: Illustrated Film Script*, Glastonbury: privately published.

Warning to Britons Against French Perfidy and Cruelty (1798), translated by Anthony Aufrére, London.

Wheeler, H. B. and Broadley, A. M. (1908), *Napoleon and the Invasion of England: The Story of the Great Terror*, 2 vols, London: John Lane, Bodley Head.

Whiting, J. (1964), *A Penny for a Song*, London: Heinemann Educational.

Winter, J. (1991), 'Imaginings of War: Some Cultural Supports of the Institution of War' in Hinde, R. A. (ed.), *The Institution of War*, Basingstoke: Macmillan.

Winterson, J. (1988), *The Passion*, Harmondsworth: Penguin Books.

Wordsworth, W. (1981), ed. Hutchinson, T., rev. by de Selincourt, E., *Poetical Works*, Oxford: Oxford University Press.

Wright, T. and Evans, R. H. (1968), *Historical and Descriptive Account of the Caricatures of James Gillray*, New York: Benjamin Blom.

CHAPTER SEVEN

War romances, historical analogies and Coleridge's *Letters on the Spaniards*

Diego Saglia

The impact of the French Revolution and the critical awareness it produced during the Romantic period have long overshadowed the facts of war in the literature produced between 1793 and 1815. Often turning to war as an effect, a function or an extension of revolution, Romantic writers represented both 'events' in interdependent fashions. Perhaps the most evident consequence of this superimposition of the texts of war and revolution is that Romantic figurations of the military displaced the actual scenes of war, representing them through other scenarios, sometimes as polysemous as the military event itself. Romantic war not only happens in a geographical elsewhere (France, Prussia, Russia, Spain or the Mediterranean), but also in a discursive one, as it is narrated through other wars, the French Revolution, legends or myths. As recently argued by Gillian Russell, from 1793 to 1815 the experience of the military was inextricably linked to such cultural practices as drama and the theatre, which aimed to describe war by various lateral manoeuvres whilst striving to avoid censorship. This phenomenon, however, was not merely a prerogative of dramatic discourse as, in many cases, the facts and events of Romantic war were generally displaced and mediated for public consumption by way of institutional, generic and rhetorical strategies which, in the process, adapted and modified them (Russell, 1995; Favret, 1994). The written discourses about Wellington's Iberian campaign, one of the climactic moments of the long anti-French conflict, are indicative of this kind of displacement and suppression of the acts and effects of war, such as the mutilated bodies, the suffering, destruction, the battlefield and military strategy, to represent the conflict by way of other discursive materials. The war that followed Napoleon's invasion of Portugal and Spain and the rebellion of the Spaniards in 1808 was intensively rewritten in Britain during the 1810s and reimagined as a bullfight, the legend of Don Rodrigo and the fall of Spain, a second French Revolution, a chivalric tournament and the Moorish rebellion against Philip II. Likewise, the war was explained in terms of fictional forms such as drama and the romance. Aiming to trace such adaptations and modifications in the version of the Peninsular War offered by Coleridge's *Letters on the Spaniards* (1809–10), this essay is primarily concerned with the fact that the Romantic writing of war often transcends the

actual scenes of warfare, dispersing them into substitutive issues and figurations. Thus although here the ostensible topic is war, nonetheless
representations of this 'event' mediate and transpose it to such an extent that
war ultimately becomes invisible in both the text and the critical reading of it.

Together with Wordsworth's tract on *The Convention of Cintra* (1809),
Coleridge's *Letters on the Spaniards* is a key prose text involved in reorganiz-
ing the Iberian campaign through a variety of narrative modes. The issue of
variety is indeed relevant, for a text with a plural title may seem a mere
collection of scattered materials. Yet, on the one hand, the plurality of the
Letters sets off the polysemy of a Spanish conflict that, like all (Romantic)
wars, was irrepresentable as a single event or a coherent series of events. And,
on the other hand, though written as eight separate letters, these were always
intended as a unity, and as such they need to be re-evaluated. Published in
instalments from 7 December 1809 to 20 January 1810 in the conservative
newspaper the *Courier*, the *Letters on the Spaniards* are formally addressed
to its editor, Daniel Stuart. The fact that his newspaper was heavily subsi-
dized by the government and always ready to accommodate its views did not
worry Coleridge, who was a regular contributor. In the past his attempts to
remain independent from its editorial policy, or to dissociate himself from its
establishmentarian discourse, had placed him in overt contrast with Thomas
George Street, Stuart's co-manager and the main link with the Tory administration. Yet, in the case of the *Letters*, Coleridge's dissension was reduced by
his sympathy with the newspaper's approval of the Iberian campaign, and
because its pages promised to be a good medium for his series of enthusiastic
essays in support of governmental foreign policy and against the onslaught of
the Opposition.[1]

After a brief spell of political consensus in the summer of 1808, most
Whigs and Radicals had turned against the British intervention in Spain, the
hostility reaching a polemical climax with the publication of Jeffrey and
Brougham's article on a document by the Spanish minister Don Pedro Cevallos
in the *Edinburgh Review* for October 1808. With the strategic aim of counter-
balancing such critiques, the *Courier* had accepted to publish Wordsworth's
tract on Cintra, inspired by the unjust terms of the settlement between the
French and British armies in Portugal in August 1808, and an essential
prologue to Coleridge's *Letters*.[2] The latter collection of essays in effect
constitutes an extended reflection on Wordsworth's final paragraphs which
point out the necessity of reviving British hope in the Spaniards and, in his
sixth letter, Coleridge states that his essays as a whole are to be read as an
'appendix' to Wordsworth's Miltonic pamphlet (*LS*, p. 77). Representing the
Iberian war in explicitly related ways, these texts are embedded in a
generational enthusiasm uniting Coleridge, Wordsworth and Stuart in a return
of their erstwhile sympathy for the Americans and the French, only this time
in line with governmental policy. Because of their committed revision of the

Iberian conflict, Coleridge's *Letters* and Wordsworth's *Convention of Cintra* are thus crucial contributions in the public debate on the Peninsular War whilst, in a more private dimension, participating in that shift of ideas which allowed the Lakers 'to realign themselves with their countrymen, their government and "Liberty", and so to close, at last, the schism that had been opened by the outbreak of the war in 1793' (Bainbridge, 1995, p. 97). Clearly laid out in the introductory paragraphs, the intention to counteract oppositional criticism becomes increasingly visible as the *Letters* progress, and by letter 7 Coleridge has his ideological targets firmly in focus:

> The opponents of the Spanish cause may be reduced to three classes. The first, those who, contemplating the tremendous power of the enemy, consider all attempts to resist it as vain ... The second class comprehends those, who (perhaps in addition to the despondency of the former) ask, *what* the Spaniards are fighting for? The third is composed of such [who] ... have thrown up the cause in consequence of the errors, defects, and vices, which they attribute promiscuously to the people of Spain and to their Government.
>
> (*LS*, p. 83)

The eight letters are organized according to a crescendo of rhetorical intensity and through an alternance of particularized analyses and digressions, historical reconstructions and generalizations, which recall the subdivisions and demarcations of the *Friend* (1809–10). The first and second letters are introductory essays which connect the series to Coleridge's periodical and programmatically announce the need for an examination of the past in order to create hopes for the future and thus vindicate the Spaniards' heroism. The section including letters 3 to 5 reconstructs and examines the insurrection of the Belgian provinces against the Spanish empire during the reign of Philip II. Finally, letters 6 to 8 re-elaborate and theorize the material set out by the historical reconstruction in order to counter the detractors of Spain and celebrate the immortal patriotic spirit which has fuelled the Spanish rebellion against France. At a structural level the *Letters on the Spaniards* shroud the events of the Iberian campaign by an array of intervening theoretical issues and facts, indicative of other types of displacement of the military towards substitutive genres and themes. Specifically through their structured rewriting of the Iberian conflict, the *Letters* offer an insight into representations of war by such strategies as historical analogy, present in the excursus into early-modern history, and the categories of the romance, intimated by the narrative of crisis and resolution. A familiar aspect of Coleridge's writings on the military, these strategies participate in a 'rhetorization' of the French wars which, as shown by Jerome Christensen, Coleridge also developed in articles about the Peace of Amiens and the question of Malta composed for the *Friend* at the same time as his essays on the Spanish war (Christensen, 1979). Reformulated by means of displacing practices, the military narrative of the *Letters* dissolves into discourses of patriotism and the national character, as well as into theorizations of politics and history. Further, the essays in the *Courier* bear out Coleridge's extended elaborations on the ethics of war which he carried out during the conclusive period of the Napoleonic conflict from 1803 to 1815. Largely influenced by Kant's philosophical reflections on international law, Coleridge's theorization of the principles of warfare ultimately dispersed the military into such issues as the ethical bases of war, the idea of a 'just' conflict, the moral differences between truce and treaty, international dialectics and national destiny as *telos* (De Paolo, 1985, p. 10). In the context of these philosophical, generic and historiographic formulations, what Marilyn Butler has named a 'commitment to story' in Romantic narratives of the French Revolution, is the decisive factor in Coleridge's rewriting of the Iberian conflict away from the actualities of war by a series of extra-military issues and images (Butler, 1989, p. 347).

The introductory remarks in the *Letters* frame the text as a vindication of the Spaniards from accusations of cowardice and ineffectiveness, setting out to narrate Spain as a nation which has 'performed and endured more than all other European nations put together' (*LS*, p. 45). And the first letter emphatically lays out the converging aims and mechanisms of Coleridge's reflections by way of both typographical and rhetorical amplification:

> I offer for insertion in your widely circulated paper, the following facts and observations – ON THE GROUNDS OF HOPE AND FEAR, WHICH THE HISTORY OF PAST AGES SUGGESTS TO US, RE-SPECTING THE WAR OF A PEOPLE AGAINST ARMIES – of an injured and insulted People struggling for Religion, national independence, and self-originating Improvements, against the numerous hosts and celebrated Commanders of a remorseless Invader, Usurper, and Tyrant.
>
> (*LS*, p. 39)

As this outline suggests, the war is approached through the materials offered by history, and thus constructed by the accumulation of historical, social and political facts, held together by an organizing principle. In particular, the *Letters on the Spaniards* retell and interpret the Peninsular War in terms of the chivalric and fantastic adventures of a romance. The programmatic statement quoted above effectively encodes the struggle of the Spanish people in terms of a heroic quest to regain their lost Grail – national independence, religion and self-determination – by overcoming the ordeals and travails presented by the French invasion. Further, the idea of retribution, central in the romance, accords well with the primacy which Coleridge more generally attributes to the ethical dimension of war. Intended in the Kantian sense of a humanistic imperative driving national and international affairs, this ethical apparatus guarantees the possibility of a 'just' war and, as in a romance,

ensures that righteous victory is achieved by the historical agent which re-
spects this moral statute (De Paolo, 1985, p. 4).[3] In addition, the use of the
romance as a scheme of reference to represent the Iberian war was a recurrent
pattern in the early stages of the conflict and, in the opening article of the first
issue of the *Quarterly Review* (1809), George Ellis and George Canning
introduced their overview of the Spanish *affaires* by observing that the unfolding of the war in Spain resembled the narrative progression of a romance:

> In surveying the transactions recorded or referred to in these papers, we
> are almost tempted to doubt whether we are reading the events of real
> history ... [The situation] presents a spectacle, certainly, not less im-
> probable than the wildest fictions of romance.
>
> (Ellis and Canning, 1809, p. 1)

As enthusiastic as the other *Quarterly* reviewers about the Iberian campaign,
Walter Scott meticulously followed the evolution of events in the Peninsula
and kept a record on a map of the battles fought by the British army. Yet, in
order to place these events in a cultural frame, he also removed them to a
fictional dimension and, in a letter to Thomas Scott of 20 June 1808, significantly remarked that 'to have all the places mentioned in Don Quixote and
Gil Blas now the scenes of real and important events ... sounds like history in
the land of romance' (Coleridge, 1932–37, vol. 2, p. 76). Cervantes's novel
here stands for the quintessential chivalric romance, as well as the novel that
marked the end of the genre itself, whereas Alain René de Lesage's *Gil Blas
de Santillane* (1715–35), a primary text in the shaping of eighteenth-century
perceptions of Spain, exemplifies picaresque adventures and an itinerant plot
with their intimate relation to the romance structure. On 14–15 July 1808
another national bard, Thomas Campbell, wrote to his friend Mayow in
resounding Whig terms of his hope to 'hear, in the language of Cervantes, all
the great principles of British liberty laid down in the future writings of
Spain', thus interweaving Cervantes's (anti)chivalric tale with the need of
narrating the military events in the Peninsula and the topos of Britain as the
birthplace of freedom (Beattie, 1849, vol. 2, p. 149). The romantic aura of the
Spanish war was then evoked in Sheridan's speech in the Commons on 15
June 1808, in which the politician and playwright urged the government to
offer British help to the Spanish insurgents and for 'the salvation of Europe'
while, at the same time, disclaiming any intention of 'prompting his majesty's government to engage in any rash romantic enterprise' (*Cobbett's
Parliamentary Debates*, 1808, p. 888).

Developing the image of the Iberian war as fictional, the *Letters on the
Spaniards* narrate it in such a way that the separate strands of international
politics, national unanimity, party political dissensions and moral imperatives
may cohere into one tale. Yet, as we have seen above, rather than collecting
all the instances of romantic exploits performed so far during the Spanish
War, the *Letters* turn the war itself into a narrative with some of the generic

requisites of a romance, such as the questing hero-nation, the obstacles to be overcome, the circular tale of retribution and the sharp contrast between good and evil, to counteract the opinions of those who saw in the Spanish War simply 'a few insulated facts' (*LS*, p. 48). The romance structure of the *Letters* is visible in their wish-fulfilment function, transfiguring the war into a resolutive plot and amplifying the prophecy of a final triumph. The romance as the narrative of a return to a lost original state is also firmly in place from the opening paragraphs, where Coleridge insists on the evidence that the Iberian war returned some essential moral quality to the English nation for, in his words, the example of Spanish patriotism 'first restored us, without distinction of party, to our characteristic enthusiasm for *liberty*', and also 'restored us to our natural good sense, and rescued us from the extravagances, into which the extremes of system and the re-action of contraries had hurried us' (*LS*, p. 38). Thus firmly embedded in a return of national values and their reinstatement in the communal identity, Coleridge's reading of the Spanish war is modelled as a 'metaphysical' romance which sees the national spirit rescued from the unnatural schematisms of 'system', here connoting the non-British extremes of French rationalism and *philosophism*, and from the chaotic misrule of clashing 'contraries'. Besides this transcendental, symbolical form of romance, Coleridge's *Letters* also develop their heroic narrative of the war on the grounds of 'exactness in historical research' because 'the history of the past is the birth-right of every present generation, and to falsify its records either positively by interpolation or virtually by omission, is a species of public robbery' (*LS*, p. 40). In the text, nonetheless, the transcendental tale of redemption and the historical reconstruction coalesce for, by incorporating details and facts, Coleridge's narrative explains the metaphysical workings of history through solid, scholarly evidence as opposed to any mechanistic interpretation of progress. In its commitment to recount the Peninsular War as an intelligible tale, this combination of quest narrative and factual reliability is presented in the following terms:

> Having thus put myself in possession of all the direct information which could be obtained by a private individual, the sole remaining light was that of analogy furnished by similar events in past ages. My general remembrances determined me to seek this light in the history of the insurrection of the Belgic provinces against Philip the Second.
>
> (*LS*, p. 49)

On the basis of these 'general resemblances' or, as seen above, what 'the history of past ages suggests to us', the *Letters* represent and comment on the war by a parallel between past and present where the romance structure combines with the analogic focus on the Spanish events. And as with the romance, the analogic structure of the *Letters* has its precedents in Romantic war literature. It was, indeed, a distinctive trait of dramatic productions during the anti-French conflict by which playwrights could circumvent censorship, composing analogical plays with indirect but not too esoteric references to the political and military events of the day. Perhaps the readiest example of this analogical drama is Sheridan's *Pizarro* (1799), a successful adaptation from Kotzebue in which the Spanish conquest of Peru might easily be interpreted as French military expansionism, constantly menacing the English coasts, and the Peruvian Indians as beleaguered Britain (Russell, 1995, pp. 54–9). In this respect, the analogical structures of fictional texts are in line with the attempt, frequent in Romantic historiography, to reconstruct and explain historical development by way of similarities and parallels between events whose differences are thus used positively to create scenarios of continuity. Indeed, as Lionel Gossmann has observed, 'by revealing the continuity between remotest origins and the present, between the other and the self, [the Romantic historian] could ground the social and political order and demonstrate that the antagonisms and ruptures … that seemed to threaten its legitimacy and stability were not absolute or beyond all mediation' (1990, p. 258; see also White, 1973, pp. 45–80). Similar analogical interpretations of history were employed in the later part of the French wars to explain the magnitude of a conflict, the end of which was nowhere in sight, as well as to envisage a possible solution. During the 1810s three poets from Coleridge's generation were composing texts on the Peninsular War, encoding their interpretations by analogic means as they described the French invasion of Spain in 1808 through the Islamic invasion in the eighth century AD. The historical parallel is the structural foundation in Walter Scott's *The Vision of Don Roderick* (1811), Walter Savage Landor's *Count Julian* (1812) and Southey's *Roderick, the Last of the Goths* (1814), which variously renarrate stories of the Arabic conquest of Spain and the adventures of the last Gothic king, Don Rodrigo, developing distinct commentaries on the Iberian campaign. Writing to James Montgomery about *Roderick*, Southey recognized that his choice of the legendary Spanish material owed much to the historical similarities with the present conflict: '[The Roderick tale] had long appeared to me a fine subject, and the deep interest which I take in Spanish affairs induced me at this time to select it because the circumstances sufficiently resemble those of the present contest to call forth the same feelings' (Southey, 1965, vol. 2, pp. 14–15). The suggestiveness of this analogy was such that Wordsworth also started a poem on the figure of Pelayo, the first Spanish king and Roderick's successor, at the same time as he was composing his pamphlet on the Convention of Cintra. Although only a short fragment remains, Wordsworth's 'Pelayo' shows that analogical interpretation rests on an organic reading of history and on the similarity of all manifestations of one national spirit through successive historical dimensions. With a quick change of perspectives, this epic fragment shifts from the eighth century AD to 1808, so that Pelayo's invocation to his people gives way to an indignant question reiterating the continuity between past and present: 'Thus spake Pelayo on his chosen hill. / And shall at this late [hour] the Heavens belie / The heroic prophecy / And put to shame the great Diviner's skill?' (Wordsworth, 1947–54, vol. 3, p. 416). The bard's voice and period replace Pelayo's, so that just as the early Spaniards' fight against the Moors led to final success, so will the present war with France. Enacting a similar leap in time, the *Convention of Cintra* proceeds by parallels in order to demonstrate that the Spaniards are supported in their struggle by symbols of continuity with the past. Here, as in the 'Pelayo' fragment, Wordsworth materializes and objectifies the invisible links between a people and its forefathers: 'There is a spiritual community binding together the living and the dead; the good, the brave, and the wise, of all ages. We would not be rejected from this community; and therefore do we hope' (1974, vol. 1, p. 339).

Beating the governmental drum in favour of the Iberian campaign, Coleridge himself employed the analogy between the French and Islamic invasions in an article for the *Courier* on 17 September 1811, where he observes that the '[The Spaniards] will succeed in driving the French from the soil, as they formerly did the Moors' (1978, vol. 2, p. 296). The narrative of the *Letters on the Spaniards* was also explicitly conceived in terms of this rhetorical formulation of history, and in a letter of 1809 to Daniel Stuart, Coleridge defined his essays as an 'interesting parallelism' which could throw light on the war and the political debate around it.[4] In particular, the parallelism of the *Letters* takes as its analogue the era of Philip II, an emblematic period which Coleridge also employed in his play *Remorse* (Drury Lane, 1813), a revised version of *Osorio* (1797) interpreted by several reviewers as a commentary on the Peninsular War. Set in sixteenth-century Spain at the time of the Moorish persecutions, *Remorse* was read as a dramatization of the Peninsular conflict, the Moors being the subjected Spaniards of the nineteenth century, and the Spaniards from the reign of Philip II corresponding to the Napoleonic armies. Coleridge's play laid bare this parallelism as openly as his *Letters on the Spaniards* and contemporary commentators, always ready to detect the political subtexts of dramatic productions, pointed out the topicality of *Remorse*, some even accusing Coleridge of taking advantage of the fashion for things Spanish to advertise his play.[5]

Developing the same historical analogue, Coleridge's *Letters* read the war back into the sixteenth-century conflict between Philip II's imperial forces and the Belgian and Dutch provinces, the reader being constantly alerted to the parallels linking the two historical planes. As Coleridge tells the editor of the *Courier*, readers are expected to order the materials of his narrative in analogical sequences: 'I trust to the recollection of your readers to fill up an imaginary column opposite to it [the sixteenth-century insurrection] with the corresponding facts of the present contest' (*LS*, p. 49). The third letter then further clarifies the grounding principles of the text's historical prophecy by explaining the mystic historical energy at work in the nation: 'The power, which raised up, established, and enriched the Dutch Republic, the same mighty power is no less at work in the present struggle of the Spanish Nation' (*LS*, p. 52). Sixteenth-century Spaniards correspond to Napoleon's *grande armée* and the French emperor himself to the notorious Spanish commander, the Duke of Alva; present-day Spaniards, by contrast, are likened to sixteenth-century Belgian or Dutch freedom-fighters. Through these shifts Coleridge's text rests on a chiasmus schematically represented in the following way:

C 16 Spain ——— 'Belgian provinces'

France ——— C19 Spain

The cross-referencing of the two conflicts is sparked off by the similarity between Philip II's and Bonaparte's empires in Europe, their extension and seemingly unshakeable solidity: 'Immense ... as the disproportion of power between Bonaparte and the Spanish nation must be allowed to be, in as great a degree was Philip the Second an over-match for the Dutch' (*LS*, p. 52). Likewise, the Spanish infiltration into the cultural and institutional structures of the Belgian provinces is compared to the subtle diplomatic stratagems with which Napoleon infiltrated his armies into the Peninsula from 1807 onwards. Depicting Philip II's military and institutional penetration into the Netherlands, Coleridge writes: 'In contempt of treaties, in contempt of a solemn oath, Philip introduced the Inquisition into the Netherlands, and placed garrisons of Spanish soldiers in the chief fortified towns' (*LS*, p. 54). Defeatism with regard to the outcome of the war is condemned by the *Letters* in both levels of the historical analogy: 'Then, as now, infamous sophists were found, who, both in conversation and from the press, declaimed on the advantages of submission, and the vanity of resistance' (*LS*, p. 54). Yet, the two planes of the historical parallel are drawn even closer together when the nineteenth-century war is prefigured, almost uncannily prophesied, by specific events from the sixteenth-century conflict. Napoleon is presented as a reincarnation of Philip II's ruthless commander, the Duke of Alva, because the latter's character showed 'a soreness of vanity, a pettiness of resentment, and a vulgarity of moral being ... strongly recalling the same traits of our contemporary, the Corsican' (*LS*, p. 58). Previously, Napoleon's military methods had been compared and assimilated to Alva's in not very flattering terms where Coleridge observes that 'Bonaparte and his agents faithfully repeat the lessons and exercises of their predecessors in the school of darkness' (*LS*, p. 56). The battle of Bailén in Andalusia (19 July 1808), the first capitulation of a Napoleonic army, is then compared to a victory gained by the Confederate army against Alva in 1568, Coleridge pointing out how this was 'an outset of the contest, which will remind the reader of the commencement of the Spanish struggle by the victory of Castanos over Dupont' (*LS*, p. 55). The resistance of the fortified towns of the Low Countries in the sixteenth century also demonstrates how a united people can successfully resist a well-trained army, because 'it is in the surprisal of towns and the maintenance of strong positions chiefly, that a *People* forced to arms can carry on a war successfully against regular troops' (*LS*, p. 59). Expanding this observation, the siege of Harlem of 1573 is analogically connected with the ancient sieges of Numantia and Saguntum and those of Gerona and Zaragoza during the Peninsular War (*LS*, pp. 61–2). Finally, 'the meeting of the states at Dordrecht', the first Dutch Parliament in 1572, is likened to the convocation of the reformed Spanish *Cortes* in May 1809 (*LS*, p. 65). And with the news of the *Cortes* being summoned Coleridge interrupts his parallels, having now presented enough data for the reader to judge favourably of the future developments of the war in the Iberian Peninsula. The analogical shifts thus completed, he confidently concludes: 'Whatever may result from the Spanish Cortes, its convocation will be welcomed with delight by every reflecting mind: for whatever this assembly may do or may not do, it will at all events furnish the best data for rational judgment concerning the fate of Spain and the event of the present struggle' (*LS*, p. 68). The 'auspicious' news in the fifth letter marks the climax of the analogical structure which closes on a vision of the Dutch and Belgian sixteenth-century triumph over the Spaniards, announcing that 'the spirit of freedom and national independence triumphed over all' (*LS*, p. 69).

The inset tale and its chiastic design contain a narrative of national resurgence which, with its successful conclusion, brings the romance quest to its solution and the hero/people to the achievement of its goal. In the fifth letter such a culmination is announced by the founding of 'the rich and powerful Republic of the United States [The Netherlands], the nurse of religious toleration, and the parent of commercial importance, to the blessing of all Europe!' (*LS*, p. 71). Yet, however pervasive, the parallel is not used indiscriminately in Coleridge's narrative. Wary of the hermeneutic problems lurking behind analogy as an instrument for historical explanation, he opens the first letter with a caveat about the use of parallels, recognizing that an analogy he had previously drawn in the *Friend* between Charlemagne's and Bonaparte's imperialism was based on 'the *factitious* resemblance of the latter to the former' (*LS*, p. 37). The italicized adjective is precisely meant to draw the reader's critical attention to itself and its complexity lies partly in the fact that, rather than merely pointing to the artificial nature of historical analogies, 'factitious' here also unveils the didactic importance of parallelism as a 'not less instructive than interesting historical document' (*LS*, p. 37). Endowed with an explicitly didactic value, the analogical trope produces reliable and truthful explanations to demonstrate and celebrate that 'a *People* forced to arms can carry on a war successfully against regular troops' (*LS*, p. 59).

Further, the educational importance of historical parallels becomes especially meaningful within the salvational value of the narratives of history for, in Coleridge's text, 'the historic muse appears in her loftiest character as the nurse of HOPE' (*LS*, p. 53).

Yet, despite the positive meanings in Coleridge's use of 'factitious', the constructedness of such explanations and inferences about the war leads Coleridge's discourse into a series of contradictions, the most obvious being that its past analogue is a period when the Spaniards ruthlessly and repeatedly quenched the Belgian rebellion. Indeed, although the similarity between Napoleon's and Philip II's power is based on the parallels between the respective supra-national empires, the *Letters* often relate Philip II's armies, politics and warfare with Spain. Thus, the text refers to 'a splendid naval victory gained by the English over the Spanish fleet' (*LS*, p. 41) and 'the Spanish soldiers' (*LS*, p. 56), while 'the Spanish oppressions' in the Low Countries were 'the object of general detestation' (*LS*, p. 59) and 'a proof and signal that God had abandoned the Spaniards' (*LS*, p. 61). This insistence on the Spanishness of Philip II's army places the *Letters*' discourse on a dubious balance because of the divided and contradictory national identities conferred upon the Spaniards in the two levels of the analogy.

Through the historical parallel Coleridge's essays extract a series of events from their immediate context and put them in relation with another set of such events. In this fashion, however, they incur the same ambiguity which Coleridge had already detected and criticized in the historical analogies employed by Foxite rhetorics. In an article for the *Morning Post* of 16 April 1800, Coleridge had attacked Charles James Fox's definition of the war with France as a 'crusade' that wanted hyperbolically to culminate with the conquest of the enemy country, an idea which the Whig leader had presented in his *Letter ... to the Electors of Westminster* (1793) and then frequently utilized by the Foxite Whigs in their anti-war interventions.[6] In his article, Coleridge accused the 'friends of liberty' of paying undue compliments to the war, and opposed their charges of imperialism and expansionism against the government's foreign policy, pointing to de-historicization as the main fallacy in their political discourse. Characteristically, he found fault with Fox's use of the term 'crusade', correcting his semantic and factual mistake by illustrating what crusades actually were. Fox and his followers thus stood accused of de-historicizing past events by taking them out of context to submit them to the ideological mandates of their own political discourse. Coleridge insisted that the war with France could not be called a 'crusade' with the meaning of a senseless war of aggrandizement. Crusades were chivalric, just wars inspired by a national consensus and inhabiting the lofty regions of the imagination rather than those of the mundane, petty advantages given by territorial conquest. In his words, a crusade 'is, perhaps, the only war in history in which defence by anticipation was no trick of Statesmen, but the demand of nations, the impulse of a general inspiration' (1978, vol. 1, p. 241). This assertion is particularly revealing as it clarifies how Coleridge deprives the Whigs of one of their rhetorical constructs to appropriate it as part of his own vision of the anti-French war as a holy, national, inspired crusade. In point of fact, Coleridge increasingly interpreted the war against Napoleon in such visionary terms, in particular after the end of the Peace of Amiens in 1803, the historical crisis from which the *Letters* take their ideological bearings, making 'the Nation unanimous in its dread of French *ambition*' (*LS*, p. 38), and the epiphanic moment when 'the war first became just and necessary' (*LS*, p. 73). The ambiguity of Coleridge's treatment of historical analogies comes into focus with his rejection of the Foxite image to replace it with a more 'historical' idea of crusade which both neutralizes Whig political rhetorics and sets itself up as a more reliable, and above all prophetic, definition of the war.

The analogical structure of the *Letters on the Spaniards* presents a similar kind of historical manipulation. Although Coleridge's reconstruction is presented as accurate, his use of the historical parallel, the analogy and supra-historical similarities function like Fox's definition of a crusade, as appears from the series of substitutions and adjustments in the article for the *Morning Post*. In the *Letters* this becomes ever more evident once Coleridge's de-historicization is considered alongside the theory of national characters as trans-historical and permanent, a theory which grounds much of the validity of his own views and predictions. Letter 8 indeed states that the national spirit interfuses and holds together all the manifestations of a nation, and that this is 'an undeniable truth, without the admission of which all history would be a riddle' (*LS*, p. 94). Consistently presenting the Spaniards as conservative, religious and loyal, the *Letters* characterize them as a people and a nation, as opposed to an army of soldiers trained to fight mechanically and not responsive to the 'patriotic imagination'. This view is emphatically spelled out in the third letter, where the nationalist energy which moves the Iberian nation is inscribed in the activity of the divine power of the state: 'A power as mighty in the rational creation, as the element of electricity in the material world … now contracted to an individual soul, and now, as in a moment, dilating itself over a whole Nation!' (*LS*, p. 52).[7] Typical of Coleridge's conjunction of natural philosophy, metaphysics and political thought, these lines anticipate the interpretation of state structure which he presented to Lord Liverpool in a letter of 28 July 1817, in which the Prime Minister was urged to take action against the dissolution of the national fabric. In Coleridge's letter the mechanisms of the state are illustrated by a comparison with atoms, galvanic phenomena and the invisible powers of electricity which had already been assimilated to a metaphysics of organicism by Friedrich Schelling in *Ideen zu einer Philosophic der Natur* (1800). Transposing organicist theories from natural philosophy to political reflection, historical evolution is explained by Coleridge through the differences between nations, whose 'spirits' are diverse by necessity, just as the natural world is powered by the reactions of different particles (1956–71, vol. 4, pp. 758–63).[8] Coleridge's letter to Liverpool thus develops the analogy between such human manifestations as character, manners, feeling, religious and political tendencies to 'the pre-dominant system of speculative Philosophy', a crucial analogy which for him cannot be understood 'unless we admit not only a reaction and interdepend-ence on both sides, but a powerful, tho' most often indirect influence of the latter on all the former' (p. 759). Yet another instance of Coleridge's didactic use of the analogical exemplum, this political-natural analogy is not so much grounded on similarity as on outright influence between the two domains. The state is then defined, in actual and not just metaphorical terms, as a 'Flux of Individuals' akin to the flux of atoms which constitutes reality. On the grounds of these reflections the state is seen to surpass and incorporate the subject, and Coleridge exhorts the Prime Minister to develop a new political approach modelled on these truths: 'It is high time, my Lord! that the sub-jects of Xtian Governments should be taught that neither historically nor morally, neither in right nor in fact, have men made the state but that the state & that alone makes them men' (p. 762). The state as a composite of atom-individuals and the national spirit as an electric charge are the analogi-cal materials with which Coleridge develops his political and historical discourses and redraws the boundaries between individual and body politic and the possibility of individual agency. At the same time, however, such analogies both construct and evacuate their referents with the result that, since history in the *Letters* progresses through the clash of such metaphysical differences, once again the acts of war disappear by being removed within a recurrent game of national characters and spirits clashing against each other in their fight for supremacy.[9]

Grounded on a rigid distribution of the categories of selfhood and otherness, the *Letters* elaborate definitions of the Spanish nation through familiar binarisms such as organicist–mechanistic, patriotic–non-patriotic or national-ist–cosmopolitan. Supporting and extending the layout of moral roles in the text, these opposites hark back to Coleridge's philosophical reflections on the 'just war' waged for national defence and inscribed in the providential des-tiny of a national community (De Paolo, 1985, pp. 4–5). Likewise, they firmly embed the *Letters* within the discourse that Coleridge had been devel-oping in the *Friend* about the moral basis of the state and the nature of the subject's duties towards it. As part of an overarching reflection on the meta-physics and ethics of war, these two issues are resolved by way of an anti-mechanistic and metaphysical view of the state as 'a mystical, or "di-vine", whole that lay behind, but at the same time constituted, the ultimate moral reality of the individuals who from time to time composed it' (Morrow, 1990, p. 81). The interrelation between state and the individual becomes evident beyond any need for further explanation. Thus, by finding patriotism on the side of the Spaniards, Coleridge's *Letters* justify and explain the war in terms of both a nationalist identity and an ethical dimension issuing forth from the very ethnic and historical continuum that is Spain. The final section in this narrative about the loss and reconquest of freedom confirms the persistence of nationalism as a spiritual attribute distinguishing peoples from multinational, overriding empires:

> there is an invisible Spirit that breathes through a whole people, and is participated by all, though not by all alike; a spirit, which gives a colour and character to both their virtues and vices, so that the same actions, such I mean as are expressed by the same words, are yet not the same in a Spaniard as they would be in a Frenchman, I hold for an undeniable truth, without the admission of which all history would be a riddle.
>
> (*LS*, p. 94)

The *Letters* depict an episode of this eternal history of the spirit, a tale of independence and the patriotic imagination. Their quasi-romance narrative of the Belgian provinces and Spanish imperialism moves from a progressive and purposive definition of history, while the structure of containment of the romance rearranges the contradictory elements of historical multiplicity into a consequential, readable tale (Ross, 1991; Jameson, 1975).

Despite these adjustments, however, the fact persists that the inset romance in the *Letters*, with its chiastic structure, paradoxically reverses the roles of the historical actors. It is difficult to overlook that Coleridge's analogical displacement stigmatizes the Spaniards as 'Inhuman invaders' and, as in *Remorse*, ransacks the repertory of the 'Black Legend' of Spanish cruelty to emphasize this nation's otherness (Maltby, 1971). The problem here is not simply one of confusion for the reader who has to imagine the Spaniards in two completely opposite roles. More importantly, this double characterization of the Spaniards subverts Coleridge's interpretation of national destiny as the uniform development of a single *Volksgeist*. This organizing principle is put forward in the *Letters* with the plainness of an act of faith: 'I hold ... that the difference of nations, their relative grandeur and meanness, all, in short, which they are or do ... [and] all in which they persevere, as a nation, through successions of changing individuals are the result of this spirit' (*LS*, p. 94). And even if Coleridge carefully points out that national spirits are present both in the virtues and vices of a people (*LS*, p. 94) he does not foresee any redistribution of the attributes of a nation along the centuries. This ideal continuity of the spirit is proved by a reference to the '*Roman character* of the Romans themselves' (*LS*, p. 97) which was the driving force of their ancient republic, but even more aptly, by recalling the endurance of the national values of the Spaniards. Despite despotic rulers, the 'worst laws', 'a blind and domineering Priesthood' and the Inquisition (*LS*, p. 97), the spirit of the Spaniards resisted and even transmuted some of these evils into virtues. Although these permutations are in keeping with the principles of organic progression, they nonetheless clash with the idea of the coherence of a continuous national character. In other words, Coleridge's scenario envisages the possibility of gradual change, but what is proper to nations, 'what they are or do', is located in spiritual immutability. This emphasis on national absolutes is repeatedly evoked in the *Letters* as Coleridge explains their aims in terms of those of the *Friend*, 'to refer the opinions of men to their proper principles, and the passions of men to their proper objects' (*LS*, p. 78). Immutable values such as 'high enthusiasm' (*LS*, p. 81) and 'faith' (*LS*, p. 82) are the axioms which may counteract the 'infectious feeling of insecurity, and the soul-sickening sense of unsteadiness' (*LS*, p. 84) affecting society in these times of war. By thus deploying immutability and changeableness, the text exposes a visible contradiction in the concept of the Spanish national spirit. Since coherence, stability and continuity are watchwords in Coleridge's discourse, present-day Spain is not the patriotic nation *par excellence* and the analogical chiasmus depicts its national ethos not so much as immutable but rather oscillating between ruthless, military imperialism and patriotic valour.

Nonetheless, despite the pressure of the analogical drive, Coleridge's rewriting of the war cannot be exhausted in terms of another example of an overriding 'organicist fallacy'. Intended as a public discourse that has to deliver closure and coherence, Coleridge's essays finally transcend the contradictions haunting their writing of history. Indeed, the effectiveness of the *Letters* as discourse on the Peninsular conflict lies in the final adjustment of their manipulations by way of a further element in their narrative structure, for, both in the sixteenth- and the nineteenth-century scenarios a third historical agent intervenes: England or, in the case of the Peninsular War, Britain. Excluded from the convoluted designs of the chiasmus, England is narrated as a fixed historical force always true to itself. Just as it is the ally of Spain and Portugal in 1808, it supported the Dutch cause in the sixteenth century, a fact that Coleridge stresses in the narrative of the capture of the Spanish *flota* in November 1573 by, as he calls them with a significant superimposition, 'the Britons or English' (*LS*, p. 64).[10] Unlike France or Spain, Britain's historical role does not need any analogical transference to be represented. Its fixed destiny seems to be that of the generous helper of subjected nations and the enemy of Continental empires and their absolutistic claims. Coleridge makes this an incontrovertible fact by asserting that 'then, as in the present day, *England* was held up to the abhorrence of the Continent, as the chief obstacle to the accomplishment of these mighty blessings' (*LS*, pp. 54–5).

The imbalances in the chiastic structure of Coleridge's romance of the Peninsular War are therefore resolved by the omnipresence of England/Britain. As an unchangeable historical actor, the writer's and reader's nation unifies the split historical panorama raised by the romance narrative, and thus confirms the crucial principle that the qualities of a people are embodied in its spirit and reappear 'through successions of changing individuals'. That Coleridge should identify this in English rather than in Spanish history shows how the ideological target of the *Letters* ultimately veers towards a definition of England/Britain as a nation and its function in the Peninsular War. Not just a prerogative of Coleridge's text, this was a constant preoccupation in the debate on the Iberian conflict, both in prose-writings such as pamphlets and articles, and in poems such as Scott's *The Vision of Don Roderick* which culminates in a paean to Wellington's army, or Southey's *Roderick, the Last of the Goths* which addresses the issues of the 'condition of Britain' in its extensive notes. The majority of Romantic attempts at defining Spain during Wellington's campaign tend to explain the role and presence of Britain on the Iberian scene, so that the war was often discussed not so much as a Spanish affair but as a primary concern for British national subsistence. Coleridge's eighth letter aptly concludes the series of essays by bringing the narrative firmly home to Britain:

> In the ultimate grounds of judgment, the Spanish cause is indeed *identi-fied* with that of Great Britain, as might have been conjectured from the known fact, that the same persons, who think a speedy *submission* to Bonaparte the best proof of wisdom, which the Spaniards could give, attempt at the same time, by every species of sophistry and misstatement, to bribe or scare Great Britain into a nominal *Peace* with the Tyrant, which is but another word for submission.
>
> (*LS*, p. 90)

What the presence of England or Britain emphasizes is that the Iberian conflict is reimagined as a romance in the name of a continuity found not in Spain, but in the author's and the reader's nation. If Coleridge's audience can have faith in the Spaniards' fight against Napoleon, this is especially because of Britain's intervention, now as in the sixteenth century. The *Letters* are then scattered with references to myths of Englishness and 'genuine English principles' (*LS*, p. 38) such as 'natural good sense' and enthusiasm (*LS*, p. 38), and the naval icon of "'the *wooden walls* of Old England"' (*LS*, p. 42). Within the mythical subtext of the romance of war, national characters are personified as historical actors fighting each other out in a conflict whose final result is a 'revolution', in the restricted sense of the word, as outlined by Jeffrey and Brougham in their article on Don Cevallos which announced that 'the Spanish revolution places the cause of freedom and reform on a much better footing than it had even at the beginning of the French revolution' (Brougham and Jeffrey, 1808 p. 223).[11] Revolution in Coleridge's reflections is rather a return to a condition that had been temporarily lost or suspended, as well as the completion of a romance in which something essential is won back. In view of this conception of revolution, the importance of the Peninsular War resides in the idea that it returns something invaluable to the English and the British nation at large: 'the Spanish contest has a separate and additional interest for Englishmen of genuine English principles: for … it was the noble efforts of Spanish Patriotism, that first restored us, without distinction of party, to our characteristic enthusiasm for *liberty*' (*LS*, p. 38). The connections between the Spanish War, the recovery of something lost and the 'genuine' meaning of revolution were so intimate for Coleridge that in the *Biographia Literaria* (1817) he briefly reconsidered the political consensus during the Peninsular War period and recalled how '[the Spanish cause] made us all once more Englishmen by at once gratifying and correcting the predilections of both parties' (1983, vol. 1, p. 189).

The literary architecture of the *Letters on the Spaniards* conveys its political message by a variety of intersecting rhetorical and generic devices. Although their primary aim is to restore faith in the Spaniards' fight, the analogical construction is convincing because it moves away from the vacillations of Spanish history and establishes Britain as a constant point of reference. Organizing the central tale in terms of a romance, the *Letters* sanction a vision of the Peninsular War as destined to success and victory over the French army, and effectively counter the detractors of the government's Iberian foreign policy. In addition, through their representation of war in terms of a 'revolution', Coleridge's *Letters on the Spaniards* also participate in the elaboration of a Romantic Conservative ideology and its revisionary work on the reformist agendas of the 1790s. History being 'a voice from the sepulchres of our forefathers' (*LS*, p. 53), the *Letters* are an attempt to come to terms with the unsolved issues of the revolutionary decade, a negotiation of Burkean theories of the nation, and that reliving of 'Jacobinism' which Deirdre Coleman (1989) has pointed out as the main concern in Wordsworth's tract on Cintra of 1809. Together with Wordsworth, Southey and many other contemporary intellectuals, Coleridge recycled the 'Jacobin' ideology of change by envisaging a return to the original balance between the individual, society and the institutions, the combination of reform and the maintenance of stability, and a firm belief in a national mission. Elaborated in different forms by these and other intellectuals, Romantic Conservatism was generally both part of mainstream Tory ideology and resistant to party politics in its analysis and theorizations of the state of the nation. Overcoming governmental policy and directives, Southey and Coleridge could elaborate both reformist and reactionary agendas in the name of what David Eastwood has termed 'a yearning for stability', which led them to campaign for greater political and social control as well as for more effective measures of poor relief and penal reform (Eastwood, 1989, p. 330).[12] In their retelling of war and revolution, the *Letters* present the ideological fixity and fluidity which underlies the political and historical discourses of Romantic Conservatism, and that revision of youthful political enthusiasm uniting the Lakers to other members of their generation. Specifically, the *Letters* succeed in creating a stable view of history and politics out of ambivalent materials and an ambiguous figurative scheme, whilst establishing a balance between forces of permanence (the unchanging spirit) and progress (through a view of post-war expansion). Thus, the text fully exploits the harmonization of discordant issues afforded by the romance which, in Fredric Jameson's definition, corresponds to a 'deep-rooted ideology which has only too clearly the function of drawing the boundaries of a given social order and providing a powerful internal deterrent against deviancy or subversion' (1975, p. 140).[13]

Because of the importance they attach to Englishness and national safety, the *Letters on the Spaniards* prefigure Coleridge's reflections on the 'condition of England' found in such later texts as *Lay Sermons* (1816–17) and *On the Constitution of Church and State* (1830). Yet, in their more immediate context, the *Letters* are indicative of the response to the war by first-generation Romantic writers and of their characteristic use of analogy. Even if Coleridge recognizes the trope as artificial, he nevertheless employs it extensively, bearing out the eagerness with which the Lakers grasped at historical analogies, in visible contrast, for instance, to Byron's interrogative use of the parallel in the first canto of *Childe Harold's Pilgrimage* (1980–93, vol. 2). There Byron questions talismanic similarities between past and contemporary events and deflates the legendary narratives, chivalric romances and feudal repertoire with which the older Romantic generation and countless occasional poets disguised the Iberian war. Byron's lines celebrate the history of Spain by evoking the traditional icon of chivalry and the Roderick legend, yet by way of the *ubi sunt* topos they also question the validity of any such historical parallel:

> Where is that standard which Pelagio bore,
> When Cava's traitor-sire first call'd the band
> That dy'd thy mountain streams with Gothic gore?
> Where are those bloody banners which of yore
> Wav'd o'er thy sons, victorious to the gale,
> And drove at last the spoilers to their shore?
>
> (II. 35)[14]

Relying on a structural scheme so liable to conflicting interpretations, the impact of the *Letters on the Spaniards* mainly resides in Coleridge's narrative strategies. Through the romance, the Peninsular War is displaced to other times and climes so that, by the sixth letter, it has virtually disappeared from the text, giving way to representations of British nationalism, the nature of the state and its relation to the individual. The material effects of war are ultimately removed from the *Letters*, where the conflict and its connected issues are played out in the realms of ethics, past history, the national spirit, natural philosophy and international law. As a consequence, for Coleridge 'the devastation effected in the moral world' by France's destabilizing historical presence is so enormous and far-reaching that 'the horrors of battle, though the miseries of a whole war were brought together before our eyes in one disastrous field, would present but a tame tragedy in comparison' (*LS*, pp. 84–5). Additionally, since Britain is inscribed within the romance of the sixteenth-century war as well as in that of the anti-Napoleonic campaign, the *Letters* validate the 'moral algebra' that the British ruling class needs to follow in the present times, a series of indications 'that assures us of the final result, though the process remains undeciphered!' (*LS*, p. 82). As with the essays in the *Friend*, the *Letters* also throw into relief the importance of the ethical education of the intellectual and political guides of the nation. Thus, the Iberian campaign is pointed out to 'every reflecting mind' (*LS*, p. 68) as a just war, a principle essential to Coleridge's idea of the state, and circumventing the unacceptable aims of defeating the enemy for territorial acquisition in favour of a conflict which expresses the national spirit and its providential destiny. This transfiguration of the war away from the battlefield and into analogy, romance and the moral dimension reassures the reader that the Iberian campaign will ultimately be victorious, prophesying that 'Spain will not be conquered by armies merely, will not be conquered while she retains her present feelings and principles' (*LS*, p. 99). But victory, as predicted by the analogy, is ensured within Coleridge's rhetorical adjustments and by British principles, so that the *Letters* turn the military campaign into a readable tale which confirms a theory of the nation as historical agent and as trans-historical essence. Coleridge's complex discourse on Spain, its national character and historical mission finally reveals that this elect nation is England and that the Iberian war is an English affair. If the inset narrative on the Belgian provinces resulted in the creation of the prosperous, tolerant and pacific Netherlands, Coleridge foresees a similar triumphant outcome from the end of the anti-French wars. Yet, this time the hero of romance awaiting retribution will be the British nation.

Notes

1. On the *Courier* see Aspinall, 1949, pp. 206–9. On 5 July 1811, the *Courier* was to publish an article by Coleridge criticizing the reappointment of the Duke of York as Commander-in-Chief of the army, following the 'Mary Anne Clarke scandal' about the corrupt sales of army commissions in January 1809. Nevertheless, the article did not appear, as the government called on Stuart to withdraw it. And, aware of the paper's political stance, in the opening to the *Letters on the Spaniards* Coleridge distanced himself from the newspaper's position by stating that: 'Whatever may be deemed, Sir, of your domestic Politics, no man, who is either Patriot or Philanthropist, will deny to the *Courier* its due praise for a steady adherence to the Spanish cause'. Samuel Taylor Coleridge, *Letters on the Spaniards* (1978, vol. 1, p. 41), henceforth *LS*. All further references will be in parentheses after the text.
2. Wordsworth's pamphlet appeared in the *Courier* from 27 December 1808 to 13 January 1809. When it was discontinued, Wordsworth arranged for it to be

published as a pamphlet in May 1809 which eventually sold very badly, although highly praised by Coleridge, Southey and the Lakers' entourage.

3.   The notion of romance used in this discussion is based on Fredric Jameson's reinterpretation of Northrop Frye (Jameson, 1975).

4.   Letter to Daniel Stuart, c. 4 April 1809: 'This I could amply illustrate by facts from the Dutch in their wars against Philip 2nd (bye the bye, I *have* written & will send you in a few days an interesting parallelism between that war & the present attempt of Spain) & the American Revolution' (Coleridge, 1956–71, vol. 3, p. 189). On parallelism as one of the dominant figures of speech in Coleridge's prose, see Grow, 1976, pp. 55–60.

5.   In 1813 the *British Review* remarked that, since 'At the present moment … any thing relating to the Peninsula is an object of interest', the managers of Covent Garden had decided to stage Coleridge's play despite its worthlessness: *British Review*, 4 (1813), pp. 361–70, reproduced in Reiman, 1973, vol. 1, p. 222. Additionally, according to Carl Woodring, 'For the audience of 1813 the Spain of the play … could be at once England and the scene of Wellington's Peninsular campaigns. The tyranny of the Inquisitors, once suggestive of the lords temporal and divine who upheld Pitt, could now oddly shadow forth Napoleon. That reviewers could think the play unfriendly toward Spain was an accident of its origins' (1961, p. 207). It is also an interesting coincidence that Coleridge first composed *Osorio* in 1797 at the request of Richard Brinsley Sheridan, whose *Pizarro* also reworked an analogical plot about Spain as an imperialistic power. And the narrative of the Belgian insurrection in the *Letters* shares one of its sources – Robert Watson's *History of the Reign of Philip II* (1777) – with *Osorio*.

6.   The article is attributed to Coleridge on the grounds that it may have been sent from Keswick and for stylistical reasons. It was reprinted in the *Courier* on 6 August 1800 (Coleridge, 1978, vol. 1, p. 240).

7.   The political and historical importance of the national character in the *Letters* relies on the theorizations of eighteenth-century anthropological and sociological discourses which, rescuing this idea from checklists of stereotypes, rephrased it as a historically active principle. From Montesquieu, through the *Encyclopédistes*, to Hume and Rousseau, the national character was defined as an important causal factor within interpretations of history and politics (Kra, 1989).

8.   On the doctrine of organic form, its philosophical import and European diffusion, see McFarland, 1981, pp. 34–42. The influence of late eighteenth-century discoveries in the fields of electricity and galvanism, especially by the Lunar Society, on Coleridge's thought is examined in Wylie, 1989, pp. 47–53, 66–7, 122–42.

9.   Much in the same vein, Wordsworth's *Convention of Cintra* announces that: 'The Spaniards are a people with imagination: and the paradoxical reveries of Rousseau, and the flippancies of Voltaire, are plants which will not naturalise in the country of Calderon and Cervantes.' Thus, rejecting what Burke termed 'the metaphysical abstraction' of French politics and culture, Wordsworth confidently announces that 'Spain has nothing to dread from Jacobinism' (Wordsworth, 1974, vol. 1, p. 332).

10. On the slow disentanglement of Britishness out of an original idea of Englishness, see Colley, 1992, pp. 101–45.

11. The conflicting meanings of 'revolution' in the Romantic period are examined by Paulson, 1983, pp. 1–10.

12. Romantic Conservatism was an eclectic fusion of Burkean theorizations, Jacobin and Godwinian principles, a strong opposition to industrialization and political economy, and a yearning for stability which posited change as a subordinate historical component. David Eastwood therefore remarks that, 'If Southey the defender of political orthodoxy recalls Burke, Southey the social critic anticipates Carlyle and even Ruskin. In short, Romantic Conservatism both reflected and itself contributed to the fluidity of intellectual debate in the early nineteenth century' (1989, p. 311).
13. On the development of the romance by Romantic authors as 'a form that privileges broad, conservative sympathies over upsetting details', see Beiderwell, 1989, p. 277.
14. On chivalry and Spain in Byron's *Childe Harold* see Duff, 1994, pp. 123–7 and Saglia, 1996, pp. 157–70.

Bibliography

Aspinall, A. (1949), *Politics and the Press c. 1780–1850*, London: Home and Van Thal.

Bainbridge, S. (1995), *Napoleon and English Romanticism*, Cambridge: Cambridge University Press.

Beattie, W. (ed.) (1849), *Life and Letters of Thomas Campbell*, 3 vols, London: Edward Moxon.

Beiderwell, B. (1989), 'Scott's *Redgauntlet* as a Romance of Power', *Studies in Romanticism*, 28 (2).

Brougham, H. and Jeffrey, F. (1808), 'Don Pedro Cevallos on the French Usurpation of Spain', *Edinburgh Review*, 13, October.

Butler, M. (1989), 'Telling It Like a Story: The French Revolution as Narrative', *Studies in Romanticism*, 28 (3).

Byron, G. G., Lord (1980–93), ed. McGann, J. J., *Lord Byron, Complete Poetical Works*, 7 vols, Oxford: Clarendon Press.

Christensen, J. C. (1979), 'Politerotics: Coleridge's Rhetoric of War in *The Friend*', *Clio*, 8.

Cobbett's Parliamentary Debates (1808), First Series, vol. 2 (11 April–4 July 1808), London: Hansard.

Coleman, D. (1989), 'Re-living Jacobinism: Wordsworth and the Convention of Cintra', *The Yearbook of English Studies*, 19.

Coleridge, S. T. (1956–71), ed. Griggs, E. L., *Collected Letters of Samuel Taylor Coleridge*, 6 vols, Oxford: Oxford University Press.

————. (1978), ed. Erdman, D. V., *Essays on his Times*, 3 vols, in *The Collected Works of Samuel Taylor Coleridge*, vol. 3, London: Routledge and Kegan Paul; Princeton: Princeton University Press.

————. (1983), ed. Engell, J. and Jackson Bate, W., *Biographia Literaria*, 2 vols, in *The Collected Works of Samuel Taylor Coleridge*, vol. 7, London: Routledge and Kegan Paul; Princeton: Princeton University Press.

Colley, L. (1992), *Britons: Forging the Nation 1707–1837*, London: Pimlico.

De Paolo, C. (1985), 'Kant, Coleridge, and the Ethics of War', *Wordsworth Circle*, 16 (1).

Duff, D. (1994), *Romance and Revolution: Shelley and the Politics of a Genre*, Cambridge: Cambridge University Press.

Eastwood, D. (1989), 'Robert Southey and the Intellectual Origins of Romantic Conservatism', *English Historical Review*, 104, April.

Ellis, G. and Canning, G. (1809), 'Affaires d'Espagne', *Quarterly Review*, 1, February.

Favret, M. A. (1994), 'Coming Home: The Public Spaces of Romantic War', *Studies in Romanticism*, 33 (4).

Gossmann, L. (1990), *Between History and Literature*, Cambridge and London: Harvard University Press.

Grow, L. M. (1976), *The Prose Style of Samuel Taylor Coleridge*, Romantic Reassessment 54, Salzburg: Institut für Anglistik und Arnerikanistik.

Jameson, F. (1975), 'Magical Narratives: Romance as Genre', *New Literary History*, 7 (1).

Kra, P. (1989), 'The Politics of National Character', *Studies on Voltaire and the Eighteenth Century*, 265.

Maltby, W. S. (1971), *The Black Legend in England: The Development of Anti-Spanish Sentiment, 1558–1660*, Durham: Duke University Press.

McFarland, T. (1981), *Romanticism and the Forms of Ruin: Wordsworth, Coleridge, and the Modalities of Fragmentation*, Princeton: Princeton University Press.

Morrow, J. (1990), *Coleridge's Political Thought: Property, Morality and the Limits of Traditional Discourse*, Basingstoke: Macmillan.

Paulson, R. (1983), *Representations of Revolution 1789–1820*, New Haven and London: Yale University Press.

Reiman, D. H. (ed.) (1973), *The Romantics Reviewed. Part A: The Lake Poets*, 2 vols, New York and London: Garland.

Ross, M. B. (1991), 'Romancing the Nation-State: The Poetics of Romantic Nationalism', in Arac, J. and Ritvo, H. (eds), *Macropolitics of Nineteenth-Century Literature: Nationalism, Exoticism. Imperialism*, Philadelphia: University of Pennsylvania Press, pp. 56–85.

Russell, G. (1995), *The Theatres of War: Performance, Politics, and Society, 1793–1815*, Oxford: Clarendon Press.

Saglia, D. (1996), '"Renown'd Romantic": Place as Text and Intertext in Byron's *Childe Harold's Pilgrimage*', in Smethurst, C. (ed.), *Romantic Geographies*, Glasgow: University of Glasgow, pp. 157–70.

Scott, W. (1932–37), ed. Grierson, H. J. C., *The Letters of Sir Walter Scott*, 13 vols, London: Constable.

Southey, R. (1965), ed. Curry, K., *New Letters of Robert Southey*, 2 vols, New York and London: Columbia University Press.

White, H. (1973), *Metahistory: The Historical Imagination in Nineteenth-Century Europe*, Baltimore and London: Johns Hopkins University Press.

Woodring, C. (1961), *Politics in the Poetry of Coleridge*, Madison: University of Wisconsin Press.

Wordsworth, W. (1947–54) ed. de Selincourt, E. and Darbishire, H., *The Poetical Works of William Wordsworth*, 5 vols, Oxford: Clarendon Press.

————. (1974), ed. Owen, W. J. B. and Worthington Smyser, J., *The Prose Works of William Wordsworth*, 3 vols, Oxford: Clarendon Press.

Wylie, I. (1989), *Young Coleridge and the Philosophers of Nature*, Oxford: Clarendon Press.

CHAPTER EIGHT

'Of war and taking towns': Byron's siege poems

Simon Bainbridge

In her futuristic *roman-à-clef The Last Man*, Mary Shelley presents a portrait of Byron as warrior hero and saviour of Greece, a role Byron aspired to but realized only in legend after his death. Shelley introduces her version of Byron, the aristocratic Lord Raymond, as the celebrated leader of the victorious Greek armies and the subject of songs adapted from traditional Greek airs 'whose themes were his glory, valour, and munificence' (1994, p. 40). Raymond's own self-conception is no less heroic. He sees himself in the martial tradition of Alexander, Caesar, Cromwell and Napoleon (p. 56), longs to be 'enregistered in the annals of nations as a successful warrior' (pp. 106–7) and in his imperial ambitions seeks to surpass the fame of Byron's own idol, stating that: 'I intend to be a warrior, a conqueror; Napoleon's name shall vail to mine; and enthusiasts, instead of visiting his rocky grave, and exalting the merits of the fallen, shall adore my majesty, and magnify my illustrious achievements' (pp. 57–8). Raymond's vision of history is one of great men performing heroic deeds, a company he aspires to join: 'The prayer of my youth was to be one among those who render the pages of earth's history splendid; who exalt the race of man, and make this little globe a dwelling of the mighty' (p. 194).

Raymond is a greatly simplified portrait of Byron. *The Last Man* is a powerfully anti-martial text in which the masculine pursuit of military glory plays a major role in the annihilation of the world's population. As the primary target of this polemic, the figure of Raymond emphasizes the heroic rather than the mock-heroic elements of Byron's martial self-conception. Similarly, Shelley's portrait of Byron does not acknowledge the complexity or ambiguity of his response to war in principle or practice, for Byron would have agreed with much of the novel's critique of militarism. Indeed, in many ways Shelley's text adopts and develops the conclusions as well as the tropes of much of Byron's own writing on war. Yet Raymond's Whiggish conceptions of history, and his ambition to play a heroic part in its course through the assumption of a martial role, have parallels in Byron's thinking and writing. The key elements of Shelley's portrait of Byron can be detected in much of his writing on war, as in his description of his cantos on the siege of Ismail in a letter to Moore of 1822:

these cantos contain a full detail (like the storm in the Canto Second) of
the siege and assault of Ismael, with much of sarcasm on those butchers
in large business, your mercenary soldiery ... With these things and
these fellows, it is necessary, in the present clash of philosophy and
tyranny, to throw away the scabbard. I know it is against fearful odds;
but the battle must be fought; and it will be eventually for the good of
mankind, whatever it may be for the individual who risks himself.

(1973–94, vol. 9, p. 191)

This passage gives a perfect expression of Byron's ambivalent attitude to
war. Beginning with an attack on mercenary soldiers that anticipates the
cantos' devastating critique of those whose 'trade / Is butchery' (*Don Juan*,
VII. 69), Byron nonetheless quickly adopts for his own martial project the
grand rhetoric and militant language that Shelley would parody through
Lord Raymond. Blurring the distinction between a literal and a figurative
battle against 'tyranny', Byron sees this battle as both beneficial to mankind in a Whiggish vision of history ('philosophy' versus 'tyranny') and as
providing a glorious, heroic and possibly self-sacrificing role for himself.
With his threat to throw away the scabbard, an allusion to Clarendon on the
republican Hampden ('Without question, when he first drew the sword, he
threw away the scabbard' (Clarendon, 1888, vol. 3, p. 63)), Byron implies
that he 'will war' in 'deeds' as well as 'words', as he would later suggest in
Don Juan (IX. 24). As Tim Webb has argued in an excellent study of the
poet's attitude to war, Byron was 'not a pacifist' and he repeatedly committed himself to what he called 'freedom's battles', those fought for a 'cause
... to which a good heart could be partial – / Defence of freedom, country,
or of laws' (1990, p. 47; *Don Juan*, VIII. 4; VII. 40). However, such causes
were difficult to find in the post-Waterloo world and Byron was often
forced to look back in history to the actions of classical heroes such as
Leonidas or forward to the New World exploits of Washington for his
examples (*Don Juan*, VIII. 5).

In addition to emphasizing Byron's martial ambitions, Shelley's portrait
of the poet is useful because of the form of action through which Raymond
seeks to gain his place in history: the taking of the Golden City, Constantinople. As early as chapter 4 Raymond announces that 'my first act when I
become King of England, will be to unite with the Greeks, take Constantinople, and subdue all Asia' (p. 57). Identifying himself more as an imperialist
and a conqueror than a liberator, Raymond puts the taking of the historic
city at the centre of his plans and he makes it a key event in his vision of
history:

in his hope of the conquest of Constantinople, he counted on an event
which would be as a landmark in the waste of ages, an exploit un-
equalled in the annals of man; when a city of grand historic association,
the beauty of whose site was the wonder of the world, which for many
hundred years had been the strong hold of the Moslems, should be

rescued from slavery and barbarism, and restored to a people illustrious
for genius, civilization, and a spirit of liberty.

(Shelley, 1994, pp. 176–7).

Here, Constantinople becomes a rich symbolic site, a place where history can
be made, whose imagined possession represents the triumph of the West over
the East and of 'civilization' versus 'barbarism' in an exemplary orientalist
vision of progress. Yet Raymond is also driven by his craving for personal
glory and it is his desire for the 'title of Victor of Constantinople' (p. 194)
which leads him to enter the plague-infested city when all advise against it.
The hollowness of both Raymond's vision of history and his personal ambition are revealed with the culmination of the siege. Raymond's solitary entry
into the deserted Constantinople is swiftly followed by an apocalyptic explosion that crushes and kills him, annihilates the city and appears to unleash on
the rest of the world the plague that destroys all of humanity except Lionel,
the eponymous Last Man. Death, not Raymond, is the Victor of Constantinople. The explosion that accompanies Raymond's entry into the Golden City
signals the end of history rather than its glorious progress; his military ambitions lead to the destruction of civilization rather than its splendid advancement.

   Shelley's choice of a siege as the central action of her novel suggests her
identification of it as a key element in Byron's treatment and understanding
of war in his writing. In the two years before she started writing *The Last
Man*, Shelley had produced fair copies of cantos VII and VIII of *Don Juan*
and *The Deformed Transformed* which contain extended treatments of sieges
and one incident in *The Last Man*, Adrian's rescue of a Muslim girl from two
soldiers during a siege, clearly recalls Juan's rescue of Leila from two Cos-
sacks during the siege of Ismail (Shelley, 1994, p. 162; *Don Juan*, VIII.
91–6). Moreover, in her use of Constantinople as a key historic city, Shelley
draws on Byron's exploitation of the symbolic potential of the siege in his
poems and his use of it to represent and investigate the narratives of history.

   In three of his most sustained descriptions of actual armed conflict between nations Byron represents war through the format of the siege. *The
Siege of Corinth*, written in stages between 1812 and 1815 and published in
1816, describes the Turkish attack on the Venetian fortress in 1715 during the
war between Venice and the Ottoman empire for control of Peloponnesus
(1980–93, vol. 3, pp. 479–82). Cantos VII and VIII of *Don Juan*, written in
1822 and published in 1823, depict the Russian assault on the Turkish fortress at Ismail of November to December 1790, part of the Russo-Turkish
war of 1787–91 (1980–93, vol. 5, pp. 714–18). *The Deformed Transformed*,
written in 1822–23 and published in 1824, dramatizes the siege of Rome of
1527 by Charles V's army of Spanish, German and Italian troops under the
leadership of Charles Duc de Bourbon (1980–93, vol. 6, pp. 725–8). None of
these three sieges could be classed as 'freedom's battles'. Rather, Byron
presents them as episodes in imperial conflicts fought for 'mere lust of

power' and 'mere conquest' (*Don Juan*, VII. 40; VIII. 3). Taken together, Byron's representations of these three 'lawless sieges', to adopt a phrase from *The Siege of Corinth* (l. 355; hereafter cited as *The Siege*), constitute one of the fullest and most powerful explorations of war in the period. The aim of this essay is to consider why Byron so frequently turned to the siege as a way of representing warfare, and to examine his use of its symbolic and allegorical potential.

Placed within the context of developments in military history during the Revolutionary and Napoleonic Wars, Byron's choice of the siege may seem rather anachronistic. As the military historian David G. Chandler has commented, though once the dominant form of warfare in Europe and still a significant feature of the military scene, particularly during the British campaign in the Spanish Peninsula, regular sieges played a considerably less important part in the warfare of the Revolutionary and Napoleonic period than they had in the mid-eighteenth century (Chandler, 1993, p. 410). Yet the siege held a prominent place in the writing and culture of war that could be traced back to Homer's *Iliad*. With its rich symbolic and allegorical potential – the fortress as a symbol for the soul, the body and the nation – the siege could be used to write about the self, the erotic and the historical. A study of the siege trope in literature would be a huge task and would need to follow it through texts like *The Castle of Perseverance*, the numerous medieval accounts of sieges, Spenser's *Faerie Queene*, Marlowe's *Tamburlaine the Great*, Shakespeare's *Henry V* and *Troilus and Cressida*, Bunyan's *The Holy War*, Richardson's *Clarissa* and Sterne's *Tristram Shandy*. Uncle Toby's obsession with siege warfare in this last text, though very much his own hobby-horse, also suggests the wider interest in the increasingly baroque design of fortifications in the eighteenth century, a period which saw the introduction of fortress modelling and war-gaming (Duffy, 1975, p. 193). In *Don Juan*, Byron writes of the 'dilettanti in war's art' and the 'dilettanti of topography / Of fortresses' (VII. 39; VIII. 74) implying that for one element of his audience the savage events of war he so graphically depicts had become transformed into a genteel, amateur pursuit. In choosing to write about sieges, then, Byron focused on a form of warfare that had important literary and cultural dimensions.

As a form of warfare, the siege can be seen as particularly suited to literary representation, offering a series of dramatic set piece actions (trenching, cannonade, assault) that had become particularly formalized during the seventeenth and eighteenth centuries (following the manuals of the French military architect Vaubon) and that contributed to a single, decisive action – the taking of a fortress and the annihilation or total surrender of the enemy. In all three poems, Byron exploits (and increasingly scrutinizes) the exhilaration of this form of combat, presenting the action of the siege from the attackers' point of view and using the structured events of the siege to structure his own works.

Despite the differences in form (verse romance, mock-epic, verse drama) and tone, all three poems follow a strikingly similar pattern of events. In *The Siege* and *Don Juan*, Byron begins with the preparatory stages of the siege, including descriptions of the besieging forces, trenching and the cannonade. *The Siege* illustrates how Byron uses these stages to generate suspense and introduce key issues, interweaving descriptions of these preparatory stages with analyses of the historical situation and the character of Alp and building to the climax of the breaching of the fortifications – 'The wall is rent, the ruins yawn' (l. 185) – that both prepares for the action of the assault the following morning and brings to a close what McGann has seen as the first part of the poem's four-part structure (Byron, 1980–93, vol. 3, p. 482). Both poems then provide an 'eve of the assault' interlude (*Don Juan*, VII. 54) with *The Siege* describing what McGann has called 'Alp's Meditation', the second part of the poem's structure (p. 482), and *Don Juan* detailing the arrival of Juan and Johnson at Ismail. In both, Byron echoes the speech of the Chorus on the night before Agincourt in *Henry V* to establish the atmosphere of suspense and expectation (*Siege*, ll. 217–19; *Don Juan*, VII. 7, 86; *Henry V*, IV. 0. 1–53). It is at this point of the 'eve of the assault' that the two main protagonists of *The Deformed Transformed*, Arnold and Caesar, arrive before the walls of Rome.

All three poems then present the action of the assault, with its mass casualties, and track the exploits of their respective heroes in the vanguard. They all follow the besiegers' entrance of the fortress and their battles with the besieged, emphasizing the 'spoil' and the 'after carnage' of siege warfare (*The Siege*, ll. 724–5). In each text there then follows an encounter with a heroic and brave defender: the Venetian Governor Minotti in *The Siege*, the Tartar Khan in *Don Juan* and Olimpia in *The Deformed Transformed*, all of whom refuse the offered quarter, the first two fighting to their deaths and Olimpia attempting suicide. The gradual capture of the city is marked by a movement inwards (emphasized in *The Deformed Transformed* by the scene divisions and stage directions), and in *The Siege* and *The Deformed Transformed* the final plundering actions of the siege are located within the sacred space of church or cathedral. In *The Siege* Minotti retreats to the church where, standing at the altar, he ignites the magazines that annihilate the garrison. In *The Deformed Transformed*, Arnold saves Olimpia from the soldiers in St Peter's, recalling Juan's rescuing of the Muslim girl Leila during the assault, though Olimpia attempts suicide by throwing herself from the altar. In each text, the taking of the town is complete (*Don Juan*, VIII. 122; *The Deformed Transformed*, II. iii. 102), though this is ironized in *The Siege* by the destruction of the city – 'Thus was Corinth lost and won!' (l. 1034). As the similarity of the poems reveals, Byron found in the siege a form that enabled him to represent war through a series of set-piece actions and recurrent narrative tropes which could be used and reused to structure an engagement with key issues such as the horrors of war, the role of non-combatants and women, the validity of the heroic and the shape of history.

If the structured pattern of siege warfare meant that it was particularly well suited to literary representation, its intense and devastating nature exemplified the horrors of war that Byron wished to expose. Chandler provides a useful account of the cost to both attackers and defenders of siege warfare:

> The old conventions of the 18th century whereby a defender could surrender with honour once a major breach had been driven through his defenses had largely disappeared, and unless disease or starvation was rampant within the position, a Napoleonic garrison commander was likely to insist on a fight to the finish. As was shown at Badajoz in 1812, even a prepared storming could be terribly expensive. Spanish garrisons, as at Saragossa, could also fight to the death. However, the besiegers could wreak a fearful penalty for a dogged defense if their storming was successful yet dearly bought – Badajoz and San Sebastian being the two prime examples, when Wellington's rank and file went out of control.
>
> (Chandler, 1993, p. 411).

The British siege of Badajoz of 1812 provides a powerful example of the brutal nature of siege warfare, costing 4670 allied casualties, of which 1800 fell during two hours within a space less than a hundred yards square (Glover, 1979, p. 160). The horror of the assault was described by one witness as follows:

> hundreds of brave soldiers lay in piles upon each other, weltering in blood, and trodden down by their own companions ... the small groups of soldiers seeking shelter from the cart-wheels, pieces of timber, fire-balls and other missiles hurled down upon them; the wounded crawling past the fire-balls, many of them scorched and perfectly black, and covered with mud, from having fallen into the *cuvette* [a trench cut into the floor of the ditch], where three hundred were suffocated or drowned; and all this time the French on top of the parapets, jeering and cracking their jokes, and deliberately picking off those whom they chose.
>
> (Duffy, 1975, p. 149)

Once the British troops had entered Badajoz, following over forty assaults, they sacked it for three days (Chandler, 1993, p. 38).

In his dedication to Wellington at the start of canto IX of *Don Juan*, Byron describes war as a 'brain-spattering, windpipe-slitting art, / Unless her cause by Right be sanctified' (IX. 4). His depictions of these three sieges, unsanctified by right, emphasize this shocking physical destructiveness of war. The horrors they describe gain added force when read in the context of the eyewitness account of the siege of Badajoz. In *The Siege of Corinth*, the bodies of the Turkish troops that lead the assault strew 'the earth like broken glass' (l. 687) and as they fall in masses are 'Heaped ... / Hand to hand, and foot to foot' (ll. 705–6). Byron's descriptions of the sacking that follows the entrance of the city echo Henry V's threats before Harfleur of the defiling of 'your shrill-shrieking daughters' (III. iv. 35) and introduces with an emphatic extra-footed line the image of streets running with blood that he draws on in all three poems:

> But the rampart is won, and the spoil begun,
> And all but the after carnage done.
> Shriller shrieks now mingling come
> From within the plundered dome:
> Hark to the haste of flying feet,
> That splash in the blood of the slippery street
> (ll. 724–9)

In *Don Juan*, Juan and Johnson are described as 'trampling' over 'dead bodies', as 'wallow[ing] in the bloody mire / Of dead and dying thousands' and, when repulsed, 'they stumbled backwards o'er / A wounded comrade, sprawling in his gore' (VIII. 19–20). When a party of grenadiers throw themselves into a ditch, their 'blood the puddle greatly did enrich' and the 'baffled heroes' 'slid[e] knee-deep in lately frozen mud, / Now thawed into a marsh of human blood' (VIII. 71, 73). Byron provides a memorable dramatization of these horrors in the incident of the Russian officer who, 'in martial tread / Over a heap of bodies', has his Achilles tendon bitten through by a 'dying Moslem' (VIII. 83–5). Again, Byron emphasizes the horrors inflicted on the civilian population: Leila is rescued by Juan as she tries to hide among the bodies in a 'yet warm group / Of murdered women' and the 'rough, tough soldiers ... / Spared neither sex nor age in their career / Of carnage' (VIII. 91, 119).

In both these texts, Byron uses natural imagery to represent the horrors of siege warfare. In *The Siege*, for example, the Turks attack like wolves, they are mown down like grass and the force of their attacks is like spring-tides pounding a cliff (ll. 678–82, 691, 694–9). Similarly in *Don Juan* the attacking army is like 'a lion' and during the cannonade 'the whole rampart blazed like Etna' (VIII. 2, 7). Yet Byron also represents the action of Ismail as so intense that it outdoes the natural world: during the assault 'Thicker than leaves the lives began to fall' (VIII. 9) and:

> so hot
> The fire was, that were red Vesuvius loaded,
> Besides its lava, with all sorts of shot
> And shells or hells, it could not more have goaded.
> (VIII. 16)

Byron's representation of the devastation of the siege of Ismail in *Don Juan* is dominated by two major tropes. One is of the sea, first used to figure the destructive potential of mankind: '"Let there be light!" said God, "and there was light!" / "Let there be blood!" says man, and there's a sea!' (VII. 41) and repeated throughout the two cantos to quantify the blood, tears, gore and slaughter produced by the siege (VII. 50, 68; VIII. 3, 122). The other is of hell (VII. 86; VIII. 6, 20, 42), Byron's use of which culminates in his final attempt to assess the events at Ismail:

> All that the mind would shrink from of excesses;
> All that the body perpetrates of bad;
> All that we read, hear, dream, of man's distresses;
> All that the Devil would do if run stark mad;
> All that defies the worst which pen expresses;
> All by which Hell is peopled, or as sad
> As Hell – mere mortals who their power abuse, –
> Was here (as heretofore and since) let loose.
>
>   (VIII. 123).

Byron's representation of the aftermath of Ismail as the result of the devil 'run stark mad' recalls one of his first uses of the siege motif in the poem 'The Devil's Drive' of 1813 in which the devil 'gazed on a town by besiegers taken, / Nor cared he who were winning' (ll. 77). It also anticipates the merging of the metaphysical and the historical in *The Deformed Transformed* which dramatizes the conceit by presenting the devilish figure of Caesar observing the bloody sacking of Rome and describing his 'sport' as 'to gaze, since all these labourers / Will reap my harvest gratis' (II. ii. 60–63).

In *The Deformed Transformed* Byron draws on the language of war he had developed in *The Siege* and *Don Juan* but uses it in a newly symbolic way to render the events of the siege in broader historical terms. For example, when Arnold arrives before the walls of Rome at the start of Act I scene ii, his comment 'my path / Has been o'er carcases: mine eyes are full / Of blood' (I. ii. 2–4) recalls the description of Juan and Johnson 'trampling' over 'dead bodies'. This literal meaning is reinforced by Caesar's instructions to him to 'wipe' the blood from his eyes (l. 3). Yet here Byron also uses this language of war to provide symbolic representations of Arnold's new-found career as 'a conqueror' (l. 4) and of the atrocities he has seen during it. This merging of the literal and the symbolic is characteristic of the play with its repeated references to the Tiber running with blood (I. ii. 85, 152), the streets of Rome red with gore (I. ii. 152; II. ii. 10–11), blood contaminating all drinking water (II. i. 167–8; II. ii. 48–52) and Arnold 'purple with the blood of Rome' (II. iii. 124). While in no way lessening the impact of the play as a representation of a particular historical event, this use of the imagery of blood suggests in broader terms not only the corruption of nature by war, as McGann has suggested (Byron, 1980–93, vol. 6, p. 746), but also war's devastation of civilization. This characteristic symbolic use of language pushes the play towards the elevated levels and grand schemas of the metaphysical dramas.

In his emphasis on the devastation done by siege warfare to the civilian population, Byron uses the format of the siege to emphasize that war is not something that can be contained within the public, professional or masculine sphere. In *The Siege*, the innocent Greek inhabitants of Corinth as well as the warring Turks and Venetians who fight for possession of the city are destroyed by the explosion of the city, as Daniel P. Watkins has pointed out (1987, p. 110). In *The Deformed Transformed*, the female figure of Olimpia acts partly as an embodiment of the Roman population who, as Arnold points out, have done nothing to deserve their fate and 'have lived in peace, / The peace of heaven, and in her sunshine of / Piety' (I. ii. 91–3). In *Don Juan*, the aim of the Russian bombardment is to 'knock down / The public buildings, and the private too, / No matter what poor souls might be undone' (VII. 23). In this way, Byron uses the siege to figure the impact of war on civic as well as military society, as when he mentions the few acts of mercy at Ismail and asks:

> What's this in one annihilated city,
> Where thousand loves, and ties, and duties grow?
> Cockneys of London! Muscadines of Paris!
> Just ponder what a pious pastime war is:
> (VIII. 124)

The siege, more than any other form, graphically illustrates war's devastation of 'loves', 'ties' and 'duties': to contemplate a siege, Byron suggests, is to consider the total impact of war.

In their studies of Byron's siege cantos in relation to their primary source, Marquis de Castelnau's *Essai sur l'Histoire-ancienne et moderne de la Nouvelle Russie,* Elizabeth Boyd and P. G. Vassallo have shown how 'Byron's purpose was to provide an ironic commentary on Castelnau's glorification of war', to quote Vassallo (1981, p. 195; see also Boyd, 1958, pp. 148–9). In revealing 'what a pious pastime war is' in his siege poems, Byron was also attacking an activity which had gained a central place in British culture and society during the Revolutionary and Napoleonic Wars. In *Don Juan* in particular, in which Byron insists upon the factual nature of his treatment of war, his 'true Muse' and 'true portrait of one battle-field' (VIII. 1, 12) are set against what he sees as the dominant ways in which war was constructed and consumed in the period. His particular targets here are the Gazettes with their lists of names which no one can remember, their mistakes and their glorification of aristocrats at the expense of the rank and file (VII. 32–4; VIII. 18), and the poetic works commemorating British victories, particularly Waterloo, with their celebrations of 'Carnage', a word used by Wordsworth in his poem on the battle which Byron constantly invokes (VIII. 9, 82, 119, 140). These forms create and feed the illusions of the 'Too gentle reader' (VIII. 1), one of the 'panters for newspaper praise' and 'dilettanti in war's art' (VII. 39) who revel in the official accounts of the war without thinking about its costs. Such readers, Byron insists, should 'Think how the joys of reading a Gazette / Are purchased by all agonies and crimes' (VIII. 125). As here, Byron constantly juxtaposes the physical actualities of war with its textual representations, asking 'if a man's name in a *bulletin* / May make up for a *bullet in* his body?' (VII. 21) and drawing attention to the 'shrieks and groans' of war 'Which few will sing' (VIII. 135).

Throughout *Don Juan*, Byron insists on the harsh realities of the language of war, a language of 'shocking sounds' (VIII. 1), 'of escalade, / Bombs, drums, guns, bastions, batteries, bayonets, bullets; / Hard words, which stick in the soft Muses' gullets' (VII. 78). As the references to 'escalade' and 'bastions' here suggests, siege warfare was a particularly suitable subject for this approach because during the seventeenth and eighteenth centuries it had developed a highly specialized language. In his account of the developments of *Don Juan* to Kinnaird, Byron emphasized this element of his treatment of the subject: 'The argument consists of *more* love – and a good deal of War – a technical description of a modern siege' (1973–94, vol. 9, p. 196). Asking the reader to 'excuse this engineering slang' in the poem (VII. 11), Byron uses the language of fortification to show his mastery of the technical details of war:

> But a stone bastion, with a narrow gorge,
>   And walls as thick as most sculls born as yet;
> Two batteries, cap-a-pèe, as our St. George,
>   Case-mated one, and t'other 'a barbette,'
> Of Danube's bank took formidable charge;
>   While two-and-twenty cannon duly set
> Rose over the town's right side, in bristling tier,
>   Forty feet high, upon a cavaliere.
>   (VII. 12)

With similar repeated references to the technicalities of siege warfare (VII. 47; VIII. 7, 37) Byron produces his credentials as a war writer and proves himself a match for the 'dilettanti in topography / Of fortresses' (VIII. 74) while also revelling in the baroque extravagances of this language of fortification.

In *Don Juan*, Byron's critique of the false construction of war is at its most powerful in his offering of 'Glory's dream / Unriddled' (VIII. 1). When this abstraction is introduced in the invocation of 'ye Goddesses of war and glory!', it is immediately undermined through a rhyme with 'gory' (VII. 14), a linking also used in *The Deformed Transformed* in which Arnold is accompanied during the siege of Rome by 'the mild twins – Gore and Glory' (II. ii. 12). Exposed as illusory – 'But Glory's Glory; and if you would find / What that is – ask the pig who sees the wind!' (VII. 84) – Glory is presented as a product of narrative – 'what story / Sometimes calls "murder," and at others "glory"' (VII. 26). Yet Byron's treatment of Glory is important because it recognizes its abstract yet pervasive power: Suvorov exploits it in his speech to his troops and during the assault Juan battles 'In search of glory' (VII. 64; VIII. 31, 52). Byron identifies the ideological force of glory, not only in the role it plays in driving soldiers into battle but in bolstering the established order:

> Yet I love Glory; – glory's a great thing; –
>   Think what it is to be in your old age
> Maintained at the expense of your good king:
>   A moderate pension shakes full many a sage,
> And heroes are but made for bards to sing,
>   Which is still better; thus in verse to wage
> Your wars eternally, besides enjoying
> Half-pay for life, make mankind worth destroying.
>   (VIII. 14)

Alluding to both Wordsworth, the 'sage' of Grasmere who had taken a governmental 'pension' as Distributor of Stamps for Westmorland, and to Wellington, the subject of numerous poems and whose pensions are alluded to in the opening of canto IX, Byron argues that the concept of 'Glory' has been used not only to justify the destruction of mankind but to maintain the positions of those individuals who have most benefitted from the recent wars.

Byron's emphasis on the realism of his treatment of war in *Don Juan* needs to be seen not only in the context of the contemporary construction of war in bulletins, gazettes and poetry but also in terms of the epic genre in which he is working. War had always been part of Byron's epic agenda for the poem (I. 200) and in canto VIII he makes a claim for the special, if ambiguous, role of 'the blaze / Of conquest and its consequences, which / Make Epic poesy so rare and rich' (VIII. 90). In choosing a siege as his subject, Byron sets up a parallel with the major epic model, 'eternal Homer', arguing that if he cannot match Homer poetically, his 'modern siege' outdoes in its devastation the great siege of classical history and literature, Troy (VII. 80–81).

Byron uses the parallel with Homer as part of the grand claims he makes for the poem and for himself as a poet. Homer's skill is registered in terms of the martial forms of his own epic: he can 'charm / All ears … By merely wielding with poetic arm, / Arms to which men will never more resort' (VII. 79). Similarly, despite Byron's savage critique of siege warfare, he uses it as a framing metaphor for his own poetic performance, introducing the subject with 'I … am about to batter / A town which did a famous siege endure' and concluding it when he is 'Worn out with battering Ismail's stubborn wall' (VII. 8; VIII. 139). Here Byron uses the metaphor of siege warfare not to present his poetic militancy but to image the power of his own poetic performance in the war cantos, suggesting it is just as spectacular and devastating in its own terms as the assault on Ismail. Similarly, when at the end of canto VI Byron introduces his martial theme with 'The Muse will take a little touch at warfare' (VI. 120), he not only echoes the Chorus's famous description of Henry V on the night before Agincourt ('A little touch of Harry in the night' (IV. I. 10)) but also recalls the 'touch' of the linstock on 'the devilish cannon' at the siege of Harfleur (III. 0. 33). Byron's dazzling display of his poetic skills in *Don Juan* is often described in terms of pyrotechnics; here he suggests it is better thought of as a cannonade, as powerful as those of the great poets of war, Homer and Shakespeare.

If Byron's use of the siege metaphor for his own poetic performance points towards the familiar idea of the narrator as the hero of *Don Juan*, his treatment of the heroic in all three siege poems is highly sceptical. All three protagonists possess conventionally heroic qualities and play major roles in the actions of the sieges. In *The Siege*, Alp is introduced in terms of his exceptional martial prowess, possessing 'deeper skills in war's black art / Than Othman's sons' (ll. 52–3). He is 'brave' (l. 265) and leads the assault on Corinth (l. 660) during which he is repeatedly represented by his powerful right arm; a symbol of both his strength and difference: 'Alp is but known by the white arm bare' (l. 785; see also ll. 660–61, 776). In both *Don Juan* and *The Deformed Transformed*, Byron uses parallels with Achilles to reinforce the presentation of his protagonists in conventionally heroic and martial terms. He informed Medwin about *Don Juan* that: 'I shall make my hero a modern Achilles for fighting' (Byron, 1986, p. 1014). Tracking 'our hero on his path of fame', the narrative follows Juan as he plays a major part in the taking of Ismail and is honoured for his 'courage and humanity' (VIII. 17, 140), the latter a reference to his saving of Leila. In *The Deformed Transformed*, the hunchback Arnold, offered the chance to adopt an alternative body, chooses that of Greece's 'best', Achilles (I. i. 281). By the time he arrives before the walls of Rome he has established himself as a 'conqueror' and is described by Bourbon as 'The beauty of our host, and as brave as beauteous' (I. ii. 4, 220). When Bourbon is killed, Arnold leads the assault and his rescue of Olimpia from the soldiers appears to ally chivalrous mercy to his martial aggression.

However, Byron's siege poems are no celebration of heroism: though all three protagonists possess the martial prowess and bravery of the conventional hero, none of them fight for a justifying 'cause' (*Don Juan*, VII. 40), or even think of themselves as so doing. Alp's motivation is specifically distinguished from that of the religious 'fanatic' and the 'burning patriot' (ll. 252–7). He is driven by the personal motives of 'revenge and love' (l. 245); revenge against Venice from which he has been exiled following unspecified accusations and love for Francesca. The early parts of the poem present Alp as a 'convert' to 'novel faith' (ll. 81, 113) but this is no conversion to Islam. As becomes clear during his 'meditation', Alp's conversion is to his own private faith of revenge: he is driven by 'all the false and fatal zeal / The convert of revenge can feel' (ll. 279–80). It is his Satan-like commitment to 'hate' and 'pride' rather than conversion to Islam which fuels Alp's martial career and prevents him from returning to the Christian faith and Venetian cause offered to him during, and symbolized by, the vision of Francesca he has on the night before the assault.

If Alp fights for private motives that are set against the religious or political causes of the 'fanatic' or 'patriot', Juan fights for no considered reason at all. He and Johnson 'arm / To burn a town which never did them harm' and fight 'thoughtlessly' (VII. 76; VIII. 19). Juan, 'a fine young lad, who fought / He knew not why' is driven on by his desire for glory and by the increasing excitement he feels during the battle (VIII. 29, 32–3, 54-5). Yet Byron's depiction of Juan in battle is also part of the poem's critique of the siege as an act of imperialism. Juan's heroics at Ismail are the product of his education as a member of the gentry class in Spain. As we were told in the opening canto, Juan has been trained in the practice of warfare:

> Then for accomplishments of chivalry,
>   In case our lord the king should go to war again,
> He learn'd the arts of riding, fencing, gunnery,
> And how to scale a fortress – or a nunnery.
>
> (I. 38)

Juan's military prowess is the product of a royalist cause and at its service. Throughout the siege cantos, Juan is presented as representative of the various aristocrats, including a large number of French émigrés, fighting in what McGann has called a 'classic instance of the imperialism of the monarchist regimes' (Byron, 1980–93, vol. 5, p. 719). Like these figures, Juan is 'delighted to employ his leisure' 'In such good company as always throng / To battles, sieges, and that kind of pleasure' (VIII. 24). For Juan, like many of the other multinational aristocrats in the Russian army, warfare is a gentlemanly pursuit, producing sensations akin to horse-riding and hunting (VIII. 54–5). So, though Juan is presented as acting without any specific motivation, Byron's treatment of him in battle makes it clear that his upbringing, his search for glory and the ways in which he responds to the excitement of war all work to the benefit of the imperialist cause.

Like Juan, Arnold fights for no explicit cause, chooses the side on which he fights seemingly by chance and becomes frenzied in battle (II. ii. 27–8). Yet if Juan, in his naivety, fights 'without malice' and with 'the best / Intentions' (VIII. 25), Arnold sees his martial spirit as the product of his deformity:

> Arnold: I ask not
>   For Valour, since Deformity is daring.
>   It is its essence to o'ertake mankind
>   By heart and soul, and make itself the equal –
>   Aye, the superior of the rest. There is
>   A spur in its halt movements, to become
>   All that the others cannot, in such things
>   As still are free to both, to compensate
>   For stepdame Nature's avarice at first.
>   They woo with fearless deeds the smiles of fortune,
>   And oft, like Timour the lame Tartar, win them.
>
>   (I. i. 312–22)

As the closing analogy with Tamburlaine implies, martial triumph becomes one way of compensating for deformity. Yet this compensation is achieved at a price. Arnold's assumption of the heroic form of Achilles is made possible through his Faustian pact with the Stranger, which is negotiated as follows:

> Arnold: But name your compact:
>   Must it be signed in blood?
> Stranger: Not in your own.
> Arnold: Whose blood then?
> Stranger: We will talk of that hereafter.
>   But I'll be moderate with you, for I see
>   Great things within you. You shall have no bond
>   But your own will, no contract save your deeds.
>   (I. i. 146–51)

Arnold's contract with Caesar is in effect signed in the blood of all those he kills during the siege of Rome. In this most bloody of all Byron's treatments of war, the achievement of fame through a martial career is represented as nothing less than a compact with the devil.

In all three poems, Byron develops his critique of military heroism through his use of secondary figures who oppose or parallel his protagonists. When Alp is suddenly and unexpectedly shot dead by a sniper in *The Siege*, the focus of the poem switches to Minotti, emphasizing his heroic defence, his motivation of revenge for the earlier death of his son in the wars, and his Byronic act of defiance in blowing up the garrison (ll. 722–73, 902–70). Similarly in *Don Juan*, the defence of a 'brave Tartar Khan' and his '*five* brave sons' is presented as a moment of genuine 'heroism' (VIII. 104–19). These episodes in the two sieges offer an alternative mode of heroism to those of the protagonists, one which is defensive and fought for familial reasons – the old mens' love for their sons – rather than for ideology, religion or glory.

In *Don Juan* and *The Deformed Transformed* Byron makes particular use of the *doppelgängers* in his investigation of the heroic. As has often been pointed out, in *Don Juan* John Johnson can be seen to function as Juan's *alter ego*, an older, more cynical version of the poem's hero. This is seen particularly strikingly in the siege cantos in which Juan's 'virgin valour' is contrasted with Johnson's more worldly-wise and 'cunning' approach to war (VIII. 35–6). If we are always aware of Juan as a literary figure in the text, a modern 'Achilles', in Johnson we are presented with a representation of a professional soldier, an Englishman who has fought for the Russians before, who knows when it is wise to retreat, who 'could kill his / Man quite as quietly as blows the Monsoon / Her steady breath' and who wants to make sure he is in on the 'first cut' of the plunder of the city (VIII. 35, 39, 101). Yet if Juan and Johnson present us with different types of heroes during the assault, the real Victor of Ismail is Suvorov, the general appointed to lead the siege. There is nothing traditionally heroic about this 'little-odd-old man, / Stript to his shirt' (VII. 49) who personally drills his troops and teaches them how to use bayonets. Yet it is this attention to detail combined with his lack of concern for life, 'deeming human clay but common dirt' (VII. 58) that leads to the taking of the city. In his efficiency, ruthlessness and willingness to expend any number of soldiers to achieve his aim, Suvorov, whose 'trade / Is butchery' (VII. 69) comes to represent both the professionalism and devastation of modern war.

In *The Deformed Transformed*, the critique of heroism is provided primarily through Caesar who, having adopted Arnold's discarded hunchback body, operates as an anti-heroic *doppelgänger* to the conquering soldier. The 'everlasting Sneerer' as Arnold calls him (I. ii. 117) offers an ongoing ironic and cynical commentary on the play's events that recalls the narrator of *Don Juan*. For example, his comment during the siege that 'I cannot find my hero' who is lost amidst the 'heroic crowd' (II. ii. 1–2) playfully echoes the opening of *Don Juan* – 'I want a hero' (I. 1) – and evokes the same issue of the devaluation of the heroic in a world in which heroism has become synonymous with butchery and heroes have become commonplace. Yet, unlike the narrator of *Don Juan* who has certain positive values, Caesar has no classical or historical agenda against which modern heroism can be judged. For him 'each Victor / From Macedon's boy / To each high Roman's picture / ... breathed to destroy' (I. i. 177–80). Julius Caesar becomes a focus for this critique of classical heroism, the stranger adopting the title Caesar because it is 'fittest for / The Devil in disguise' (I. i. 539–40: see also I. i. 204–6; I. ii. 76). Caesar provides a debunking commentary throughout the siege and, ultimately, in his cosmic vision, he sees 'Heroes and chiefs, the flowers of Adam's bastards!' as nothing more than 'poor puppets' and 'pismires' (I. ii. 315, 320, 326). *The Deformed Transformed* also uses Caesar to provide a critique of heroism through its dramatic action as well as through his commentary. Though unfinished, it appears from fragments and notes that Byron intended to continue the drama by setting up Caesar and Arnold as rivals for Olimpia's love, with the possibility of her preferring the intellectual, though hunchback figure of the former to the 'beautiful and brave' form of the latter (III. 53). If so, the dramatic action of the play would suggest that the qualities of intellect and wit are to be valued above those embodied by the 'Conqueror' (III. 92).

In all three poems there is a gendered element to this critique of martial heroism which draws on the traditional symbolism of the siege as the assault on the woman's body. In his excellent book *The Medieval Siege*, Malcolm Hebron quotes W. Calin's comment that 'the assault on a fortress is a fundamental image of love-conquest' (1997, p. 150). This is an idea which could be traced from Ovid's *Amores* through texts such as *Roman de la Rose* and *Henry V* to Richardson's *Clarissa*. Byron's use of this erotic symbolism is seen most clearly in *The Siege* in which Alp besieges Corinth not only out of revenge but because it contains Francesca: 'Within these walls a maid was pent / His hope would win' (ll. 136–7). Before his exile Alp and Francesca had been in love, but after he was forced to flee she accompanied her father, Minotti, when he became Governor of Corinth. Alp's assault on the city is an attempt to win her back:

> None, save thou and thine, I've sworn
> Shall be left upon the morn:
> But thee will I bear to a lovely spot,
> Where our hands shall be joined, and our sorrow forgot.
> There thou yet shalt be my bride,
> When once again I've quelled the pride
> Of Venice

(ll. 540–46)

During the first two sections of the poem (to follow McGann's structural outline) the fortress stands for the Venetian and patriarchal authority that Alp must overcome if he is to win Francesca from her father. But during the third part, Alp's encounter with the visionary Francesca, it also comes to represent her own resistance. Francesca is a deeply conventional figure who does not want to be rescued or liberated from her Venetian values and Christian faith but wants Alp to re-embrace them. The narrative of the poem is as critical in its treatment of Alps's attempted sexual conquest of Francesca as it is of the Turk's territorial imperialism: if the assault on Corinth leads only to the city's annihilation, Alp's attempts to gain Francesca lead only to his knowledge of her death and his own destruction.

The image of the siege is used throughout *Don Juan* to focus one of the poem's major themes, the equation of the martial and the erotic: Juan is trained to 'scale a fortress – or a nunnery', 'cunnus' becomes the best cause of war and reason to 'batter down a wall', and the women of society erect 'palisades' to protect their virtue (I. 38; IX. 56; XIV. 61). In the siege cantos, war and love provide not only the subject of the poem – 'Oh Love! O Glory!' (VII. 1) – but are deliberately conflated in Byron's invocation: '"Fierce loves and faithless wars" … I sing them both' (VII. 8). Parodying Spenser's *Faerie Queene*, 'Fierce warres and faithfull loues shall moralize my song' (Spenser, 1978, p. 39), Byron not only cynically updates Romance values, but suggests a likeness between the martial and the erotic in contemporary society. As in *The Siege*, Byron's critique of imperialism links sexual and territorial aggressiveness, in the figures of Catherine the Great with her excessive appetite for new lands and new lovers and Potemkin – 'a great thing in days / When homicide and harlotry made great' (VII. 37). At the level of action the poem links the martial and the erotic urges, as in the depiction of the death of the Tartar Khan's son (VIII. 111–16).

We might expect Juan, the naive, feminized hero and saviour of Leila, to be exempted from this linking of the martial with the erotic but his valour is frequently equated with his virility. This idea is first introduced by Johnson who, speaking within the context of Juan's adventures in the Harem, responds to Suvorov's questions as follows:

> 'And this young fellow – say what can he do?
> He with the beardless chin and garments torn?'
> 'Why, General, if he hath no greater fault
> In war than love, he had better lead the assault.'
> (VII. 62)

Despite appearances, Johnson suggests, Juan has proved himself 'man enough' to be in the front of the fight. This linking of Juan's erotic and military adventures is developed by the narrator, who states that:

> if he warr'd
> Or loved, it was with what we call 'the best
>   Intentions', which form all mankind's *trump card*,
> To be produced when brought up to the test.
> (VIII. 25)

In equating Juan's martial impulses with his erotic ones here, the narrator puts an interesting critical gloss on Juan's sexual adventures throughout the poem. He implies that just as Juan is a 'thing of impulse' in battle (VIII. 24), fighting for no reason, he is unthinking in his love affairs, following his instinct regardless of the consequences for himself or his lovers. Despite acting with 'the best intentions', Juan is presented as complicit in the savagery of Ismail and this is paralleled with the devastation caused by his romantic adventures to the lives of those involved, such as Donna Julia or Haidee. In a comment that recalls the original trajectory of Don Juan's career in which he is 'Sent to the devil' (I. 1), the narrator points out: ' 'Tis pity that [the best intentions] should pave Hell' (VIII. 25). In *Don Juan*, the manly instincts behind both 'Fierce loves and faithless wars' are destructive.

In *The Deformed Transformed*, Byron reworks the dramatic situations of *The Siege* and *Don Juan* to further explore the fortress–woman symbolism and the love–war analogy. Again, the play explicitly links the worlds of love and war – 'the world' is presented as 'thickest' where there is 'War / And Women in activity' and in taking an aristocratic title Arnold assumes an identity that equates the lover with the warrior: 'Count Arnold' will 'look well upon a billet-doux' and 'in an order for a battle-field' (I. i. 493–6, 544–6). Recalling Alp's erotic reasons for his assault on Corinth, in *The Deformed Transformed* the assault on Rome becomes focused on the figure of a single woman, Olimpia, who operates partly as a symbol for Rome itself. In an action that echoes Juan's saving of Leila, Olimpia is saved from the rampaging soldiers by Arnold, but as both Caesar and the soldiers observe, he has as little right to her as they have (II. iii. 73–4, 86–7). Their critique is developed by Olimpia who is equally suspicious of Arnold's actions, attempts suicide to avoid being taken by him and even when married to him withholds her love. Through its spirited and independent heroine who refuses to love the 'beautiful and brave' figure of Arnold, *The Deformed Transformed* offers a powerful critique of masculine physical force.

In all three texts, then, the erotic symbolism of the siege is used to reinforce the critique of military heroism. *The Siege* and *The Deformed Transformed* invoke the parallel of the taking of the town with the conquest of the woman only to undermine it. In both the use of force to attain either territory or the object of desire is destructive and self-defeating. If the symbolic dimensions of the siege present war as an assertion of masculinity, equating the martial and erotic instincts, *Don Juan* points to the devastation that results from the unthinking unleashing of these urges.

If Byron exploits the siege's erotic symbolism to add an extra dimension to his critique of warfare, he also explores its potential to act as an allegory for history itself. As Hebron has shown in *The Medieval Siege*, the siege is a form of action which particularly lends itself to the representations of supposed truths about history: it 'appears not only as an event in history but as the model for history itself' (1997, p. 90). In this model the siege becomes both a key event in the shaping of history – the end of a great city marking a decisive moment – and a symbol of history's shape. The shape given to history through the symbol of the siege usually takes two forms, either a cyclical and dynastic pattern of the rise and fall of great kingdoms or states in a secular vision or a teleological narrative working towards a given end in a divinely ordained scheme.

One instance in *Don Juan* provides an excellent example of Byron's allegorical use of the siege. When Ismail is entered, Byron makes the town, as opposed to the countryside, a symbol of civilization with a narrative structured by a sequence of sieges:

> The town was entered. Oh Eternity! –
>   'God made the country, and man made the town',
> So Cowper says – and I begin to be
>   Of his opinion, when I see cast down
> Rome, Babylon, Tyre, Carthage, Nineveh,
>   All walls men know, and many never known;
> And pondering on the present and the past,
> To deem the woods shall be our home at last: –
>   (VIII. 60).

The great sieges of the past here represent a model of history as a series of falls; the siege of Rome, the first example in this list, provides Byron with the subject for his dramatic exploration of the sacking of the city in *The Deformed Transformed*. In this play the great historic city of Rome becomes 'a theme for pity' (II. i. 62); a figure for this pattern of history as a sequence of falls. Throughout the play, Rome is presented as the 'World's Wonder' (II. i.

87), the high point of Western civilization, that is destroyed by the siege. But it also becomes symbolic of the world itself. Arnold and Caesar choose Rome as a place where they can observe 'the world ... in / Its workings' (I. i. 493–6). As McGann has pointed out, Bourbon's comment during the siege that 'the world is winning' (II. i. 154) means that the world is being won (Byron, 1980–93, vol. 6, p. 744). As these examples reveal, in the play the 'work' of the siege (I. ii. 36) becomes representative of all human activity; the siege operates as an image of 'Where the world / Is thickest' (I. i. 494).

However, Byron uses the dramatic structure of *The Deformed Transformed* to offer different perspectives on the siege of Rome. By contrasting different understandings of the event he reveals both the ambiguities in how history is understood in the play, its 'Gore and Glory' (II. ii. 12) and the ways in which models of history serve particular ideologies. For Arnold, Rome represents the centre of Christianity and the epitome of historical grandeur, symbolized for him by St Peters – 'the Giant / Abode of the true God' (I. ii. 37–8) – and the Colosseum – 'those scarce mortal arches, / Pile above pile of everlasting wall' (I. ii. 49–50). For him, modern Romans are innocent and undeserving of their impending destruction (I. ii. 90–93). Yet for Caesar, their deaths and the near total destruction of Rome are part of the cycle of history: Rome was founded in blood with Romulus's murder of Remus and its sacking will only replay the devastation it has itself caused:

> Rome's earliest cement
> Was brother's blood; and if its native blood
> Be spilt till the choked Tiber be as red
> As e'er 'twas yellow, it will never wear
> The deep hue of the Ocean and the Earth,
> Which the great robber sons of Fratricide
> Have made their never-ceasing scene of slaughter
> For ages.
>
> (I. ii. 83–91)

In this model, history is a 'reckless roundelay' like the soldiers' song (I. ii. 95), a repeated refrain of destruction. On the night before the assault, Bourbon presents his impending sacking of Rome in terms of this vision of history:

> The world's
> Great capital perchance is ours to-morrow.
> Through every change the seven-hilled city hath
> Retained her sway o'er nations, and the Caesars
> But yielded to the Alarics, the Alarics
> Unto the Pontiffs. Roman, Goth, or Priest,
> Still the world's masters! Civilized, Barbarian,
> Or Saintly, still the walls of Romulus
> Have been the Circus of an Empire. Well!
> 'Twas *their* turn – now 'tis ours; and let us hope
> That we will fight as well, and rule much better.
>
> (I. ii. 274–84)

Bourbon presents the history of Rome as cyclical, a series of 'turns'. Again, the symbolic dimensions of Rome are stressed: as McGann has observed, the reference to 'Circus' involves an 'allusion to the Circus Maximus of ancient Rome, suggesting the walls have always enclosed both a seat of power and an arena for the spectacles of history' (Byron, 1980–93, vol. 6, p. 743). But in his hope that he will 'rule much better', Bourbon, who shortly after describes Rome as his 'treasury' (I. ii. 303), shows how this model of history can be used to serve his own purpose and justify his invasion of Rome. A similar, self-justifying construction of history is given by the dying Lutheran soldier who represents the sacking of Rome not as an exercise in plunder (despite the looting of St Peters) but as part of a divine teleological scheme:

> 'Tis
> A glorious triumph still; proud Babylon's
> No more; the Harlot of the Seven Hills
> Hath changed her scarlet raiment for the sackcloth
> And ashes!
>
> (II. iii. 24–7)

These contrasting mortal understandings of history are also set against Caesar's cosmic vision in which he uses the image of the siege to represent the pattern and absurdity of human history:

> 'Twere a jest now
> To bring down [a star] amongst them, and set fire
> Unto their ant hill: how the pismires then
> Would scamper o'er the scalding soil, and, ceasing
> From tearing down each other's nests, pipe forth
> One universal orison! Ha! ha!
>
> (I. ii. 324–9)

The Deformed Transformed is primarily concerned with Western history and an action in which 'Christians war against Christ's shrine' (II. i. 39). In *The Siege* and *Don Juan*, Byron uses the siege to represent the cultural and religious clash of East and West. In *The Siege*, the martial encounter of the Venetians and the Turks replays on a national scale the action of *The Giaour* with its fight between the nameless Venetian aristocrat and the Turk Hassan for possession of Leila. Corinth takes the place of Leila as the figure for Greece, represented throughout the poem as a symbolic site: 'A fortress formed to Freedom's hands' (l. 4). But if Corinth, like Greece, remains a symbol of long-departed freedom (l. 333), it has also become a site of the struggle of history, of 'desperate conflict … / On that too long afflicted shore' (II. 983–4). Byron represents the present conflict as a clash of signs, the crescent against the cross (ll. 30, 93–4, 253, 672), making the two opposing forces representative of broader cultural and religious ideologies. As in *The Giaour*, the contest for possession of the desired object leads to its destruction along with all those involved, here represented in the staggering apocalyptic explosion of the magazine that annihilates the city and destroys the difference of the two opposing forces: 'Christians or Moslems, which be they?' (l. 996). As Watkins has pointed out, if the early parts of the poem seem to favour the Venetian cause, the concluding scenes reveal that Christianity is just as much an ideological weapon as Islam in the exercise of power and the fight for colonial gain (1987, pp. 114–17). Anticipating both Mary Shelley's *The Last Man* and his own visions of the end of the world in 'Darkness', Byron uses the action of the siege to dramatize a profoundly anti-imperial message. In *The Siege*, the destructive potential of war fought for conquest is so great it can bring about the end of the world.

In *Don Juan* Byron again uses the siege to represent the clash of East and West but reverses the situation of *The Siege* as if to emphasize the two powers' similarities in their 'mere lust of power' and warring for 'mere conquest' (VII. 40; VIII. 3); now it is the Russians who besiege the Turkish Fortress. As in *The Siege*, Byron uses the imagery of the crescent and the cross to symbolize the religious and ideological conflict:

> Ismail's no more! The crescent's silver bow
> Sunk, and the crimson cross glared o'er the field,
>   But red with no *redeeming* gore: the glow
> Of burning streets, like moonlight on the water,
> Was imaged back in blood, the sea of slaughter.
>   (VIII. 122)

The blood-besmeared cross, presiding over the scenes of devastations in Ismail, becomes a symbol of the perversion of Christianity, representing not Christ's redemptive sacrifice through crucifixion but the destructiveness of religiously endorsed imperialism.

It is through the figure of Suvorov that Byron represents the force of history as it enacts itself through war, and it is in response to this figure that he offers his own alternative vision of it. Suvorov is one of the 'great men' who makes history, possessed of 'the spirit of a single mind [that,] / Makes that of multitudes take one direction' (VII. 48). Yet Suvorov's ability to make history is the product of a limited understanding of it. Byron describes Suvorov's historical vision as follows:

> Suwarrow, – who but saw things in the gross,
>   Being much too gross to see them in detail,
> Who calculated life as so much dross,
>   And as the wind a widowed nation's wail,
> And cared as little for his army's loss
>   (So that their efforts should at length prevail)
> As wife and friends did for the boils of Job
>   (VII. 77)

The limitations of Suvorov's vision are re-enacted by 'History' itself, as described in the next canto:

> History can only take *things in the gross*;
>   But could we know them *in detail*, perchance
> In balancing the profit and the *loss*,
>   War's merit it by no means might enhance,
> To waste *so much* gold for a little *dross*
>   As hath been done, mere conquest to advance.
>   (VIII. 3; emphasis added)

It is against this 'gross' vision of history that Byron writes in *Don Juan*. Throughout the cantos, as here, he counters history's Suvorovian values by offering his reader an account 'in detail' of the true cost of war, redefining territory rather than human life as 'so much dross'.

Jerome McGann has convincingly argued that Byron's choice of the siege of Ismail at the moment he was reconceiving his poem was 'extremely important' because it gave his 'epic narrative a specific historical and socio-political dimension context at this juncture. Such a decision indicates the point and seriousness with which he undertook to rededicate *Don Juan* to its new beginnings – that is to say, to its new, self-conscious, and more comprehensive aspirations towards political and ideological commentary and commitment' (Byron, 1980–93, vol. 5, p. 718). This new seriousness and militancy is seen in the way Byron defines his own role as a poet against Suvorov's embodiment of history enacted through war. In his description of Suvorov's victorious message to the Empress Catherine, Byron presents him as 'a poet' who 'Could rhyme, like Nero, o'er a burning city' (VIII. 134 and note). Just as Suvorov's embodiment of history's 'gross' vision prompts Byron's alternative detailed vision, so the fatuous and inappropriate 'couplet' of this 'Russ so witty' stimulates Byron's climatic statement of his own poetic role in the siege cantos:

> He wrote this Polar melody, and set it,
>   Duly accompanied by shrieks and groans,
> Which few will sing, I trust, but none forget it –
>   For I will teach, if possible, the stones
> To rise against Earth's tyrants. Never let it
>   Be said that we still truckle unto thrones; –
> But ye – our children's children! think how we
> Showed *what things were* before the world was free!
>   (VIII. 135)

Defining his own song against Suvorov's 'Polar melody', Byron here gives his most ambitious statement of the function of his poetry and the part it will play in the bringing about of a 'free' world in the future. Adapting the 'things as they are' slogan and aesthetic of the English Jacobin novelists, Byron presents his role as an educative one that will lead to change: he will 'teach' by showing '*what things were*'. While Byron uses the disasters of the sieges of Corinth and Ismail to reveal the pattern of history as shaped by 'thrones, / And those that sate upon them' (VIII. 137) he presents as startlingly different the ultimate outcome of this pattern of history in the two texts. Despite its occasional wishing for 'better days' (l. 341), *The Siege* ends on an apocalyptic note of total destruction with no envisioning of a world after the apocalypse. By contrast, the account of the siege of Ismail in *Don Juan* concludes with a millennial vision of an ideal, republican world to come (VIII. 135–7). The factor that will make the difference between these two outcomes, Byron suggests, is his own insistence on singing the 'shrieks and groans' of war and his decision to 'throw away the scabbard' in the 'present clash of philosophy and tyranny' (1973–94, vol. 9, p. 191).

Bibliography

Boyd, E. F. (1958), *Byron's Don Juan: A Critical Study*, London: Routledge and Kegan Paul.

Byron, G. G., Lord (1973–94), ed. Marchand, L., *Byron's Letters and Journals*, 13 vols, London: John Murray.

————. (1980–93), ed. McGann, J. J., *Lord Byron, Complete Poetical Works*, 7 vols, Oxford: Clarendon Press.

————. (1986), ed. McGann, J. J., *Byron: The Oxford Authors*, Oxford and New York: Oxford University Press.

Chandler, D. G. (1993), *Dictionary of the Napoleonic Wars*, London: Greenhill Books.

Clarendon, E., Earl of (1888), ed. Dunn Macray, W., *The History of the Rebellion and Civil Wars in England, begun in the Year 1641*, 6 vols, Oxford: Clarendon Press.

Duffy, C. (1975), *Fire and Stone: The Science of Fortress Warfare, 1660–1860*, London and Vancouver: David and Charles.

Glover, M. (1979), *The Napoleonic Wars: 1792–1815, An Illustrated History*, London: Book Club Associates.

Hebron, M. (1997), *The Medieval Siege: Theme and Image in Middle English Romance*, Oxford: Clarendon Press.

Shakespeare, W. (1992), ed. Gurr, A., *King Henry V*, Cambridge: Cambridge University Press.

Shelley, M. (1994), ed. Paley, M. D. *The Last Man*, Oxford and New York: Oxford University Press.

Spenser, E. (1978), ed. Roche, T. P. and O'Donnell jr., C. P., *The Fairie Queene*, Harmondsworth: Penguin.

Vassallo, P.G. (1981), 'Casti's *Animali Parlanti*, the Italian Epic and *Don Juan*: The Poetry of Politics' in Stürzl, E. A. and Hogg, J. (eds), *Byron: Poetry and Politics: Seventh International Byron Symposium, Salzburg 1980*, Salzburg: Institut Für Anglistik und Amerikanistik.

Watkins, D. P. (1987), *Social Relations in Byron's Eastern Tales*, London and
     Toronto: Associated University Presses.
Webb, T. (1990), 'Byron and the heroic syllables', *Keats–Shelley Review*, 5,
     Autumn.

CHAPTER NINE

Leigh Hunt and the aesthetics of post-war liberalism

Philip Shaw

The intoxication of triumph

On 18 June 1815 the Allied Forces, under the command of the Duke of Wellington and Field Marshall Blücher, attained a decisive victory over the imperial army of Napoleon Bonaparte. The first 'Great War' of Europe had come to an end. From the outset, the Battle of Waterloo was depicted in British culture as an event of peerless, even transcendental significance. As Lord Castlereagh summarized in his address to Parliament, mere hours after the news of victory reached London:

> It was an achievement of such high-merit, of such pre-eminent impor-
> tance as had never perhaps graced the annals of this or any other country
> till now … it must be felt that it opened to our view a prospect so
> cheering, and so transcendentally bright, that no language could do
> justice to the feelings it must naturally inspire.
>
> (*Cobbett's Parliamentary Debates*, p. 980)

At the end of the year Castlereagh's hyperbole was reciprocated in the opening pages of the *Annual Register* with its description of Waterloo as the most important happening, not only of the year 1815 but indeed of the entire history of modern warfare. Language, it seems, could not do justice to the magnitude of this victory; Waterloo was too big or too sublime to lend itself to cognition. Somewhat perversely, therefore, the acknowledgement of this matchless victory was accompanied by a pervasive sense of uneasiness: a feeling of incredulity at the 'near run thing' that is history and a corresponding anxiety about the inability of language to substantiate its significance. True, the victory was 'brilliant and complete' – Scott described it as a 'grand finale' (1932–57, vol. 4, p. 74) and Wordsworth as 'this closing deed magnificent' ('Ode. 1815', l. 6)[1] – but the assertion of narrative closure masked an underlying feeling of incredulity, as if, to adopt a Hegelian figure, Waterloo had revealed itself as a moment of rupture rather than as an instance of self-definition.

A frequently cited passage from the diary of Haydon provides us with a clue to the structure of this feeling:

> How this Victory pursues my imagination! I read the Gazette four times
> without stopping … I read the Gazette again, the last thing [before]
> going to bed. I dreamt of it & was fighting & waking all night. I got up
> in the morning in a steam of intense feeling. I read the Gazette again,
> ordered a Courier for a month, called at a Confectioner's shop, & read
> all the Papers till my stomach aked. The more I think of this Glorious
> Conflict, the more I glory in it …

> There is something to me infinitely imposing, sublime, & overwhelming
> in the present degraded state of France & Napoleon Buonaparte …
> One's imagination is oppressed with [Waterloo's] brightness, one's fac-
> ulties dulled by [its] remembrance.
>
> (1960, vol. 1, pp. 458, 462–3)

Haydon's support for the victory is accompanied by a feeling of imaginative
instability – a feeling that was to haunt the painter for the remainder of his
life. In this case, to adopt a Kantian register, even as reason attempted to
qualify the sublime 'shock' of Wellington's triumph, every presentation of an
object designed to 'make visible' this absolute greatness would prove to be
painfully inadequate.

Yet despite the risible nature of Haydon's attempts to give form to Waterloo, the experience of radical negativity, of the radical inadequacy of all
phenomena to the Idea (Kant, 1989, pp. 106, 119), provided a useful support
for governmental attempts to elevate the battle to the status of a peerless
event, beyond the reach of public representation. In the state-sanctioned
press, victory over the detested French was presented as an incomparable
event in national history; its sublime import derived not from its tendency to
crush the imagination but, rather, from its ability to enhance a supersensible
Idea of collective genius. Thus, in Parliament, the concept of 'transcendent'
victory was deployed by Castlereagh as a means of silencing the opposition.
At the conclusion of the minister's vote of thanks Sir Francis Burdett stood
up to announce 'he thought it was not fair in the noble lord to hold such
language with respect to that which he knew such different opinions pre-
vailed'. Those who 'denied the justice of the case must either seem to acquiesce
in the description thus given of it, or be compelled to appear unwilling to
assent to the motion for a vote of thanks where it was so deemed' (*Cobbett's
Parliamentary Debates*, p. 988).

For those outside Parliament the disciplinary effect of this positioning, as
William Cobbett describes it in his 'historical notice' for Saturday 24 June, a
mere two days after the initial announcement, would prove to be overwhelm-
ing:[2]

> The *Times* newspaper says, that the campaign has opened with 'a great
> and glorious victory; that Bonaparte's reputation has been wrecked, and
> his last grand stake has been lost in this tremendous conflict; the fabric
> of rebellion is shaken to its base.' The *Morning Chronicle*, that pink of

hypocrisy, tells us, that it has been 'a brilliant and complete victory, which will for ever exalt the glory of the British name; that it is the grandest and most important victory ever obtained.' The *Courier*, in the height of its frenzy, declares, that there could not have been 'a greater victory in point of glory, more vital to the real interests and safety of Europe, big with more important political consequences'. – Of course, as this same *Courier* says, 'the city is a scene of complete confusion; business is entirely neglected; the immortal Wellington is the universal theme; the streets and Exchange are crowded to excess – all anxious to hear the details of the glorious victory obtained by our noble country-men.'

(p. 783)

It is worth looking at Cobbett's text in detail. As the passage proceeds, the radical's qualifying language – 'that pink of hypocrisy', 'in the height of its frenzy' – is overwhelmed by the inflationary rhetoric of greats, grands and grandest. The deployment of state-sanctioned hyperbole suggests the creation of a new and seemingly indisputable consensus, one that Cobbett, as a repre-sentative of the counter-public sphere, seems powerless to critique. By the time the final sentence is reached, the passage has turned into a performance of the very power that the radical must 'speak through'. What he is faced with, however, is the incontrovertible force of a 'universal theme' – in this case the sublime fiction of the 'immortal Wellington'.

Unlike Haydon, however, Cobbett's encounter with the textual sublime found its check a week later through the reimposition of the rational lan-guage of socio-economic critique. In the following passage it is satire that establishes a clearer perception of the effect of Waterloo:

MY LORD, – The intelligence of this grand event reached me on Satur-day last, and in the following manner. I had been out very early in the morning, and, in returning home to breakfast, I met a populous *gang of gypsies* … upon a nearer approach to them, I perceived the whole caravan decorated with *laurel*. The blackguard ruffians of men had *laurel* boughs in their hats; the nasty ferocious looking women, with pipes in their jaws, and straddling along like German trulls, had *laurel* leaves pinned against their sides. The poor assess, that went bending along beneath the burdens laid on them by their merciless masters, and that were quivering their skins to get the swarms of flies from those parts of their bodies which the wretched drivers had beaten raw, had their bridles and halters and pads stuck over with *laurel*. Somewhat staggered by this symbol of victory, I, hesitating what to do, passed the gang in silence, until I met an extra-ordinary ill-looking fellow, who, with two half-starved dogs, performed the office of rear-guard. I asked him the meaning of the laurel boughs and he informed me, that they were hoisted on account of the '*glorious victory obtained by the Duke of Wellington over Bony*;' that they were furnished them by a good gentle-man, *in a black coat and big white wig*, whose house they had passed the day before, between Andover and Botley, and who had given them several pots of ale, wherein to drink the Duke's health. – 'And, to be

sure,' added he, 'it is glorious news, and we may hope to see the gallon
loaf at a *grate* again, as 'twas in my old father's time.'

                                         (*Political Register*, 1 July 1815, p. 801)

To Cobbett, the victory of Waterloo stood for the triumph of the establishment over the people. Since a sizeable portion of that people had been
slaughtered in the campaign, the muted reception of the news amongst the
labouring classes seems entirely credible. In this aggressive parody, Cobbett
implies that to wear the laurel is to rescind one's claim to true nationality.
The gypsies are a feckless race, duped into acting the part of 'rude mechanicals'
by a ruthless aristocracy, intent on transforming the nation into a picturesque
backdrop as a distraction from the effects of invidious economic policies.

Despite Cobbett's best efforts, London at the close of June 1815 was
widely depicted as a scene of universal celebration. On the morning of the
22nd, Edward Smirke reported to Joseph Farington that he 'had been to the
Park, and found the People [we may speculate over the composition of this
group] everywhere rejoicing at the intelligence' (1922–28, vol. 3, p. 12). The
following evening illuminations, reminiscent of those seen the previous year,
appeared at the public offices and at houses on the north side of Oxford
Street. In such an atmosphere it was difficult to imagine any form of constructive questioning. As Wellington's sublime status was proclaimed over
London, literally so in the form of a giant illumination depicting a mounted
figure, sword held aloft, in pursuit of a fleeing dwarf, the best that confirmed
Napoleonists such as Whitbread, Byron and Charles Blagdon could register
was a form of blank astonishment (Lean, 1970, p. 108). In the *Examiner* for 2
July, Leigh Hunt offers the following reflection on the state of unreality: 'The
changes that now take place in the world have really more the look of
pageants or shews than anything else' (p. 430). Successive articles struggle to
get behind the 'vacant airiness' of the times: 'The daily events of our time are
like the wildest dreams of a century back. *Dartineuf*, the epicure … never had
a nightmare more oddly compounded in its visions' (2 July, p. 417). But, in
an 'age which has seen Kings and Emperors made and unmade … in the
twinkling of an eye, – and, in short, has been familiar with infernal machines,
massacres, revolutions, restorations, revolutions again, and all sorts of great
and remarkable changes' (30 July, p. 431), perhaps Hunt could be forgiven
for failing to perceive the distinction between the virtual and the actual. So
'oddly compounded' was the present state of affairs that all but the most
dogged ideologue would be disturbed, as Cobbett himself came to realize:
'While this delirium continues at its height, it would be useless in me to
attempt to bring the public back to reason … I might as well expect that a
drunken man could discuss, with calmness and perspicuity, an argument in
mathematics or moral philosophy' (*Political Register*, 24 June 1815, p. 783).
The effects of the 'great exhibition of political things', as Bagehot was to
express it, had permeated the whole of society (Sales, 1983, p. 117).

Before long, however, the great burst of intoxication was to be followed by a protracted period of depression. As Coleridge puts it, in the course of a discussion of the 'unprecedented prosperity' of the war years:

> It was one among the many anomalies of the late War, that it acted, after a few years, as a universal stimulant ... and to all this we must add a fact of the utmost importance in the present question, that the war did not, as was usually the case in former wars, die away into a long extended peace by gradual exhaustion and weariness on both sides, but *plunged* to its conclusion by a concentration, we might almost say, by a *spasm* of energy, and consequently by an *anticipation* of our resources ... The first intoxication of triumph having passed over, this our 'agony of glory,' was succeeded, of course, by a general stiffness and relaxation.
>
> (Coleridge, 1972, p. 159)

Compared with the present state of economic slump, the war years were charged with energy and vigour. The frankly sexual metaphors with which Coleridge invests his description are revealing, not only of the author's psychopathology (they draw, of course, on the rhetoric of addiction) but also of the extent to which Romantic discourse in general benefited from the culture of conflict. The radical Cobbett, with his hard-driving commitment to socio-economic analysis, would find plenty of resources for the continuation of his combat in other spheres. But for Hunt, the liberal and poet, the ensuing period of slackening would be experienced an altogether different level: '"Wonder," he writes, "grows unactive by excesse" ... For some years past we have been fed with astonishments; the last eighteen months have fairly surfeited us; and the consequence is, that one almost longs to be refreshed with common-places, or like Squire Western after dinner, to have some old tune played to us, familiar as our names, upon which our senses might go placidly to sleep' (*Examiner*, 2 July 1815, p. 417). Thus, where Coleridge raises a sublime elegy for the loss of mental (and economic) stimulation, and Cobbett wields renewed fire in political critique, Hunt seeks relief in a form of benevolent quietism.

But lest we be tempted into accusing Hunt of evading Waterloo, he is quick to point out the emotional reality that his post-prandial stupor obscures: 'We talk not this out of mere pleasantry. There is a feeling of seriousness which must relieve itself; and we feel too well, that when we jest at a season like the present, it is in an English and not a French spirit; – a gravity, which must be lightened, – not a levity, which can never be grave'. Hunt, in short, is appalled by the suffering of Waterloo: 'What are to us the common feelings of hostility or of triumph, when we think of all those men cut down with irreverent violence?' The passage goes on to decry the loss of 'those [who] have nothing about them, as it were, to warrant the seriousness of death, or to fit them with an answer for its sudden changes, – walking about in all the lighter susceptibilities of happiness' (*Examiner*, 2 July 1815, p. 417). This is a far cry from the agonistic poetics of Coleridge's victory or, one might add, the vulgar materialism of Cobbett. With its emphasis on inadequacy and incongruity it speaks rather of the stark reality of sudden death, unrelieved, we might say, by mythical truth or economic critique. This brings me to the central concern of this essay. Could it be that Hunt, alone amongst his contemporaries – with the possible exception of Lord Byron – comes closest to understanding what is really at stake in the representation of war: that the corporeal alteration demanded by conflict is exacted on the bodies of private individuals, not on the abstract or immortal body of the state? And, by extension, should we not see in Hunt's measuring of the pathos of Waterloo the promise of a humane alternative to the sublime poetics of official post-war culture? A means, even, of speaking against the social production of triumphalism? To address these questions we must look more closely at Hunt's political writings.

The gentle genius

Between 23 January 1814 and 13 August 1815 Hunt wrote a number of articles on the nature of education and its effects on the development of civilised society. They can be read, in part, as an instance of Hunt's ongoing dialogue with his fellow journalist and liberal thinker, William Hazlitt. Hunt's aim is to create a sociological context for Hazlitt's claim that man is 'naturally a lover of kings' (Hazlitt, 1932, vol. 7, p. 149). In Hunt's view, the origins of this passion are to be found in the current system of education which promotes 'admiration … for wars and soldiers in general':

> The causes of such men as Bonaparte are not to be found in the vicious-ness of the individual, nor are their effects to be done away by singling him out for abuse, to the impunity of all others resembling him. The causes are to be found … in that admiration which these very complain-ers persist in keeping up for their own purposes – in early habits of education – and in books of all kinds, school-books in particular, in Homer, in Plutarch, in Caesar, in Zenophon, and a hundred others which grave Christian divines continue to teach all over Europe. Edifying no doubt were the sermons which these reverend persons preached in all the churches in behalf of the Waterloo subscription, and grevous their denunciations against the lust of conquest and the unbridled violence of the passions … But what then? The next morning these very persons are as didactic as ever in behalf of the Caesars and Alexanders, are giving out themes upon the glories of the Greeks and Romans, and flogging their scholars or their children for not knowing that *virtue* in the Latin language is the same as *valour*.
>
> (*Examiner*, 13 August 1815, p. 512)

By maintaining a system of education which places so much value on mili-tary achievement, culture has produced, and will continue to produce,

Alexanders, Caesars and Napoleons. Hunt's thinking on the origins of violence owes a great deal to the utilitarian philosopher and pacifist Jeremy Bentham, whom Hunt quotes in his *Remarks On War and Military Statesmen*:

> Of all that is pernicious in admiration, the admiration of heroes is the most pernicious ... The crimes of heroes seem lost in the vastness of the field they occupy ... Is it that the magnitude of the evil is too gigantic for entrance? ... Our schoolmasters, and the immoral books they so often put into our hands, have inspired us with an affection for heroes; and the hero is more heroic in proportion to the numbers of the slain ... In that better and happier epoch, the wise and the good will be busied in hurling into oblivion, or dragging forth for exposure to universal ignominy and obloquy, many of the heads we deem *heroic*; while the true fame and the perdurable glories will be gathered around the creators and diffusers of happiness.
>
> (Hunt, 1923, pp. 693–4)

In their support of the march of progress, neither Hunt nor Bentham would have felt any sympathy with the Freudian view that we are mentally predisposed to invest our desires in heroes and hero-worship (Freud, 1985, pp. 85–8). Yet, when examining Bentham's prose one cannot help but notice the curious appeal of the martial: the 'evil' of war is vast and grand; peace is merely happy, it lacks gravity. When faced with the imaginative appeal of a Coriolanus, or for that matter a Wellington or Napoleon, how is society to overcome its love of war?

The force of this question is implicit in Hunt's ambiguous response to Byron's 'Ode to Napoleon Bonaparte', published in the *Examiner* for 17 April 1814. In the form in which it first appeared, the poem was printed alongside an article by Hunt criticizing those who wished to see the Emperor dead, the idea being that public execution or suicide would merely perpetuate the image of Napoleon as a tragic figure. Hunt, however, was sailing against the tide of public opinion. In different forms, and at different times, poets as diverse as Wordsworth, Southey, Coleridge and Shelley would argue for the death of the anti-hero, but the 'Ode' is noticeable for the way in which it incorporates this feeling into a sustained meditation on the suicidal impulse of classical tragedy. Where Satan 'in his fall preserved his pride, / And, if a mortal, had as proudly died' (Byron, 1980–93, vol. 3; ll. 143–4) or Caesar 'dared depart in utter scorn / Of men that such a yoke had borne' (ll. 59–61), Napoleon, by clinging to life, has manifestly failed to be himself with the result that a career that ought to be perceived as tragedy can now be seen only as banal: 'To think that God's fair world hath been / The footstool of a thing so mean' (ll. 80–81). Henceforth, as the appended epigram from Gibbon makes clear, human history enters the domain of ambiguity: 'By this shameful abdication, he protracted his life a few years, in a very ambiguous state, between an Emperor and an Exile, till –' As Byron curtailed quotation indicates, the 'till' of Napoleon awaits fulfilment in a future that may never arrive.

In a gesture comparable to the Hegelian critique of art, what Byron cannot accept in the Napoleonic story is an unforeseen reliance on the irrational and the incoherent. For Hegel, art is an insufficient ground for the realisation of self-consciousness; art can never be transparent in the way that pure thought requires (1989, pp. 375–6). Similarly, in Byron, what occurs in both the life and the poem (as if one could continue to speak of such a distinction) is a form of ambiguity that cannot be converted into profit. Through his failure to die, Napoleon becomes a 'nameless thing', present in the poem only as an unrelenting circuit of exchange: never quite Satan, never quite Caesar, and certainly not the father, Napoleon is everything and nothing by turns. His absence leaves only a 'ghastly gap', a hole in the real that no signifier can plug. Thus, as Jerome Christensen observes, the process of mourning, like the work of the poem, is indeterminate. This leaves the poet caught in the same circuit of exchange; Byron can no more 'kill' Napoleon than Napoleon can kill himself, for he recognises his alien-ness as internal to his own ego, as part of his own, empty relationship with himself (Christensen, 1993, p. 129).

Liberal politics, however, would not rest content with such a view: as the *Examiner* makes clear, there is more value to the cause of liberty in the life of a disgraced tyrant than in the death of a romantic hero (17 April 1814, pp. 258–9). Thus, where Byron, first in the 'Ode' and then in Canto III of *Childe Harold's Pilgrimage*, betrays his fascination with the great 'disturbers of mankind' such as Julius Caesar, Augustus and Napoleon, Hunt places more emphasis on the 'great names of wit and *utility*, – with Petrarch, Milton, Shakespeare, Columbus, Bacon, Newton, Voltaire' (*Examiner*, 23 January 1814, p. 49; my emphasis). The contest is between a tragic and a utilitarian view of history or, at another level, between the aristocratic ideals of the private sphere and the democratic principles of the public.

But even in Hunt, sacrifice is never far away. Although he does not espouse the official view of the Allied victory, he nevertheless ascribes to a form of sacrificial logic, utilitarianism, which enables him, despite his avowed hatred of war, to rationalize its long-term effects.[3] Thus, in an echo of his critique of Byron's 'Ode', he praises the 'perseverance of the British soldier' over the 'aristocratical ... enlargement ... upon the names of an individual ... It is truly the *English* who have won this great victory, and not one man of merit among them nor one hundred ... let us hope that good will come out of the evil, though of a different complexion from what the Allied Sovereigns may contemplate'. By replacing the name of Wellington – or, for that matter, the Napoleon that a Foxite Whig such as Byron might have preferred – with 'the solid strength of the [English] national character, and of [its] constitutional causes', Hunt can look forward to a period when 'civil power, intellect and rights of the community at large, [may] be heard and felt in their own cause' (*Examiner*, 25 June 1815, p. 413). Put another way, even as Hunt gestures to a time when the despotic simulacra of pageants and 'shews' will give way to the democratic reality of the ideal speech situation – the time, that is, when a poetics of justice and understanding replaces the degraded forms of tragedy and sensation – he is unable to imagine this community on the basis of anything other than a civil or military conflict.

This much is shown in Hunt's patriotic poem the 'National Song', first printed in the *Examiner* for 25 June 1815:

> Hail, England, dear England, true Queen of the West,
> With thy fair swelling bosom and ever-green vest,
> How nobly thou sitt'st in thine own steady light,
> On the left of thee Freedom, and Truth on the right,
> While the clouds, at thy smile, break apart, and turn bright!
> The Muses, full voiced, half encircle the seat,
> And Ocean comes kissing thy princely white feet.
>   All hail! all hail!
> All hail to the beauty, immortal and free,
> The only true goddess that rose from the sea.
> Warm-hearted, high-thoughted, what union is thine
> Of gentle affections and genius divine!
> Thy sons are true men, fit to battle with care;
> Thy daughters true women, home-loving and fair,
> With figures unequalled, and blushes as rare:
> E'en the ground takes a virtue, that's trodden by thee,
> And the slave, that but touches it, starts, and is free.
>   All hail! all hail!
> All hail, Queen of Queens, there's no monarch beside,
> But in ruling as thou dost, would double his pride.
>
>   (p. 415)

According to Hunt the poem was written, not as Cobbett thought 'in allusion' to Waterloo but rather 'in contemplation of that general character of the natives, which keeps our country altogether the freest in Europe, and is the true secret why it is victorious even when it may be on the best side of the question' (preface to 'Hail England', p. 415). It is important to keep in mind Hunt's own estimation of his poem, for it goes some way to correcting a persistent reading of the work which sees it as unambiguous 'celebration' of victory. In fact, the poem's real concern is with the recovery of the popular rights won during the Civil War and placed in contempt by the wanton authority of the Regency. Thus, Hunt's England is not the land of Castlereagh and Croker, but of Hampden, Milton and Sydney: 'On the left of thee Freedom, and Truth on the right'. As the poem proceeds the language struggles to contain its prior investment in internal strife by foregrounding images of national unity. Thus, in a return to the idealized merry England of the Elizabethan period, England becomes the 'true Queen of the West', at whose feet the unity 'Of *gentle* affections and genius divine' (my emphasis) is sanctioned by a universal 'hail!'. This 'gentle genius' is a figure not only of an anti-Romantic creative power (though, for

that matter, it is antipathetic towards virtually all hegemonic ideas of genius) it is also symptomatic of an attempt to redefine the political significance
of nationhood: away from the bellicose nationalism of the Regency and
towards a restitution of the unifying ideals of the Constitution, albeit filtered through the ubiquitous image of the hearth and home (l. 14). But, in a
sense, the poem falls victim to the author's indefatigable meliorism, rendering Waterloo the means by which Napoleon, the pervertor of liberty, is
thrown into 'obloquy'. Therefore, whilst it is possible to read the 'National
Song' as a fulsome response to the victory (and clearly this is what Cobbett
believed), to do so one must overlook not only the immediate context of
Hunt's politics, but also the extent to which the poem presents Waterloo as
an essential element in the *telos* of universal happiness.

Hunt is therefore brought to the uncomfortable recognition that violence
is indeed 'endemic to the very constitution of society'. The attempt to
assimilate the magnitude of Waterloo, to reduce it to a key stage in the
gradual progress of enlightened humanity brings with it a recollection of
the impossible origins of civilized society, the very 'thing' that Hegel, in
anticipation of Freud, warns against (1962, pp. 209–10; see Shapiro, 1997,
pp. 41–3). Yet despite the inevitable return of antagonism, Hunt's resistance
to the tragic origins of social relations is sufficiently robust to mark his
work out as a progressive response to the violent poetics of Hazlitt and
Byron. It might also be seen as a proleptic response to the agonistic labours
of Keats, who gave up his progress poem, *Hyperion*, to concentrate on the
fall of the reactionary Titans. Hunt, by eschewing sympathy with the dead
fathers, be they of the ancient or the new regime, could incorporate Waterloo into a larger pattern which embraced redemption and made the 'victory'
fortunate, *felix culpa*. Alone amongst his contemporaries, therefore, Hunt's
view of the conflict is, I would suggest, a potentially comic one; it is
certainly the sensibility that is most dominant in the narrative poems of this
period: from the Spenserian pathos of *The Story of Rimini* to the theatrical
extravagance of *The Descent of Liberty*. And it also explains, I think, why
his own poetic response would prove to be as inadequate as that of his
peers.

The poetics of peace: 'a common property in style'

At the beginning of 1814 Hunt announced that he was attempting a narrative
poem: 'a piece of some length, with which he is varying less agreeable
studies, and in which he would attempt to reduce to practice his own ideas of
what is natural in style, and of the various and legitimate harmony of the
English heroic' (Blunden, 1930, p. 79). The key words 'natural' and 'heroic'
signify Hunt's dialogue with his two most influential contemporaries:

Wordsworth and Byron. Hunt's critique of Byron is contained in the first separate edition of *The Feast of the Poets*, issued by James Cawthorn at around the same time as work was beginning on *The Story of Rimini*. In sufficiently lofty tones, the older poet urges the lord:

> to habituate his thoughts as much as possible to the company of those recorded spirits and lofty countenances of public virtue, which elevate an Englishman's recollections, and are the true household deities of his country – or to descend from my epithets, that he would study politics more and appear oftener in Parliament; – secondly, that he would study society, not only in its existing brilliance or its departed grandeur, but in those middle walks of life, where he may find the most cordial sum of his happiness, as well as the soundest concentration of its intelligence; – and thirdly, that though he has done a good deal already, he would consider what he has done as too full of promise to warrant his resorting at any time to a common property in style, or his use of such ordinary expedients in composition, as a diligent student of our great poets will be too proud to adopt.
>
> (Blunden, pp. 79–80)

Hunt's concerns are with the decidedly un-Byronic virtues of the English household, public 'utility' and the suburban middle class. Added to this is Byron's deleterious flirtation with the Tory poetics of Alexander Pope. Again, it is the singularity of this interest in the elevated and artificial that marks Byron out from the 'common property in style'. In Hunt's view, Byron's literary 'difference' is at odds with the democratic leanings of his politics. It is to the advantage of *Childe Harold's Pilgrimage* that the full implications of this advice were left unheeded. For Hunt, however, it would play a crucial role in the attempt to align political and aesthetic considerations.

A few attempts have been made to place *The Story of Rimini* in a political context. Most recently Vincent Newey has pointed out how, in revising Dante's story of the adulterous and incestuous love of Paulo and Francesca and their tragic deaths, 'Hunt shifts the emphasis over from sin to sympathy, and to the conditions that engendered the fatal act' (1995, p. 168). Again, the focus on the social causes of sin is on a par with the philosophy of cheerfulness with which Hunt responded to the Battle of Waterloo. As the 'Preface [to *Foliage*], Including Cursory Observations on Poetry and Cheerfulness' makes clear:

> my creed, I confess, is not only hopeful, but cheerful; and I would pick the best parts out of other creeds too, sure that I was right in what I believed or chose to fancy, in proportion as I did honour to the beauty of nature, and spread cheerfulness and a sense of justice among my fellow-creatures. It was in this spirit, though with a more serious aspect, that I wrote the *Story of Rimini*, the moral of which is not as some would wish it to be – unjust, and bigoted, and unhappy, sacrificing virtue under pretence of supporting it – but tolerant and reconciling, recommending men's minds to the *first* causes in misfortune, and to

> see the danger of confounding forms with justice, of setting authorized
> selfishness above the most natural impulses, and making guilt by mis-
> taking innocence.
>
> (Hunt, 1956, p. 132)

Hunt's 'first cause', as he writes in the preface to the collected edition of
1832, is not original sin but rather

> the habit of falsehood which pervade[s] society ... in other words, [it] is
> the great social mistake, still the commonest among us, arising from
> want of better knowledge, and producing endless mistake, confusion,
> and a war of principle, in all the relations of life. Society lied, and taught
> lying, with contradictory tenets that drove the habit to desperation.
>
> (Hunt, 1923, p. xxiv)

The poem, then, 'was intended to inculcate a sense not only of true justice but
also of possible improvement in human affairs, since suffering is shown to
arise out of "want of knowledge rather than defect of goodness"' (1923, p.
xxiv). And as in Rimini, so in Regency England. To those Tory Romantics
who attacked Hunt for daring to represent Napoleon as anything other than
Satanic, he replies: 'in all cases [to avoid aggrandizing Bonaparte] we pro-
tested ... against the causes that tend to produce such men, than the effects
which naturally result from them' (*Examiner*, 6 August 1815, p. 498). As the
behaviour of the protagonists in *The Story of Rimini* is shown to be the result
of a 'great social mistake', so Napoleon is depicted as the product of an
absolutist monarchy and a brutish educational system. Two somewhat pat
conclusions follow from this: firstly, there is nothing innately evil in the
poem or the world; secondly, the behaviour of fictional sinners and actual
tyrants is 'natural'. We can extend our sympathy because, in the end, for them
as for us, it is society that is at fault.

A more charitable view, however, would maintain that Hunt's comic purpose is vindicated by the extraordinarily pressing circumstances in which the
poem was composed. Yet the lines that follow, from canto IV, seem particularly repulsive when set in the context of Hunt's more sober response to the
slaughter of Waterloo:

> Sorrow, to him who has a true touched ear,
> Is but the discord of a warbling sphere,
> A lurking contrast, which though harsh it be,
> Distils the next note more deliciously.
> E'en tales like this, founded on real woe,
> From bitter seed to balmy fruitage grow:
> The woe was earthly, fugitive, is past;
> The song that sweetens it, may always last.
> And even they, whose shattered hearts and frames
> Make them unhappiest of poetic names,
> What are they, if they know their calling high,
> But crushed perfumes, exhaling to the sky?

Or weeping clouds, that but a while are seen,
Yet keep the earth they haste to, bright and green?
(ll. 17–30)

If Waterloo was to be assimilated within the journalism under the utilitarian creed of the greatest happiness for the greatest number, its suffering is transmuted in the poetry 'as the discord of a warbling sphere / A lurking contrast'. By allowing the pastoral rhetoric of 'balmy fruitage', 'crushed perfumes' and 'weeping clouds' to overlay the 'shattered ... frames' of earthly woe, Hunt falls short of the ironic contrasts of Byron's treatment of the battle (see Wilson, 1992); moreover, he risks collapsing the distinction between an aesthetic view and a political one.

From a certain point of view, therefore, there is something troubling about Hunt's transumption of social space in the name of 'feary' or 'mental space' (Coleridge, 1836–39, vol. 1, p. 94), but I think there is a way of addressing this tendency in Hunt without lapsing into the dreary predictability of sociological critique. In both cases, Hunt falls back on the cognitive pleasures of the 'happy prison' (Brombert, 1973); the compensatory strategy that allows the poet to find satisfaction in deprivation. In the third canto of *The Story of Rimini* there is the example of the enchanted pavilion where Paulo and Francesca make love:

a delicious sight,
Small, marble, well-proportioned, mellowy white
With yellow vine-leaves sprinkled, – but no more, –
And a young orange either side the door.
The door was to the wood, forward, and square,
The rest was domed at top, and circular;
And through the dome the only light came in,
Tinged, as it entered, with the vine-leaves thin.
(ll. 448–55)

The sexual topos of this 'delicious sight', with its 'young orange' and domed ceiling is a form of the *tromp l'oeil* with which Hunt transformed the Horsemonger gaol. But it also looks out to the comparison between the 'delicious dreaming' of the poet and the arrested progress of the conqueror (see the *Examiner*, 17 April 1814, p. 243): both '[a] Place of nestling green, for poets made' (l. 430) and 'a beauteous piece of ancient skill, / Spared from the rage of war' (l. 457). In terms of the language of orality, Napoleon is identified with the exponential logic of greed, Hunt with the suspended delights of savouring. The use of such language cannot be denounced simply as mawkish or infelicitous, still less can it be seen as a negation of politics; it points rather to a desire to refashion the political sphere in terms other than those of master and slave, conqueror and conquered. By focusing on the pleasures of repose, Hunt is asking us to reconsider the Romantic investment in sacrifice, tragedy and the Napoleonic will. The contrast, if you like, is between the gentle armour of the suburbanite and the executive strength of the conqueror: between Hunt and Byron, Captain Pen and Captain Sword.

Hunt's anti-Napoleonic imagination is perhaps best illustrated in the conclusion of his 'Ode for the Spring of 1814', first published in the *Examiner*, 17 April 1814 and later reprinted in the *Descent of Liberty: A Mask*. Inspired by the fall of Napoleon, the poem, as Edmund Blunden points out, 'is an idealisation of the world's political drama, and at the same time the dream and fancied escape of a captive, whose wall'

> If wrongly round him, like a curtain flies;
> The green and laughing world he sees,
> Waters, and plains, and waving trees
> (ll. 62–4; cited in Blunden, p. 82)

As well as contributing to the developing significance of the happy-prison motif, the lines also look forward to their place in the *Descent of Liberty*, the work in which Hunt comes closest, I feel, to marking his difference from Byron and, as we shall see, Wordsworth.

In form, *The Descent of Liberty* is an experiment with the mask tradition of Beaumont, Carew and Browne. It departs from this tradition, however, in signalling and making a virtue of its unperformability: 'It may seem strange to some readers, that a drama professedly full of machinery should be written exclusively for the closet ... In a word ... the present piece was written to indulge the imagination of one who could realize no sights for himself' (Hunt, 1950, pp. 116–33). These words are strangely suggestive for, in a sense, they comment on the unrealizable nature of the liberal project itself. As Hazlitt might have put it, in both its literary and political forms, liberty is present, if at all, only in the theatre of the mind: 'who ... does not feel that he can raise much better pictures in his own mind than he finds in the theatre?' By virtue of its resistance to the Burkean forms of the sublime, the language of liberty is denied access to the real; it becomes, as Hunt inadvertently admits, a liberty only of poetic licence; a 'mixed drama ... essentially given up to the fancy' where the 'violation of rules and probabilities' is symptomatic of the subordinate status of liberalism (1950, pp. 131–2).

That Hunt would disagree with this estimation of his work is made clear in his own response to the Burkean language of power. Reviewing Hazlitt's *Plain Speaker*, Hunt points to the dangers of conflating rhetorical force and political truth: 'we suspect even Mr. Hazlitt's love of power to be more on a par with his love of truth than he may chuse to discover ... he has a real reverence for those very sophistications and petty lordly authorities which we are called upon, in his pages, at once to think great and little' (1956, p. 244). The same deconstructive principle that undoes the binary opposition of truth and power in the critic's appreciation of Burke, is also shown to be at work in Hazlitt's stubborn allegiance to Napoleon, the power of action to Burke's power of thought: 'Very foolish were they who put any faith in the Allies; but the interests of freedom were not to be identified with those of Bonaparte, who was a turncoat from the cause'. Here, once again, is the reactive force that impels Hunt's critique of the alignment of truth and power: 'Freedom will have gained more ... from the weakness of the lesser men than it would from the strength of the greater one' (p. 253).

The problem for Hunt, as the masque makes clear, is that liberty, unlike Napoleon, is real only at the level of allegorical representation. In a sense, it has to be, for if liberty is to remain aloof from the strength of great men it can only exist in the imaginary space of literature. Here at least, music, poetry and painting can be shown to effect change without acceding to the power of the sublime, the rhetorical conduit between the world of fiction and the world of reality. The retrenchment from political actuality is further accentuated by the predominance of the pastoral-romance motif. Just as the 'Ode' closes with the image of a rejuvenated 'green and laughing world', so the play opens with the idealizing vision of 'the flowering Spring' where liberty 'lead[s] a lovelier period for mankind' ('Prologue', ll. 35–8). In the first scene the setting for the reception of liberty is suitably bucolic: as eloquent shepherds discourse on the 'gloomy weight' of war that 'Has visited so long our weary land' 'like a disease of nature' (ll. 34–6), pan pipes herald the dawning of 'a new freshness' (l. 77). At first this is taken to be a trick of the 'Enchanter' Napoleon, but as the music reaches a climax it is shown to be the work of spirits, 'Couriers of Liberty' who urge the shepherds to rejoice. In this adaptation of the faery land of Shakespeare's *Tempest*, nature is so full of 'promise' that it can even restore the dead; as the paternalistic Eunomus, a version of Prospero, discovers when he is reunited with his missing son in scene three: ''Tis he! 'Tis he! / Risen out of buried thousands to come back to us!' (ll. 186–7).

Hunt's better purpose, then, is not to bemoan the suffering of war so much as to celebrate 'The pleasures that perfect victorious times' (III, 414). It is an optimistic philosophy, one that allows him to usher in the allegorical forms of the allied powers, figured in this case as harbingers of liberty rather than as agents of oppression (the masque was completed before the Congress of Vienna). Thus, in the drama's most didactic moment the leaders of nations are instructed in the ways of constitutional freedom. Tellingly, their state is 'well-earned'; a gift bestowed by the people rather than by divine right (III. 277).

Liberalism's endless summer

But if social amelioration is the guiding ethos of the work, it is Hunt's contest with Wordsworth that provides its literary-critical interest. The issue turns on the question of who, in the wake of Waterloo, is God's true 'daughter'. For

Wordsworth (1989), in a statement that was to prove decisive in promoting the idea of the poet's apostasy, it is 'Carnage' ('Thanksgiving Ode', ll. 278–82). For Hunt, it is 'Liberty'. Hazlitt recognized in this phrase the elements of Wordsworth's aristocratical power, the Burkean flavour that prevents him from speaking in the name of truth, utility and freedom; once again, 'Poetry is right-royal ... It has its alters, sacrifices, human sacrifices' (1932, vol. 4, p. 214). By contrast, as I have argued, Hunt aims for the goodness and proportion of a republican poetics. What Hunt's relationship with Wordsworth reveals is both the weakness and the strength of this ambition.

Before 'Carnage' entered the public sphere, two sonnets by Wordsworth were to appear in the *Examiner*. 'How clear, how keen, how marvellously bright' was published on 28 January 1816; 'While not a leaf seems faded' a fortnight later. On 18 February, however, Wordsworth became the subject of an indignant leader article by Hunt: 'Heaven made a Party to Earthly Disputes – Mr. Wordsworth's Sonnets on Waterloo'. The sonnets, 'Inscription for a National Monument, in Commemoration of the Battle of Waterloo', 'Occasioned by the Same Battle' and the 'Siege of Vienna Raised by John Sobieska' were printed in John Scott's *Champion*. More overtly political than the poems offered to the *Examiner*, they raised the question of the relation between Wordsworth's genius and his political unreliability; a question that, for Hunt, could be extended to the poet's treatment of his great precursor, John Milton. Specifically, Hunt's attack centred on the sonnet 'Occasioned by the Same Battle' in which the Wordsworthian 'Bard' claims the sole power of 'comprehending this victory sublime'. Elsewhere I have argued that Wordsworth's most strident celebration of 'Victory Sublime' hides an agonistic, self-conscious purpose (Shaw, 1995), but for Hunt, writing in the wake of Waterloo, the lines were proof enough that Wordsworth had perverted the true spirit of Milton: 'We hope to see many more of Mr. Wordsworth's sonnets, but shall be glad to find them, like his best ones, less Miltonic in one respect, and more so in another' (*Examiner*, 18 February 1816, p. 98).

In what sense, then, did Hunt wish that Wordsworth would be more Miltonic? To approach this question let us return to a poetic distinction we noted earlier. In his article on pacifist education, it is interesting to note that Hunt does not include Homer or Virgil in the role of 'wit and utility'. Unlike, say, Byron and Keats who give (qualified) assent to the traditional Virgilian path from pastoral to epic, Hunt seems doggedly attached to the virtues of the lesser forms, specifically to the sonnet, the bucolic and the romance. Indeed, even Hunt's praise of Milton is qualified by his '"secret preference for his minor poems" over *Paradise Lost*, which in spite of its poetic intensity and its superlative imagination and musical qualities, everywhere conveys a "certain oppressiveness of ambition and conscious power"' (1956, p. 23). I want to put this criticism in the context of Hunt's republicanism. For whilst it may be the case that, at one level, he writes in support of the democratic values of the progress poem, at another he seems more perversely attracted to the regressive lyricism of the Cavaliers, to Suckling and Carew rather than to Dante and Milton. Thus, in *Imagination and Fancy*, even as Hunt claims that Keats's 'greatest poetry' is to be found in the forward-looking *Hyperion*, he makes the decision to omit all but a small portion of this poem in favour of generous selections from the odes, romances, sonnets and lyrics. Although Hunt would go on to qualify this preference by raising the imagination above the fancy, in terms of poetic achievement, he would nevertheless remain paradoxically committed to the 'values' of the superficial, the picturesque and the beautiful. Literature which indulged these states, as a recent editor of Hunt puts it, offered 'an escape ... in time of trouble'. What the poet and critic desired, therefore, whether the subject be the fall of man or the fall of Napoleon, was 'not an excitement, but a balm', not the sublime lament but the reverie (Hunt, 1956, p. 27).

The Descent of Liberty is, of course, a development of the masque tradition in which *Comus* is inscribed. A product of 'the exuberance of an age of real poets', its wit and extravagance is contrasted with the Puritan ideology that impels the 'oppressiveness' of *Paradise Lost*; it is the same oppressiveness that stands behind the poet of 'Occasioned by the same Battle'. A throw-away comment of Wordsworth's in a letter to Haydon gives a sense of what is at stake in the contest between the poets. A few months before Wordsworth composed his Waterloo sonnets, he received from Hunt a copy of *The Descent of Liberty*. This is his judgement on it: '[Hunt's] Mask has been read with great pleasure by my Wife and her Sisters under this peaceful Roof. They commend the style in strong terms; and though it would not become *me* to say that their taste is correct, I have often witnessed with pleasure and an entire sympathy, the disgust with which in this particular they are affected by the main part of contemporary productions' (1970, vol. 2, p. 273). The *Descent*, in other words, is a work that should be considered by women, not poets. In this we can detect the gendered distinction between Fancy and Imagination that Wordsworth had introduced in his 1815 'Preface': Imagination is 'conscious of an indestructible dominion' (recall Hunt's 'conscious power'), Fancy is 'given to quicken and beguile the temporal part of our nature'. In Wordsworth's view, therefore, Hunt's work belongs to the sphere of the 'playful', the 'amusing' and the 'tender'; above all, it is 'fleeting': it will not 'incite ... and support the eternal' (1974, vol. 3, pp. 36–7).

Hunt himself admits as much in the preface to the masque, but his defence of fancy is based on the premise that such works combine poetic licence with 'primitive feelings, and natural language' (1950, p. 119). This is a refashioning of the ideas expressed in the preface to *Lyrical Ballads*, so that natural language encompasses not only the austere power of *Paradise Lost* but also the 'sports and extravagances' of *Comus* (p. 130). The preface to *The Descent of Liberty* can be read as an earnest attempt to unify two competing sides of

Milton: the sententious bard who spoke contemptuously of 'Mixed Dance, or wanton Mask' and the delightful poet who counted '"Mask and antique Pageantry" among the rational pleasures of cheerfulness' (pp. 119–30, *passim*). In considering Hunt's own experiments with the sonnet form, it is possible to trace the rudiments of an aesthetic entirely opposed to the draconian sublimity invoked by the later Wordsworth. With the Gothic grandeur of Milton reduced to the domestic simplicity of the leafy Hampstead suburb, Hunt is able to begin the process of pacifying the high Romantic imagination. Within this space, as Stuart Curran argues, even the 'brave Kosciusko' is 'transformed from Coleridge's martial hero, as one who, faced with swearing allegiance to Napoleon or the Holy Alliance, forswears both, substitutes rhymes (spade for blade), and heroically tends to his garden: both warrior and nature are quietly methodized' (1986, p. 50). The 'stormier fields' of romantic excess, in other words, are replaced by the 'calm green amplitudes' of peace and humanity (Hunt, 1923, p. 239); a figure for the very forms of liberal understanding that Wordsworth, in his bid to establish himself as a cultural authority, has betrayed.

Wordsworth may well have read some of Hunt's sonnets. It is therefore somewhat puzzling that Hunt thought well enough of Wordsworth's own sonnets to include them in the *Examiner*, for in many ways they form an implicit critique of the Miltonic ideal he sought to promote. Let us define this in summary as the pastoral idyll of *Comus* opposed to the martial shadings of Pandemonium. Where Wordsworth endorses the tragic cycle of death and renewal, Hunt looks forward to a period of pastoral stasis:

> And all this burst of out-o'-door enjoyment,
> Just like a new creation, – Spring and Summer
> Married, and Winter dead to be no more
> *(The Descent of Liberty*, III, 153–4)

I would suggest that what would be life for Hunt would be death for Wordsworth, and that the sense of this difference is what impels the significance of his sonnets.

The first poem to be published in the *Examiner* is the serene 'How clear, how keen, how marvellously bright'. The poem is a meditation on ideas of permanence and tranquillity, focused on the sight of a 'distant mountain's head', its snowy beauty 'destined to endure' (ll. 2, 11). But lest we be tempted into reading this quotidian scene as a figure for the imagination, the couplet is quick to remind us that it is in fact a work of fancy; the snow will live 'Through all vicissitudes, till genial Spring / Has filled the laughing vales with welcome flowers'. Winter and spring, that is, are part of a wider pattern of 'multitude, / With order and relation' (ll. 12–14). The seasons are transitory and therefore fanciful, but in succeeding to each other they signify the imaginative presence of 'Composure and ennobling harmony' (*The Prelude*, 1805, VII, 741; Wordsworth, 1984).

The political context of this poem becomes clearer when one considers its sequel, 'While not a leaf seems faded'. Here the poet draws upon the image of the 'ripening harvest':

> this nipping air,
> Sent from some distant clime where Winter wields
> His icy scimitar, a foretaste yields
> Of bitter change – and bids the flowers beware;
> And whispers to the silent birds, 'Prepare
> Against the threatening Foe your trustiest shields'
>
> (ll. 3–8)

As the sonnet continues it is evident that Wordsworth has something other than natural processes in mind. Just as the masque contains its reference to the defeat of Napoleon in the bitter cold of the Russian winter, so Wordsworth presents his winter as both dirge and promise:

> For me, who under kindlier laws belong
> To Nature's tuneful quire, this rustling dry
> Through leaves yet green, and yon crystal-line sky,
> Announce a season potent to renew,
> 'Mid frost and snow, the instinctive joys of song, –
> And nobler cares than listless summer knew.
>
> (ll. 9–14)

On one level the sonnet can be read as a song of literary potency, a prayer for the quickening of poetic powers – the production of new 'leaves' – after the listlessness of summer. On another it becomes a homage to the natural force that defeated the advance of the conqueror. Still further it becomes a slight at Hunt's state of perpetual peace. When faced with the comfortable encroachment of liberalism's endless summer, Wordsworth counters with the reassertion of death and renewal. By a strange twist, then, it is Wordsworth rather than Hunt who pre-empts the Shelley of 'Ode to the West Wind'. But Wordsworth's version of the death-as-quickening trope is set firmly within a loyalist rather than a republican tradition, a point that is substantiated when we consider that the sonnets were eventually included in the *Thanksgiving* volume.

But lest we be tempted into dispensing with Hunt let us return to the journalism that spurred the poetic contest. For all the talk of the aesthetic weakness of liberalism, Hunt's literary criticism, I would suggest, is as stridently materialist as anything published in the wake of *The Romantic Ideology*. In his analysis of the 'Siege of Vienna Raised by John Sobieska. February, 1816', for instance, Hunt points to the significance of the poem's concluding line with its reference to 'Filicaia's Canzone, addressed to John Sobieska, King of Poland, upon his raising the siege of Vienna' (Wordsworth, 1989, p. 173). In the first place, Filicaia was a Catholic poet which means, somewhat unfortunately, that 'Mr Wordsworth is longing for the flame that inspired Catholic superstition'. Secondly, Sobieska, unlike the newly restored monarchs of post-war Europe, was an elected king. 'In short, Filicaia, though a devotee, and inclined well enough to praise a despotic sovereign where religion was concerned, was also a lover of freedom in the abstract' (*Examiner*, 18 February, p. 98). Hunt concludes that Wordsworth has missed the point of his own citation: Filicaia was the poet of Italian independence and would certainly have raised his voice against the restoration of despotic monarchies in Italy, Poland and Spain – just as, by extension, Milton would have. In Hunt's view, the bard of the English revolution has more in common with the republican poetics of Tasso, Ariosto and Petrarch, than Wordsworth is willing to admit. This criticism is intended as an ironic barb at the poet's political stance, but on a formal level it also gestures towards the discovery of a nascent poetical sensibility, one that is opposed to the Gothic chiaroscuro displayed elsewhere in the *Thanksgiving* volume.

Where, then, does this leave the relationship between liberal poetics and politics? In moving between the roles of poet, literary reviewer and political commentator, Hunt foregrounds the intertwining of the aesthetic and the political. But his particular contribution, in my view, is to emphasize the irreconcilability of a progressive politics with a sublime or tragic view of art. For the liberal imagination to realize itself outside the Arcadian vistas of Hampstead and Rimini, it must accede to the political real. This, however, would imply a recourse to either the violent poetics of Byron and Wordsworth – the very discourse that liberalism, in the name of truth, utility, justice and proportion would eschew – or the disputatious rhetoric of Cobbett. However, that Cobbett provides a materialist solution to this dilemma in no way detracts from Hunt's real achievement, which is to demonstrate the yearning gulf between political actuality and imaginative transformation. It is fitting, therefore, that Hunt's final statement on the miseries of war, *Captain Sword and Captain Pen* (1835), should derive its power from the trope of allegory, a figure that, in Paul de Man's view, renounces 'the nostalgia and the desire to coincide' (1983, p. 207). There is not the space in this essay to consider the poem in detail. It is enough to say that Captain Pen, the archetype of the gentle genius, armed only with 'a letter calm and mild' defeats Captain Sword in bloodless combat. After facing up to the horrors of war (the poem is unstinting in its depiction of the devastation of civilian communities), and after satirizing the efforts of victorious states to secure sublime consensus, the reader is invited to contemplate the birth of a golden age of peace and prosperity. Thus where Byron, in *Don Juan*, qualifies the prospect of social redemption, Hunt ends by embracing the possibility of a millennial transformation; the satire that marks the poem out as a powerful riposte to the military governance of Britain is suspended for an ennobling vision of unity and synthesis.

As the 'new-faced world' is 'born', so closes the reign of Captain Sword; the oppressive hegemony of the military state disappears with 'the level[ing] dawn' of civil polity (VI, 489–517, *passim*). Yet it is an unintentional irony of the piece that the birth of the new age can be imagined only through an evocation of the primal violence that resides at the core of civic society. It is the symbolic potential of poetic language that reveals Hunt's underlying fascination:

> A sound as of cities, and sound as of swords,
> Sharpening, and solemn, and terrible words,
> And laughter as solemn, and thunderous drumming,
> A tread as if all the world were coming.
>   (V, 487–500)

The (s)word that Captain Pen releases is as violent, in its way, as the sword wielded by his opponent. For, as the combat winds down, its descent is in tune with the rhythms of sex, 'Such as Love knows, when his tumults cease' (l. 507). The clash of tumult and calm, man and nature, pastoral and sublime; Hunt, like the author of 'Why War?' (Freud, 1985, pp. 341–62), cannot conceive of peace on any other terms.

A truly liberal aesthetic, therefore, must struggle against the imaginative legacy of high Romanticism. Like the mighty instruments of Hunt's late poem, 'The Trumpets of Dollkarnein', Romantic verse, at its best, is 'stern' and 'imperious' (ll. 28–30), and when the sound is stopped by 'Nature's least and gentlest courses' (l. 68) we may well 'smile' (l. 70) but there is also disappointment that the 'great' and 'stormy music' has been 'stilled' (l. 63).

Notes

An earlier version of this essay first appeared as 'Leigh Hunt and the Battle of Waterloo: British Culture in Transition, 1815–1816' in Baschiera, S. D. and Everson, J. (eds), *Scenes of Change: Studies in Cultural Transition* Pisa: Edizioni Ets.

1. Unless otherwise stated all quotations from Wordsworth's poetry will be taken from Wordsworth, 1989.
2. Within opposition circles, the news of the Allied victory was greeted with a mixture of bafflement, incredulity and despair. Byron was 'damned sorry for it'; Thelwall and Hazlitt were reportedly 'stunned' (Lean, 1970, p. 108). Not even Godwin, so vigorous in his warnings against the impending conflict, could inform *Mandeville* with anything approaching a coherent critical view (Crabbe Robinson, 1872, vol. 2, pp. 256–7).
3. Bentham's *Plan for an Universal and Perpetual Peace*, though written in 1789, was not published until 1843. Hunt, however, like many pacificists writing in the wake of Waterloo, was well aware of the congruence of humanitarian and utilitarian arguments. See Ceadal, 1996, pp. 67–8, 238–45.

Bibliography

*The Annual Register or a View of the History, Politics and Literature for the
    Year 1815* (1816), London: Baldwin, Craddock and Joy.
Blunden, E. (1930), *Leigh Hunt: A Biography*, London: Cobden-Sanderson
    Press.
Brombert, V. (1973), 'The Happy Prison: A Recurring Romantic Metaphor',
    in Hartman, G. and Thorburn, D. (eds), *Romanticism: Vistas, Instances,
    Continuities*, Ithaca: Cornell University Press, pp. 52–70.
Byron, G. G., Lord   (1980–93), ed. McGann, J. J., *Lord Byron, Complete
    Poetical Works*, 7 vols, Oxford: Oxford University Press.
Ceadal, M. (1996), *The Origins of War Prevention: The British Peace Move-
    ment and International Relations, 1730–1854*, Oxford: Clarendon Press.
Christensen, J. (1993*), Lord Byron's Strength: Romantic Writing and Com-
    mercial Society*, Baltimore: Johns Hopkins University Press.
Cobbett's Parliamentary Debates (1815), vol. 31 (2 May–12 July), London:
    Hansard.
Coleridge, S. T. (1836–9), ed. Coleridge, H. N., *The Literary Remains of
    Samuel Taylor Coleridge*, 2 vols, London: Pickering.
————. (1972), ed. White, R. J., *Lay Sermons*, in *The Collected Works of
    Samuel Taylor Coleridge*, vol. 6, London: Routledge and Kegan Paul;
    Princeton: Princeton University Press.
Crabbe Robinson, H. (1872), ed. Sadler, T. H., *The Diary, Reminiscences,
    and Correspondence of Henry Crabbe Robinson*, 2 vols, London and New
    York: Macmillan.
Curran, S. (1986), *Poetic Form and British Romanticism*, New York and
    Oxford: Oxford University Press.
De Man, P. (1983), *Blindness and Insight: Essays in the Rhetoric of Contem-
    porary Criticism*, London: Methuen.
The *Examiner* (1814–17), London.
Farington, J. (1922–28), ed. Greig, J., *The Farington Diary*, 8 vols, London:
    Hutchinson.
Freud, S. (1985), ed. Dickson, A., *Civilization, Society and Religion: Group
    Psychology, Civilization and its Discontents and Other Works, The Pelican
    Freud Library, vol. 12*, Harmondsworth: Penguin.
Haydon, B. R. (1960), ed. Pope, W. B., *The Diary of Benjamin Robert
    Haydon*, 2 vols, Cambridge, Mass.: Harvard University Press.
Hazlitt, W. (1932), ed. Howe, P. P., *The Complete Works of William Hazlitt*.
    21 vols, London and Toronto: J. M. Dent and Sons.
Hegel, G. W. F. (1962), ed. Knox, T. M., *Philosophy of Right*, Oxford: Oxford
    University Press.
————. (1989), ed. Inwood, M. J., *Hegel: Selections*, London: Macmillan.

Hunt, L. (1923), ed. Milford, H. S., *The Poetical Works of Leigh Hunt*, Oxford: Oxford University Press.

————. (1950), ed. Huston Houtchens, L. and Washburn Houtchens, C., *Leigh Hunt's Dramatic Criticism, 1808–1831*, London: Oxford University Press.

————. (1956), ed. Huston Houtchens, L. and Washburn Houtchens, C., *Leigh Hunt's Literary Criticism*, New York: Columbia University Press.

Kant, I. (1989), trans. Meredith, J. C., *Critique of Judgement*, 2 vols, Oxford: Clarendon Press.

Lean, E. T. (1970*), The Napoleonists: A Study in Political Disaffection, 1760–1960,* Oxford: Oxford University Press.

Newey, V. (1995), 'Keats, History, and the Poets' in Roe, N. (ed.), *Keats and History*, Cambridge: Cambridge University Press, pp. 165–93.

The *Political Register* (1815), London.

Scott, W. (1932–57), ed. Grierson, H. J. C., *Letters of Walter Scott*, London: Constable.

Sales, R. (1983), *English Literature in History: 1780–1830: Pastoral and Politics*, London: Hutchinson.

Shapiro, M. J. (1997), *Violent Cartographies: Mapping Cultures of War*, Minneapolis: University of Minnesota Press.

Shaw, P. (1995), 'Commemorating Waterloo: Wordsworth, Southey, and "The Muses' Page of State"', *Romanticism*, 1 (1).

————. (1996), 'Leigh Hunt and the Battle of Waterloo: British Culture in Transition, 1815–1816' in Baschiera, C. D. and Everson, J. (eds), *Scenes of Change: Studies in Cultural Transition*, Pisa: Edizioni Ets, pp. 281–95.

Wilson, M. (1992), 'Byron and the Battle of Waterloo' in Kneale, J. D. (ed.), *The Mind in Creation: Essays in Honour of Ross G. Woodman*, Quebec: McGill Queen's University Press.

Wordsworth, W. (1970), ed. Moorman, M. and Hill, A. G., *The Letters of William and Dorothy Wordsworth: The Middle Years. Part 2. 1812–20*, Oxford: Clarendon Press.

————. (1974), ed. Owen, W. J. B. and Worthington Smyser, J., *The Prose Works of William Wordsworth*, 3 vols, Oxford: Clarendon Press.

————. (1984), ed. Gill, S., *The Oxford Authors: William Wordsworth*, Oxford: Oxford University Press.

————. (1989), ed. Ketcham, C. H., *Shorter Poems, 1807–1820*, Cornell Wordsworth Series, Ithaca and New York: Cornell University Press; Brighton: Harvester Press.

CHAPTER TEN

Marriage and the end of war

Eric C. Walker

I

In the autumn of 1814, the following advertisement ran in the London papers, over the names of its patroness, the Duchess of York, and (not inappropriately denominated) her several vice-patronesses, including the Duchess of Richmond and the Marchionesses of Buckingham and Landsdowne: 'SUBSCRIPTION of the WOMEN of GREAT BRITAIN and IRELAND, to commemorate the SERVICES of the DUKE OF WELLINGTON, by an appropriate monument.' Of the advertised goal of £3136, the Countess of Eglinton was down for £20 at the head of the list; at the other end appeared a 'Mrs. W. Shakeshaft, Leegomery', at £2.10 (*The Times*, 29 October 1814). Linda Colley has recounted the subsequent misadventures of this scheme and its negotiations of the body parts selected for the Hyde Park display (1992, pp. 285–6); I would only supplement her fine account of this curious episode in the history of war and gender by underscoring the brazen irony of the word 'services' in the advertisement, which in Wellington's philandering case implodes the barrier between conquests on the battlefield and in the bedroom. When the Cato Street conspirators a few years later defended themselves by equating Wellington's mistreatment of his wife with his authoritarian politics – the Duke is to nation as the Duke is to spouse – the billboard on which Wellington's conjugal life had been plastered since the Duke of York scandals in 1808–1809 became at last an eyesore. In this essay, I will examine some of the stories told about conjugality in the immediate wake of war. A governing assumption of the inquiry is that romantic war will come into better focus not just by scrutinizing the war years themselves, but also by attending closely to the narratives that soon circulated to try to make meaning of the war experience. Jerome Christensen has contributed especially important work to direct attention to the several meta-narratives that began to compete in the half-decade following Waterloo; his observation that the war years constituted in Britain a two-decade 'suspension of dailiness' (1996, p. 603) prompts my investigation into the ways in which 'dailiness' tries to sputter back to life in the second half of the Regency. In a series of studies, Stanley Cavell has argued that the central figure in Western discourse for dailiness, for the quotidian – a central component of what Cavell calls the ordinary – is marriage. I want to suggest that a foundational argument justifying a quarter-century of national emergency, a rationale so pervasive as to remain generally unstated this side of Hegel, runs like this: What is the war all about? To make the world safe for conjugality.

The emptiness of this fiction is nowhere more apparent than in the history of the bad marriage in 1795 between Frederick George Augustus, Prince of Wales and Princess Caroline Amelia Elizabeth of Brunswick-Wolfenbûttel, which turned tabloid bad at the start of the Regency and roiled for a decade to notorious boil in the divorce trial of Queen Caroline in 1820. Yet the fiction remains powerful enough to continue to shape our own narratives about the war. Mary Favret's excellent work to demonstrate how war culture contributed to the construction of domestic sphere ideology by building a myth of the (virtuous) public male warrior defending the (virtuous) private female home assumes that this very myth was not always seen as threadbare. There is much evidence in the culture that this fiction circulated precisely as a palpable fiction, a myth that was simultaneously demythologized. The cultural scene is deeply ironic, in other words, replayed in our own time by the spectacularly impudent ironies of one of the most notoriously philandering US chief executives signing in 1996 a 'Defense of Marriage Act', sponsored by a group of male legislators all of whom had indulged in at least one divorce. For the conjugal myth to work as myth, it needs its fantasy forms: Prinny and Caroline collapsing after Waterloo in each other's blissful state arms, the Duke of Wellington retiring devotedly to the Pemberley world of Stratfield Saye with a devoted Kitty. War is, infamously, anti-conjugal: spouses die, separated spouses sleep around and split up. But the cultural cover story is that these threats to marriage are the necessary price to pay, precisely to ensure peacetime marriage. The immiscibility of war and marriage purchases a peace the sign of which is a matrimonial paradise regained.

Post-war nuptial celebrations are strangely lacking where we might expect to find them, however, or the celebrations that do occur begin to look very strange. There is, of course, much anti-conjugal discourse in the wake of the war, culminating in William Thompson's and Anna Doyle Wheeler's 1825 tract *Appeal of One Half of the Human Race, Women, Against the Pretensions of the Other Half, Men, to Retain them in Political, and Thence in Civil and Domestic, Slavery*. This steady stream of post-Godwinian attacks on matrimony illustrates an obvious point, that the war had settled nothing about what Godwin had scorched in 1793 as 'a system of fraud' and 'the worst of all laws' (1926, vol. 2, p. 272). Rather than replay the debates between the polemically conjugal and the polemically anti-conjugal, however, I aim to focus on a different type of marriage writing that, after Cavell, I find it useful to call the antithalamic. Cavell floats the neologistic balloon 'antithalamion' as a way of thinking about marriage and the scepticism in 'The Rime of the Ancient Mariner' (1988, p. 65). Instead of celebrating or attacking marriage, the antithalamic is writing that, finding itself inescapably at sea about marriage, would seek to figure out conjugality, in several senses, but confesses itself in a variety of forms perplexed, stymied or otherwise balked by the nuptial, for better or for worse. Antithalamic writing may be replete with marriages – Jane Austen's fiction, to take an obvious case – but constitute on the whole a pervasively ironic contest with conjugality, a relationship between representational form and social practice of a different order than the idiom of endorsement or attack. Or marriage may appear to be generally absent from antithalamic writing – William Wordsworth's post-Waterloo poetry, to take an obscure case – but therein constitute a series of formal attempts to wrestle with compulsory conjugality on its baffling grounds of ubiquity and silence.

A crucial form of cultural perplexity in 1815 is the intractability of one of the key narratives necessary to make sense of the war. The commentary that follows is part of a larger argument that, at greatest stretch, takes this abbreviated form: modern marriage – that is, post-sacramental, post-war marriage – is the site of a representational crisis that can seem as wide as writing itself. To sketch that crisis in the terms of an impossible dilemma, the tendency of modern marriage is to lodge this doubly outrageous bid: marriage is the only tale there is to tell and, as if that insult could be topped, it is a tale that is untellable. To glimpse this crisis as it takes shape in late-Romantic theory on the Continent, consider the unpromising union of Hegel's assertion that marriage is 'life in its totality' (1942, p. 111) and Kierkegaard's observation that 'conjugal love does not come with any outward sign' (1987, vol. 2, p. 142). The double bind is that modern marriage strives to be the name of the place where in one form or another, inside or outside, coming or going, all must live, or, terrifyingly, not at all – what D. A. Miller terms the 'conjugal imperative' (1995, p. 1). But it gets worse: the very claim of ubiquity works to deny this necessary dwelling-place a language that, because distinct and set apart, can be understood as a language, and marriage thus eludes or thwarts representation. No wonder Austen's novels end when they do. No wonder De Quincey claimed that Wordsworth never wrote about marriage.

Marriage as, ideally, the constitutive sign of peace – the end of war, in a double sense – is marked by an earlier moment in the lives of the two writers I will discuss here. In 1802, during the brief interval of peace that followed the Treaty of Amiens, William Wordsworth married. Jane Austen became engaged during the very same wartime lull – but only for the course of one long and unhappy night. The bulk of this essay takes up two sets of post-war texts from Wordsworth and Austen. After a review of the odd circumstances and forms of Wordsworth's 1816 *Thanksgiving Ode* volume, I offer a reading of Wordsworth's most important Waterloo text, 'Dion', as a tragedy in the special sense suggested by Cavell, as the narrative form scepticism takes when figured as an assault on marriage. My comments on Austen feature *Emma* and *Persuasion*. *Persuasion* is typically read as the very post-war epithalamion that I am arguing is unavailable; by reading the Anne Elliot–

Frederick Wentworth marriage in close tandem with *Emma*, I hope to sketch a way to think of both novels more usefully under the sign of the antithalamic. Read with and against one another, the post-war publications of Austen and Wordsworth bring to attention the inscrutability of modern marriage at precisely the moment when the conjugal myth fails to supply the justification for a war nominally fought to restore it triumphant.

II

For Wordsworth, the war ended with a wedding – but it was, characteristically, a ceremony he did not attend. He was, however, the father of the bride. On 28 February 1816, Caroline Wordsworth-Vallon, the twenty-four-year old daughter of Annette Vallon and William Wordsworth, married Jean-Baptiste Baudouin in Paris. Annette and Caroline had hoped the wedding would occur immediately after the war, in the autumn of 1814, as soon after the engagement as possible. Dorothy Wordsworth, who planned to be there on behalf of the English branch of the family, managed to put them off until the spring of 1815, when she could better arrange her travels; the return of Bonaparte then scotched that among many other itineraries. In the event, no one from the Wordsworth family made it to Paris until 1820, but the war did provide the Wordsworths their most recent direct link to the wedding party: Baudouin's brother, Eustace Baudouin, was a post-Peninsular prisoner of war in Britain and visited the family at Rydal Mount before returning to France, helping to re-establish contact between the Lake District and Paris. In lieu of an album or a video, the Wordsworths had to make do with Annette's epistolary account of the festivities, as circulated by Dorothy:

> Thirty persons were present to dinner, ball and supper. The deputies of the department and many other respectable people were there – the Bride was dressed in white Sarsenet with a white veil. – 'was the admiration of all who beheld her but her modesty was her best ornament.' She kept her veil on the whole of the day – how truly French this is!
>
> (Wordsworth, 1970, p. 296)

The problem facing the bride's absent father was how best in verse to ornament a palimpsest of distant military victory and distant matrimonials.

In his correspondence, Wordsworth remarks that the poem prominent in his mind at this very time was Spenser's *Epithalamion*. Instead of writing an explicit nuptial celebration for his daughter, however, he composed a set of Waterloo victory odes and other miscellaneous pieces that were published in May 1816 in a thin octavo volume titled *Thanksgiving Ode*. Philip Shaw (1995) has skilfully investigated the relevance of Spenser's text to the form and rhetoric of Wordsworth's poems as a model of public, national discourse;

the private, nuptial connection is crucial to keep in mind as well, however, because Wordsworth in these poems transfigures the epithalamic occasion into an antithalamic performance directed in an extraordinarily oblique manner at Wellington. I have elsewhere traced the history of Wordsworth's semi-public quarrel with Arthur Wellesley, arguing that, after a first skirmish in the *Convention of Cintra* pamphlet in 1809, Wordsworth's attack on Wellington emerges full-blown in the *Thanksgiving Ode* volume as a pervasive antinomic rhetoric that performs a shaped unwillingness to join in the conventional ceremonies of heroic naming, ceremonies on prominent display in productions such as Walter Scott's *The Field of Waterloo* and Southey's laureate performance, *The Poet's Pilgrimage to Waterloo* (Walker, 1990a, 1990b). Wordsworth's poems instead regularly offer structures in which the verse simultaneously invites and withholds the blessing of the proper name. To recirculate just two brief examples, in its third stanza the title poem (Wordsworth, 1989, pp. 180–89) turns to the causes of Allied victory:

> Have we not conquered? – By the vengeful sword?
> Ah no, by dint of Magnanimity;
> That curbed the baser passions, and left free
> A loyal band to follow their liege Lord,
> Clear-sighted Honour
>
> (ll. 56–61)

The enjambed appositive, 'honour', defeats the wish that the 'liege Lord' will be given human name. Later in the same stanza, it again seems that the poet is preparing to name:

> Who to the murmurs of an earthly string
>   Of Britain's acts would sing
>   He with enraptured voice will tell
> Of One whose spirit no reverse could quell;
> Of One that mid the failing never failed
>
> (ll. 66–71)

In his 1896 edition of Wordsworth's poetry, William Knight named the absent 'One' with an asterisk and a footnote: Wellington. Wordsworth himself never did so, and the subsequent verses make it clear that 'Britain' alone is the antecedent. In like manner throughout the volume, the desire to hear the warrior's celebrated name is regularly thwarted. Stephen Gill rightly observes that the *Thanksgiving Ode* poems are 'empty of human beings' (1989, p. 320), but his remark has the tone of puzzled complaint. That vacancy, however, is precisely their point. The 'Thanksgiving Ode' is simultaneously about a victory whose human hero Wordsworth refuses to name and about a ceremony he did not attend.

Larkin, on his Whitsun journey south, supplies a nuptial image that to my mind helps make sense of what strikes every reader as the peculiar excess of the victory poems in the *Thanksgiving Ode* volume: 'fathers had never known /

Success so huge and wholly farcical' (1988, pp. 114–16). Kitted up in an ill-fitting tuxedo to celebrate both Waterloo and a wedding, the proud father stumbles his way – much to Shelley's glee – into infamously astonishing rhetorical pits such as 'Yea, Carnage is thy Daughter!' The title poem's sustained refusal to name real heroes and real daughters builds enormous pressure for simple human signification by its end, a pressure only partly relieved by the publication in 1820 of the poem written at the same time as Wordsworth's other Waterloo verse in which the war years are brought to focus in the person of a single human being. That person, however, is disconcertingly remote, a figure from classical history, Dion. This chief Wordsworthian exercise in the well-trod late Enlightenment genre of 'parallel history' has long occasioned its share of scholarly ink-spilling in pursuit of Dion's contemporary referent: Napoleon? Beaupuy? Nelson? John Wordsworth? the poet himself? Wellington? I compound previous sins on this score by returning to the fray: in the light of Wordsworth's severe judgement of Wellington's habits as a spouse, I offer here a reading of the narrative that is 'Dion', a tale of a bright warrior's failure, as an antithalamic tragedy in the special sense put forward by Cavell in his readings of Shakespeare and film (1994, p. 141). In this key Wordsworthian post-Waterloo instance, marriage fails to perform the celebratory post-war role the culture demands.

Wordsworth calls careful attention to his source text with the notation 'See Plutarch' immediately below the poem's title (1989, p. 217). Dion's tale in brief runs this way: Plato's pupil Dion of Syracuse is the virtuous rival to the tyrant Dionysius. After his triumphant return from exile, Dion yields to the temptation to allow his allies to assassinate his new rival, Heraclides. Tormented by guilt, Dion is then himself assassinated. These bare bones of the narrative have drawn attention to public, world-stage events – such as Napoleon's complicity in the plot to assassinate the Duc D'Enghien – in the quest to fill the contemporary blank that is Dion's name. What has not been remarked is the extent to which Plutarch's narrative is shaped as a domestic tragedy, and it is thus worth the time to track the passages in which Dion's tragedy hangs on the question of marriage.

The final breach between Dion and Dionysius is occasioned by the maltreatment of Dion's wife. In the language of North's 1579 translation that Wordsworth used:

> These things went to Dion's harte [Plato's low opinion of Dionysius], so that shortly after he shewed him selfe an open enemie unto Dionysius, but specially when he heard how he had handled his wife … After Dion was exiled, Dionysius returning Plato back againe, he willed him secretlie to feele Dions minde, whether he would not be angrie that his wife [Arete] should be married to an other man: *bicause there ranne a rumor abroade (whether it were true, or invented by Dions enemies) that he liked not his marriage, and coulde not live quietlie with his wife.*
>
> (1896, vol. 6, p. 145; emphasis added)

In spite of Plato's advice that Dion 'would be marvelous angrie' if he pursued his plan, Dionysius marries Arete 'against her will, unto one of his friends called Timocrates' (p. 145). The plot then seems firmly to install the martial form of the conjugal myth, that the end of war is to preserve, protect, and defend marriage: 'Dion from thenceforth disposed him selfe altogether unto warre' (p. 146). But the Plutarchian/Wordsworthian twist to the conjugal myth is that the threatened marriages that war ostensibly defends are themselves always already less than satisfactory: 'there ranne a rumor abroade … that he liked not his marriage, and coulde not live quietlie with his wife' (p. 145).

The tale swerves back onto conventional conjugal tracks with a tearful post-war reunion between the victorious Dion and Arete:

> [T]he women within the castell, would not tarry till [Dion] came into the house, but went to meet him at the gates, Aristomache [Dion's sister] leading Dion's sonne in her hand, and Arete following her weeping, being verie fearefull how she should call and salute her husband, having lyen with an other mann. Dion first spake to his sister, and afterwards to his sonne: and then Aristomache offering him Arete, said unto him: Since thy banishment, O Dion, we have led a miserable and captive life: but now that thou art returned home with victorie, thou hast ridde us out of care and thraldom, and hast also made us againe bolde to lift up our heades, saving her here, whom I wretched creature have by force (thy selfe alive) seene married unto an other man. Now then, sith fortune hath made thee Lord of us all, what judgement givest thou of this compulsion? Howe wilt thou have her to salute thee, as her Uncle [Arete is also Dion's niece], or husbande? As Aristomache spoke these wordes, the water stoode in Dions eyes: so, he gently and lovingly taking his wife Arete by the hand, so he gave her his sonne, and willed her to go home to his house where he then remained, and so delivered the castell to the Syracusans.
>
> (pp. 174–5)

So Princess Caroline would be called home from her Italian rambles to the regal hearths of Carlton House and Brighton Palace; so Arthur Wellesley and Kitty Pakenham would together choose fabrics to decorate the country mansion bestowed by a grateful nation. It seems no accident that one of the most widely-circulated photographic images in the history of that medium is an end-of-war icon, the 1945 Alfred Eisenstaedt Times Square photograph that stages a spontaneously eager 'V-J Day Kiss' between returning sailor and home-front nurse.

But Plutarch's tale does not end in blissful reunion. Conjugality regained and Dion's virtue are incompatible, and the narrative spirals downward into multiple deaths and betrayals. After Dion's death, the text ends with a bleak series of images of broken families. Its final words:

> Now for Aristomache and Arete, they were taken out of prison: and Icetes Syracusan, that sometimes had bene one of Dions frends, tooke

them home to his owne house, and used them verie well and faithfully
for a certaine time, but afterwards was wonne and corrupted by Dions
enemies. So he caused a shippe to be provided for them, and bare them
in hande that they would send them into Peloponnesus: but he gave them
charge that caried them away, to kill them as they went, and to throw
them over bord into the sea. Some say, that the two women, and the little
young boy, were cast alive into the sea. But this reward of the sinfull act
that he committed, returned againe upon him selfe, as it had done before
unto others. For he was taken up by Timoleon that put him to deathe:
and besides, the Syracusans did also kill two of his daughters in revenge
of the unfaithfulness he had shewed unto Dion.

(p. 181)

Framed as the wholescale destruction of families, the narrative's tragic end
figures the incommensurability of marriage and the very peace it is taken to
signify. What is at issue is not the social consequences of infidelity, but
something more fundamentally epistemological: marriage fails to sustain the
post-Cartesian burden to break the prison of the doubting self by forging
satisfactorily the foundational communitarian unit, the couple. Why could
Dion 'not live quietlie with his wife'? No philanderer, Dion's failure is quite
the opposite: he is too enamoured of his solitude. Plutarch notes that Dion
'by nature had a certeine hawtinesse of mind and severitie, and he was a
sower man to be acquainted with'. Plato thus warns Dion 'that he should
beware of obstinacie, the companion of solitarinesse, that bringeth a man in
the ende to be forsaken of everie one' (p. 134). But Dion's 'severity' and
'obstinacy' persist after his victorious return, and the nightmare visions that
come upon him after the assassination of his rival are represented as the
torments of solitude: 'sitting late one evening all alone … being in a deep
thought with him selfe … he saw a monstrous great woman, like unto one of
the furies shewed in playes, and saw her sweeping of the house with a
broome' (p. 178). Wordsworth was very taken by this image and amplified it
at elaborate length in his poem: it occupies nearly 40 of 130 lines in the
poem's first draft. The image of tormented domesticity – a Fury with a broom
– signifies not the torments of domesticity but the failure of conjugality to
resolve the failures of solitude, of severity, of obstinacy. In the published
poem's vexed opening stanza (Wordsworth later removed it and later regret-
ted the removal), Dion is represented in extended metaphor as a majestic
swan 'on Locarno's lake' where 'Winds the mute creature without visible
Mate' (l. 2). The problem of identity is framed as the sufficiency of solitude;
in Wordsworth's final version, Plato helps Dion before his fall steer the
moderate course where he is 'not too elate / With self-sufficing solitude' (ll.
31–2). Wordsworth turns the tearful reunion with Arete in Plutarch into a
triumphal entry celebration that resembles nothing so much as that wedding
ceremony he missed in Paris; Dion enters Syracuse 'in a white, far-beaming,
corslet clad!' (l. 44), recalling Wordsworth's first-born child 'dressed in

white Sarsenet with a white veil'. Nevertheless, solitude remains for Dion the
elation that is also ultimately and simultaneously his abjection, the blessing
and the curse that 'bringeth a man in the ende to be forsaken of everie one.' In
the poem's first draft, Wordsworth indicates that the disappointments of
conjugality are simultaneously, at this post-Waterloo moment, a sign of the
failure of the war to accomplish its end; Dion's tale is 'Proof, for the historian's page and poet's lays, / That Peace, even Peace herself, is fugitive' (ll.
35–6).

Haughty of mind, severe, sour, obstinate, solitary: Wellington? Wordsworth
himself? Keats, for one, was alert to the ways in which the careers of writer
and warrior tracked each other: 'I begin to think that detracting from [Wel-
lington] as well as from Wordsworth is the same thing' (1958, vol. 1, p. 144).
Although it is almost certain that Keats was thinking chiefly of Tory politics,
I want to hold open the possibility that a point of twinned identity a poet
would have been especially alert to is language. In the extended metaphor
that opens the original text of the 'Dion' verses, the nuptial solitude of the
swan is yoked with silence: 'the mute creature without visible Mate' (l. 16).
Wellington was, of course, famously taciturn and blunt; his official dis-
patches recounting Waterloo, widely circulated in the press as soon as they
hit London, were faulted rhetorically for their flat understatement. Almost
lost among the headline post-battle debates (did Napoleon surprise Wellington? if the Prussians had not appeared, was Wellington done for?), a comic
issue in the contest for fit language was Wellington's choice to name the
battle Waterloo – Waterloo!? – when the splendid topographic alternative 'La
Belle Alliance' offered itself euphoniously, as Southey privately complained
(1850, vol. 4, p. 119). Yet Southey publicly praised the 'noble simplicity' of
Wellington's language (1815, p. 522). Wordsworth, another taciturn sort and
master of litotes, would have nothing of this party line. Where Wellington's
language falls short of his subject, Wordsworth's language in the *Thanksgiving Ode* poems surprises readers as it falls compensatorily beyond it in
rhetorical excess. The poems tumble all over themselves to supply the words
the hero of the hour is unable to speak, and to supply antithalamic shadows of
parental words not spoken at the Paris wedding that brought to a nuptial close
the poet's own lived history with revolutionary France. Wellington has too
few words and Wordsworth too many: there seem to be no fit words to signify
peace, and wedded bliss, and victory.

Southey in his *Quarterly Review* essays on Wellington and Waterloo not
only dismissed the attacks on Wellington's generalship but issued a blanket
blessing: '[he exhibited] personal behaviour, on all occasions, as perfect as
his conduct as general' (1815, p. 470). Wordsworth would also have nothing
to do with this absolute form of the party line. The 1977 recovery of the lost
1810 and 1812 letters between Wordsworth and his wife Mary made it clear
that Wordsworth's lifelong beef with Wellington, which began with his dis-

dain for the political misjudgements of Cintra, was soon after compounded by his disapproval of Wellington's conduct as a spouse. In the spring of 1812, Wordsworth in London reported to Mary in Wales that he had been in company with 'the Countess of Wellington', whom he refers to as 'Wife or rather Widow bewitched'. This celebrity snapshot is surrounded by a litany of complaint about Wellington as a 'debauchee', as 'licentiously connected', and as 'that profligate man Lord Wellesly' (1981, p. 208). Accustomed to reading such bits of evidence as biographical fodder that builds the picture of the cold Wordsworth of 'a pretty piece of paganism' fame, we are now in a position to read these comments otherwise, as figures in a cultural text of great perplexity. What is ruffling Wordsworth's feathers is less male infidelity than the failure of marriage itself to hold steady as a necessarily stable sign. If the representational system demands conjugal harmony as the sign of victory and peace, where are the signs of victory? Where are the signs of peace? In the late winter weeks of 1816 when Wordsworth was missing his first-born's wedding and composing his Waterloo poems, London chatter was full of Captain James Wedderburn-Webster and his wife, Lady Frances (of Byronic fame), who were suing the *St James's Chronicle* for libel for spreading the gossip of her affair with Wellington, a trial that was a dress rehearsal for the pyrotechnics of the divorce trial of Queen Caroline in 1820. Just when peace needs a good wedding, the presiding cultural form is instead the antithalamion.

III

Much like a younger Bennet sister, Jane Austen is still typically presented as an enthusiast for military life. Anne Mellor supplies what persists as the summary case in *Romanticism and Gender* in 1993: Austen is 'positively disposed to the military, and portrays her naval officers in *Persuasion* and William Price, the young midshipman in *Mansfield Park*, with unqualified approval of their industry, courage, and domestic virtue' (p. 62). One might suspect that the 'viciousness' of Admiral Crawford in *Mansfield Park* (1998c, p. 36) would cast some sort of qualifying shadow over William Price's chosen profession, at the very least. A biographer as canny as Claire Tomalin as recently as 1998 keeps spinning the old myth of a sheltered Austen; on the subject of war, writing of Austen's relationship with her sailor brother Francis, Tomalin asserts that 'she could have no opinion of what she did not know, of shipboard brutality, of clandestine services to the East India Company, or high-handed dealings with foreign powers; she saw a sober, sensible, well-conducted brother who served his country single-mindedly at sea and deserved a happy life at home' (1998, p. 144). The martial form of the conjugal myth seems alive and well in Austen studies. Popular interpretations are also stuck in an epithalamic rut. Emma Thompson ends her screenplay of *Sense and Sensibility*, for example, with straightforward images of untroubled nuptial celebration, whereas the novel's last sentence performs something very different by means of a typically sly litotes: the language directs the departing reader to puzzle through the epithalamic proclamation of the happiness of the Dashwood sisters in terms of the absence of qualities that belong to the anti-conjugal brief, 'disagreement' and 'coolness'. To call a marriage 'not unhappy' is a quintessentially antithalamic manoeuvre, sidestepping both the epithalamic 'happy' and the anti-conjugal 'unhappy' (1998e, p. 335). The novels perform this trope writ large as they stage antithalamically ironic contests with cultural conjugal imperatives, such as the demand that marriage and peace be commensurable. My comments on Austen will take up two novels briefly in an effort to sketch a way to locate these two post-war texts under the sign of the antithalamic. I read conjugality in *Emma* as skewered by the buried narrative of Jane Fairfax's mother, and I read conjugality in *Persuasion* as calling into question a particular form of the marriage fantasy, the domiciliary refuge that in its fixity would mirror the stability of marriage itself in the representational system.

If the spate of recent films of *Emma* did not clinch the point that the novel still circulates under the under the sign of the epithalamic, recall the long arm of Wayne Booth's formidable judgement in *The Rhetoric of Fiction* in 1961: 'Marriage to an intelligent, amiable, good, and attractive man is the best thing that can happen to this heroine, and the readers who do not experience it as such are, I am convinced, far from knowing what Jane Austen is about' (p. 260). To think otherwise, Booth suggests, is the interpretive equivalent of ridiculing poor Miss Bates, and such a reader, like Emma, will be properly humiliated. To read *Emma* epithalamically is to see its anti-conjugal impulses deflectively ironized within the text in the person of Mr Woodhouse, whose unhappiness at the departure of Miss Taylor at the opening of the novel issues in absolute principle: 'Matrimony, as the origin of change, was always disagreeable' (1998a, p. 5). But in spite of this comic encapsulization of the anti-conjugal as just another piece of valetudinarian whimsy, Mr Woodhouse's plea to Emma, 'pray do not make any more matches' (p. 9), performs antithalamically an echo of Hamlet's despair at the wreckage of what he once knew as home: 'Let there be no more marriages!'

Claudia Johnson's recent work on *Emma*, both in her book on Austen (1988) and in the final chapter to *Equivocal Beings* (1995), demonstrates with great skill the complex negotiations of gender in the novel, which in Johnson's account is a multifaceted, sustained meditation on masculinity. Conjugality in this reading, instead of the constitutive *telos* of the narrative, is very nearly irrelevant, and the book in Johnson's hands begins to look extra-conjugal. Chiefly because of the distance it needs to put between itself and those prevailing readings that inscribe conjugality as the defining structure of the novel, Johnson's interpretation tends to elide conjugality as a new postwar problem. In other words, whereas Johnson historicizes *Emma* as a belated tribute to the discourse of gender in the fiction of the 1790s, I want to locate it more directly in the historical moment of its composition and publication in 1814 and 1815. Conjugality in *Emma* is undone by the nearly buried narrative of one of the very few war casualties in Austen's major fiction, Jane Fairfax's father. Jane Fairfax the elder, one of the most elusive of Austen's many tantalizingly fugitive off-stage characters, is, remarkably, the one war widow in Austen's novels, and I argue that her almost unnoticed fate is recast as the novel's refusal to embrace or endorse conjugality in simple, untroubled forms.

Claudia Johnson herself supplies the paradigm for this way of thinking about *Emma*, in her remarks on the redundancy of the tales of the two Elizas in *Sense and Sensibility* (1988, pp. 55–8). (These are the narratives of the mother and daughter, both named Eliza, who have been abused and discarded, the first by Col. Brandon's brother and the second by Willoughby.) Johnson's superb point is that we actually need only one of these tales to convey the argument about the unhappy fate that threatens romantic young women like Marianne Dashwood; the effect of the double narratives, however, underscored by the identical names, is that all women in the world of this book might as well be called Eliza. It seems to be the only tale there is to tell. Although it is almost always a fool's errand to rush into the territory of an Austen sequel, we can predict with some confidence that Willoughby's love-child is fated to be named, like her mother and grandmother, Eliza.

There is a very similar narrative structure in *Emma*, and it is surprising that Johnson does not seem to want to make much of it in the later novel. There are two Jane Fairfaxes in the book; all readers recall the younger, jerked around mercilessly by Frank Churchill, but how many recall her mother, also Jane Fairfax? Here is the text, just a few sentences at the opening of the second chapter of the second volume:

> Jane Fairfax was an orphan, the only child of Mrs. Bates's youngest daughter. The marriage of Lieut. Fairfax, of the — regiment of infantry, and Miss Jane Bates, had had its day of fame and pleasure, hope and interest; but nothing now remained of it, save the melancholy remembrance of him dying in action abroad – of his widow sinking under consumption and grief soon afterwards – and this girl.
>
> (1998a, p. 145)

That is it. But the redundant names point to what is at work: the long crisis of identity that is Jane Fairfax the younger's life, is war by another name. Just as in *Sense and Sensibility* all the women might as well be called Eliza, so all the women of Highbury might as well be named Jane Fairfax. The logic of these naming strategies argues that the heralded crisis of identity that is an Austen novel – what is a girl to do, other than marry? – is not a peacetime condition, but a state of wartime emergency. *Emma* puts into question antithalamically the logic of the national agenda of the previous quarter-century: what was all that fighting all about, if not to make the world safe for marriage?

Austen's naming strategies are often finessed so openly that they defy belief. Does it not strike closer to the authorial home that these Fairfax women happen to be named Jane? If any suspicions linger that the national agenda is not at issue in the novel, we need only go to Knightley himself, that object of Wayne Booth's intense affection, whose Christian name is of course George. As the novel was in press, Austen learned, to her simultaneous pleasure and discomfort, that the Prince Regent – George, of course – was an interested reader of her fiction, and that he would not be displeased to receive the dedication of her next work. Austen is on record in her correspondence as considering the Prince Regent, conjugally, as the 'Big Creep'. In February 1813 she wrote to Martha Lloyd:

> I suppose all the World is sitting in Judgement upon the Princess of Wales's letter. Poor Woman, I shall support her as long as I can, because she *is* a Woman, & because I hate her Husband – but I can hardly forgive her for calling herself 'attached and affectionate' to a Man whom she must detest – & the intimacy said to subsist between her & Lady Oxford is bad, – I do not know what to do about it; – but if I must give up the Princess, I am resolved at least always to think that she would have been respectable, if the Prince had behaved only tolerably by her at first.
>
> (1995, p. 208)

In the autumn of 1815, she nervously allowed the dedication to go forward, in the anxious confidence that what the dedication gave, the now spectacular irony of the novel's final words – 'the perfect happiness of the union' (1998a, p. 440) – would simultaneously take away so cleanly that George himself would hardly notice (you might as well call all the men of this world George). If the end of war is to make the world safe for conjugality, the spectacularly broken marriage of the Prince Regent and Princess Caroline rendered that fiction palpably empty, and the opportunity to engraft the image of the royal conjugal mess on the happy nuptials of Emma Woodhouse and George Knightley was clearly too good to resist.

Among Austen's books, these topics place *Persuasion* most urgently at issue. The Anne Elliot–Frederick Wentworth marriage, most often taken to be a celebratory sign of peace, constitutes instead a reinscription of marriage as a new kind of peacetime puzzle. In addition to a characteristic mix of comically imperfect pairs and more menacing matches, *Persuasion* invites attention for its unusual degree of apparently epithalamic energy. The Croft marriage in event and the Wentworth marriage in prospect both look very inviting. Unlike the epithalamic fantasy that *Pride and Prejudice* becomes, however, the epithalamic as constituted in *Persuasion* contests antithalamically the very grounds of conventional nuptial celebration. Marriage in *Pride and Prejudice* invests hugely in the rootedness of conjugality, in the idea that marriage signifies a domiciliary refuge that in its fantasy forms, such as Pemberley, would refuse mutability. Marriage in *Persuasion*, on the other hand, is always on the move; the Crofts are never long in any one place and the Wentworths seem bound for that sea that Coleridge in 'The Rime of the Ancyent Mariner' foundationally figures as antithalamic for romantic discourse. What *Persuasion* celebrates, in other words – peripatetic marriage – is antithalamically oxymoronic. In her last finished novel, Austen balks the elusiveness of modern marriage by figuring a set of elusive marriages.

Persuasion was published in a four-volume set with *Northanger Abbey*, where the fantasy of the marital home as fixed domiciliary refuge is on prominent display just on the edge of parody. Late in the novel, Catherine Morland visits what all signs suggest will be her new matrimonial home, the Woodston parsonage where Henry Tilney is already installed. Master of hyperbole, Catherine judges the sitting room to be 'the most comfortable room in the world' on her way to the drawing-room, which is 'the prettiest room in the world' (1998b, p. 189). But the house itself, where the party moves from interior to interior, is not the ultimate retreat. From the drawing-room windows, Catherine catches sight of the refuge within the refuge: 'Oh! what a sweet little cottage there is among the trees – apple trees too! It is the prettiest cottage!' (p. 190). Catherine Morland's vision of the nuptial home as fixed refuge is set vividly against the celebrated rootlessness of the Croft marriage in *Persuasion*:

> 'What a great traveller you must have been, ma'am!' said Mrs. Musgrove to Mrs. Croft. 'Pretty well, ma'am, in the fifteen years of my marriage; though many women have done more. I have crossed the Atlantic four times, and have been once to the East Indies, and back again; and only once, besides being in different places about home – Cork, and Lisbon, and Gibraltar.
>
> (1998d, p. 288)

'Home' in Sophia Croft's definition is any temporary European port, which effectively scatters the myth of the domiciliary refuge. In the penultimate paragraph of the novel, we are told in a single phrase of Anne Elliot's and Frederick Wentworth's 'settled life' that: 'their marriage, instead of depriving [Mrs. Smith] of one friend, secured her two. She was their earliest visitor in their settled life' (p. 455). The remarkable thing about this image is that the text offers no information whatsoever about what 'settled' signifies. Settled where? Settled how? This is not a question that Austen usually leaves hanging: we know that Elizabeth Bennet will gain Pemberley, and we know that Emma Woodhouse – in a different kind of antithalamic disruption – will remain at Hartfield instead of moving to Donwell Abbey. To read *Persuasion* as supplying Austen's epithalamic period to a quarter-century of war is to miss the fact that the celebrated nuptial space – the *thalamos*, the bridal chamber – is nowhere to be found. The Roger Michell film of the novel gets it right, I think, in its liberties with the text: the final images of the film put the married couple on board ship, at sea, based on the solid interpretation that the model for the Elliot–Wentworth marriage is the Croft marriage, a marriage that has been spent in no fixed peacetime spot but on the wartime move.

Even when the Crofts rent a nominally peacetime port, they cannot stay at Kellynch-hall long and soon hit the road, which simply continues their wartime habits. On the streets of Bath – crucially, not an interior – Anne Elliot and the text contemplate at length their model of marriage:

> They brought with them their country habit of being almost together. He was ordered to walk, to keep off the gout, and Mrs. Croft seemed to go shares with him in every thing, and to walk for her life, to do him good. Anne saw them wherever she went. Lady Russell took her out in her carriage almost every morning, and she never failed to think of them, and never failed to see them. Knowing their feelings as she did, it was a most attractive picture of happiness to her. She always watched them as long as she could; delighted to fancy she understood what they might be talking of, as they walked along in happy independence, or equally delighted to see the Admiral's hearty shake of the hand when he encountered an old friend, and observe their eagerness of conversation when occasionally forming into a little knot of the navy, Mrs. Croft looking as intelligent and keen as any of the officers around her.
>
> (p. 377)

The dominant image is motion, the walking human pair, which refigures the rootedness of marriage – especially for a woman – not in degree but in kind. The antithalamic manoeuvres of this text may be glimpsed at the syntactic level, in the splendid puzzle that is the second sentence of the passage: 'He was ordered to walk, to keep off the gout, and Mrs. Croft seemed to go shares with him in every thing, and to walk for her life, to do him good.' The two infinitive phrases at the beginning of the sentence, which have a clearly subordinate grammatical relationship ('He was ordered to walk [in order] to keep off the gout'), suggest that the final two infinitive phrases should be read the same way: 'Mrs. Croft seemed ... to walk for her life [in order] to do him good'. But the first infinitive of that pair strikes a semantically odd note: just what – in a pre-aerobics age – does 'to walk for her life' exactly mean? The echo of 'run for your life' adds a curious whiff of something not unlike desperation to the puzzling sense, and raises the possibility that the final two infinitives are co-ordinate: Sophia Croft both walked for her life (whatever that means) and (also, by the way) did Admiral Croft good. One form of the sublime of Austen's style is that the syntax finesses both readings, which might signify this about marriage: a new way of figuring conjugality, peripatetic marriage manages to be both subordinate (the old) and co-ordinate (the new). If such a formulation sounds suspiciously utopian, the quiet enigma of 'to walk for her life' should discourage the temptation to view the Croft marriage as an uncomplicated mystification of companionship.

The whole paragraph emphasizes the togetherness of the conjugal couple: 'almost always together', the Crofts 'walked along in happy independence'. But independence from what? This couple on the move manages together to be independent of cultural norms (the Crofts are also childless, having ducked, apparently, the procreative imperative), but the text leaves open the possibility that independence is also independence from each other, what Cavell calls 'the mutual acknowledgement of separateness' (1988, p. 178). This glimpse of a new kind of marriage is a far cry from the companionate ideal overly familiar from social histories of marriage in this period, and is closer to the complex account of identity formation in Hegelian marriage, where conjugality produces three new persons (not only the corporate pair, but two new individuals as well), all engaged in a struggle for recognition – war by another name. But to follow this account into Hegelian thickets would be to leave the topic at hand unfinished. Contrary to prevailing accounts, *Persuasion* does not inscribe marriage as the sign and seal of peace. Just as the tribulations of Jane Fairfax and Emma Woodhouse are war by another name, the penultimate sentence of *Persuasion*, as it sketches Anne Elliot's future, suggests that war is not over and done with: 'the dread of a future war [was] all that could dim her sunshine' (p. 455). We are left at the end of *Emma* and *Persuasion* with images of happy couples, and what Austen novel does not end that way? But the novels also refuse to tell us the tales of these marriages, in part because there would be far too many stories to try to tell all at once, some if not all of which we have no language for. Rather than the pleasing epithalamic solution of Janeite tradition, the final fixation in these novels on the inscrutable couple signifies antithalamically the unavailability of other narratives that might, in another time, satisfy more.

By his own account, E. P. Thompson met harsh criticism from audiences on the North American lecture circuit in the late 1970s when he tried to present his conclusions about the topic he at last published in 1993 as 'The Sale of Wives'. Constructed by these audiences as an especially brutal instance of the patriarchal marriage system operating a system of chattel slavery, wife-selling, Thompson tried to argue, is better understood as a form of working-class divorce ritual purposefully and necessarily outside the legal system. One of the problems of this debate is the skimpy evidence; a pseudonymous contribution to *Notes and Queries* in 1863 argued a connection between wife-selling and the end of war:

> There have been several notices of wife-selling in your columns, but I do not remember seeing any account of the peculiar circumstances under which the customer became a settled legal point in the minds of the labouring population. When the war was over in 1815, and a great number of soldiers disbanded, many of them found, on reaching what had been

their homes, that their wives had married again, and that a new family had
sprung up to which the unfortunate soldier or sailor had no claim. In some
of these cases certainly nobody was to blame. The wife had heard from
more or less certain sources that her husband had been killed in such a
battle, and after a decent interval had got another; all parties were in the
wrong; all were to be pitied, but what was to be done? I don't suppose that
the thing originated then, for such events must have occurred in former
wars; but any way, the fact of taking a wife to the market, and selling her
by auction was considered as effectual a way of dissolving the *vinculum*
as if it had been done in the House of Lords itself. The second husband
became the purchaser for a nominal sum, twopence or sixpence, the first
was free to marry again, and all parties were content. In the manufactur-
ing districts in 1815 and 1816 hardly a market-day passed without such
sales month after month. The authorities shut their eyes at the time, and
the people were confirmed in the perfect legality of the proceeding, as
they had already been satisfied of its justice.

(p. 450)

Like a tale soon to come from Hardy, let such a scene stand as the image of
the relationship between marriage and the end of war. In spite of the contributor's assertion that 'all parties were content', I find it impossible to call such
ceremonies epithalamic. But the especially odd thing is that they are not
exactly anticonjugal either: as bad as it may look, marriage keeps limping
along, undaunted, like a bad habit simultaneously unbearable and irresistible.
Adam Phillips puts the post-Christian blind trust in conjugality this way:

Like a magnet that collects our virtues and vices, monogamy makes the
larger abstractions real, as religion once did. Faith, hope, trust, morality;
these are domestic matters now. Indeed, we contrast monogamy not
with bigamy or polygamy but with infidelity, because it is our secular
religion. God may be dead, but the faithful couple won't lie down.

(1996, no. 10)

In a similar mood, Cavell suggests that we dwell in an in-between time, after
religion (because, as Cavell puts it, nothing is any longer common to our
Gods), and before philosophy, because, again in Cavell's words, we are not
yet interested in our new lives. The name of that in-between time, after
religion and before philosophy, is marriage (1988, p. 63). It comes into
telling focus in characteristically inscrutable antithalamic forms in 1815, at
the end of war.

Bibliography

Austen, J. (1995), ed. Le Faye, D., *Letters*, Oxford: Oxford University Press.
———. (1998a), ed. Kinsley, J., *Emma*, Oxford: Oxford University Press.
———. (1998b), ed. Davie, J., *Northanger Abbey, Lady Susan, The Watsons,
and Sanditon*, Oxford: Oxford University Press.

————. (1998c), ed. Kinsley, J., *Mansfield Park*, Oxford: Oxford University Press.

————. (1998d), ed. Davie, J., *Persuasion*, Oxford: Oxford University Press.

————. (1998e), ed. Kinsley, J., *Sense and Sensibility*, Oxford: Oxford University Press.

Booth, W. (1961), *The Rhetoric of Fiction*, Chicago: University of Chicago Press.

Cavell, S. (1988), *In Quest of the Ordinary*, Chicago: Chicago University Press.

————. (1994), *A Pitch of Philosophy*, Cambridge, Mass.: Harvard University Press.

Christensen, J. (1996), 'The Detection of the Romantic Conspiracy in Britain', *South Atlantic Quarterly*, 95 (3).

Colley, L. (1992), *Britons: Forging the Nation, 1707–1837*, New Haven: Yale University Press.

Favret, M. A. (1994), 'Coming Home: The Public Spaces of Romantic War', *Studies in Romanticism*, 33 (4).

Gill, S. (1989), *William Wordsworth: A Life*, Oxford: Oxford University Press.

Godwin, W. (1923), ed. Preston, R. A., *An Enquiry Concerning Political Justice and its Influence on General Virtue and Happiness*, 2 vols, New York: Alfred A. Knopf.

Hegel, G. W. F. (1942), ed. Knox, T. M., *Philosophy of Right*, Oxford: Oxford University Press.

Johnson, C. (1988), *Jane Austen: Women, Politics, and the Novel*, Chicago: University of Chicago Press.

————. (1995), *Equivocal Beings: Politics, Gender, and Sentimentality in the 1790s*, Chicago: University of Chicago Press.

Keats, J. (1958), ed. Rollins, H. E., *The Letters of John Keats, 1814–1821*, Cambridge, Mass.: Harvard University Press.

Kierkegaard, S. (1987), ed. Hong, H. and Hong, E., *Either/Or*, 2 vols, Princeton: Princeton University Press.

Larkin, P. (1988), ed. Thwaite, A., *Collected Poems*, London: Faber and Faber.

Mellor, A. (1993), *Romanticism and Gender*, London: Routledge.

Michell, R. (1995), *Persuasion* (film), Sony Corporation.

Miller, D. A. (1995), 'Austen's Attitude', *Yale Journal of Criticism*, 8 (1).

Notes and Queries (1863), 3rd series, 4, 5 December.

Phillips, A. (1996), *Monogamy*, London: Faber and Faber.

Plutarch (1896), ed. Henley, W. E., *Plutarch's Lives of the Noble Grecians and Romans Englished by Sir Thomas North Anno 1579*, London: David Nutt.

Shaw, P. (1995), 'Commemorating Waterloo: Wordsworth, Southey, and "The Muses' Page of State"', *Romanticism*, 1 (1).

Southey, R. (1815), 'Life of Wellington', *Quarterly Review*, 13 (25).

————. (1850), ed. Southey, rev. C. C., *Life and Correspondence of the Late Robert Southey*, 6 vols, London: Longman, Brown, Green and Longmans.

The Times (29 October 1814), London.

Thompson, E. P. (1993), *Customs in Common*, New York: New Press.

Thompson, E. (1995), *The Sense and Sensibility Screenplay and Diaries*, New York: Newmarket Press.

Tomalin, C. (1998), *Jane Austen: A Life*, New York: Alfred A. Knopf.

Walker, E. C. (1990a), 'Wordsworth, Warriors, and Naming', *Studies in Romanticism*, 29 (2).

————. (1990b), 'Wordsworth, Wellington, and Myth' in Behrendt, S. C. (ed.), *History and Myth: Essays on English Romantic Literature*, Detroit: Wayne State University Press, pp. 100–115.

Wordsworth, W. (1896), ed. Knight, W., *The Poetical Works of William Wordsworth*, London: Macmillan.

————. (1970), ed. Moorman, M. and Hill, A. G., *The Letters of William and Dorothy Wordsworth: The Middle Years, Part 2, 1812–20*, Oxford, Clarendon Press.

————. (1981), ed. Darlington, B., *The Love Letters of William and Mary Wordsworth*, Ithaca and New York: Cornell University Press.

————. (1989), ed. Ketcham, C. H., *Shorter Poems, 1807–1820*, Cornell Wordsworth Series, Ithaca and New York: Cornell University Press; Brighton: Harvester Press.

Index